Grace A. Ellis

A Selection from the Poems and Prose Writings of Mrs. Anna

Laetitia Barbauld

Grace A. Ellis

A Selection from the Poems and Prose Writings of Mrs. Anna Laetitia Barbauld

ISBN/EAN: 9783744669849

Printed in Europe, USA, Canada, Australia, Japan

Cover: Foto ©Thomas Meinert / pixelio.de

More available books at **www.hansebooks.com**

A

SELECTION

FROM THE

POEMS AND PROSE WRITINGS

OF

MRS. ANNA LÆTITIA BARBAULD,

BY

GRACE A. ELLIS.

" Wisdom, discipline, and liberal arts ;
Th' embellishments of life ; virtues like these
Make human nature shine, reform the soul."
ADDISON.

BOSTON:
JAMES R. OSGOOD AND COMPANY,
LATE TICKNOR & FIELDS, AND FIELDS, OSGOOD, & CO.
1874.

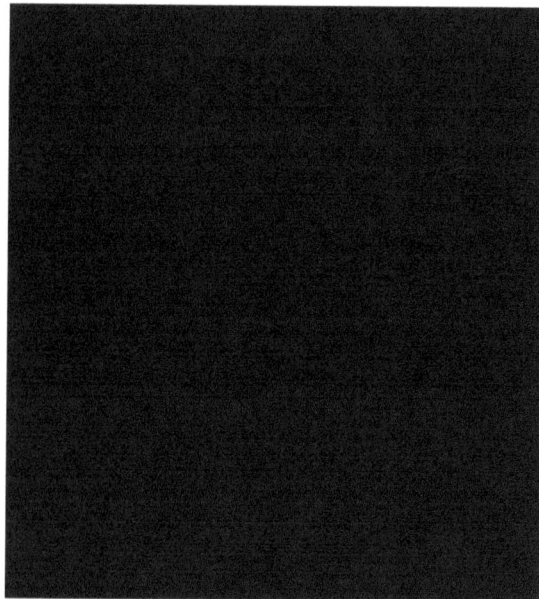

UNIVERSITY PRESS: WELCH, BIGELOW, & CO.,
CAMBRIDGE.

CONTENTS.

POEMS.

PROSE WORKS.

MISCELLANEOUS.

LEGACY FOR YOUNG LADIES.

Works of Mrs. Barbauld.

THE INVITATION.

TO MISS B . . . . .

HEALTH to my friend, and long unbroken years,
   By storms unruffled and unstained by tears:
Winged by new joys may each white minute fly;
Spring on her cheek, and sunshine in her eye:
O'er that dear breast, where love and pity springs,
May peace eternal spread her downy wings:
Sweet beaming hope her path illumine still,
And fair ideas all her fancy fill!
From glittering scenes which strike the dazzled sight
With mimic grandeur and illusive height,
From idle hurry and tumultuous noise,
From hollow friendships, and from sickly joys,
Will Delia, at the Muse's call, retire
To the pure pleasures rural scenes inspire?
Will she from crowds and busy cities fly,
Where wreaths of curling smoke involve the sky,

To taste the grateful shades of spreading trees,
And drink the spirit of the mountain breeze ?

When Winter's hand the roughening year deforms,
And hollow winds foretell approaching storms,
Then Pleasure, like a bird of passage, flies
To brighter climes, and more indulgent skies ;
Cities and courts allure her sprightly train,
From the bleak mountain and the naked plain,
And gold and gems with artificial blaze
Supply the sickly sun's declining rays.
But soon, returning on the western gale,
She seeks the bosom of the grassy vale :
There, wrapt in careless ease, attunes her lyre
To the wild warblings of the woodland quire :
The daisied turf her humble throne supplies,
And early primroses around her rise.
We 'll follow where the smiling goddess leads,
Through tangled forest or enamelled meads ;
O'er pathless hills her airy form we chase,
In silent glades her fairy footsteps trace :
Small pains there needs her footsteps to pursue,
She cannot fly from friendship, and from you.
Now the glad earth her frozen zone unbinds,
And o'er her bosom breathe the western winds.
Already now the snow-drop dares appear,
The first pale blossom of the unripened year ;

As Flora's breath, by some transforming power,
Had changed the icicle into a flower :
Its name and hue the scentless plant retains,
And winter lingers in its icy veins.
To these succeed the violet's dusky blue,
And each inferior flower of fainter hue ;
Till riper months the perfect year disclose,
And Flora cries exulting, See my Rose!

The Muse invites ; my Delia, haste away,
And let us sweetly waste the careless day ;
Here gentle summits lift their airy brow,
Down the green slope here winds the laboring plough ;
Here, bathed by frequent showers, cool vales are seen,
Clothed with fresh verdure and eternal green ;
Here smooth canals across the extended plain
Stretch their long arms to join the distant main:*
The sons of toil with many a weary stroke
Scoop the hard bosom of the solid rock ;
Resistless, through the stiff opposing clay
With steady patience work their gradual way ;
Compel the genius of the unwilling flood
Through the brown horrors of the aged wood ;

---

* The Duke of Bridgewater's canal, which in many places crosses
the road, and in one is carried by an aqueduct over the river Trewell.
Its head is at Worsley, where it is conveyed by deep tunnels under
the coal-pits, for the purpose of loading the boats.

'Cross the lone waste the silver urn they pour,
And cheer the barren heath or sullen moor.
The traveller with pleasing wonder sees
The white sail gleaming through the dusky trees,
And views the altered landscape with surprise,
And doubts the magic scenes which round him rise.
Now, like a flock of swans above his head,
Their woven wings the flying vessels spread;
Now meeting streams in artful mazes glide,
While each unmingled pours a separate tide;
Now through the hidden veins of earth they flow,
And visit sulphurous mines and caves below;
The ductile streams obey the guiding hand,
And social plenty circles round the land.

But nobler praise awaits our green retreats;
The Muses here have fixed their sacred seats.
Mark where its simple front yon mansion rears, —
The nursery of men for future years!
Here callow chiefs and embryo statesmen lie,
And unfledged poets short excursions try;
While Mersey's gentle current, which too long
By fame neglected, and unknown to song,
Between his rushy banks — no poet's theme —
Had crept inglorious, like a vulgar stream,
Reflects the ascending seats with conscious pride,
And dares to emulate a classic tide.

Soft music breathes along each opening shade,
And soothes the dashing of his rough cascade.
With mystic lines his sands are figured o'er,
And circles traced upon the lettered shore.
Beneath his willows rove the inquiring youth,
And court the fair majestic form of Truth.
Here Nature opens all her secret springs,
And heaven-born Science plumes her eagle-wings.
Too long had bigot rage, with malice swelled,
Crushed her strong pinions, and her flight withheld;
Too long to check her ardent progress strove, —
So writhes the serpent round the bird of Jove;
Hangs on her flight, restrains her towering wing,
Twists its dark folds, and points its venomed sting.
Yet still — if aught aright the Muse divine —
Her rising pride shall mock the vain design;
On sounding pinions yet aloft shall soar,
And through the azure deep untravelled paths explore.
When science smiles, the Muses join the train,
And gentlest arts and purest manners reign.
Ye generous youth who love this studious shade,
How rich a field is to your hopes displayed!
Knowledge to you unlocks the classic page,
And virtue blossoms for a better age.
O golden days! O bright unvalued hours!
What bliss — did ye but know that bliss — were yours!
With richest stores your glowing bosoms fraught:

Perception quick, and luxury of thought ;
The high designs that heave the laboring soul,
Panting for fame, impatient of control ;
And fond enthusiastic thought, that feeds
On pictured tales of vast heroic deeds ;
And quick affections, kindling into flame
At virtue's or their country's honored name ;
And spirits light, to every joy in tune ;
And friendship ardent as a summer's noon ;
And generous scorn of vice's vernal tribe,
And proud disdain of interest's sordid bribe ;
And conscious honor's quick instinctive sense,
And smiles unforced, and easy confidence ;
And vivid fancy, and clear simple truth,
And all the mental bloom of vernal youth.

How bright the scene to Fancy's eye appears,
Through the long perspective of distant years,
When this, this little group their country calls
From academic shades and learned halls,
To fix her laws, her spirit to sustain,
And light up glory through her wide domain !
Their various tastes in different arts displayed,
Like tempered harmony of light and shade,
With friendly union in one mass shall blend,
And this adorn the State, and that defend.
These the sequestered shade shall cheaply please,

With learned labor and inglorious ease;
While those, impelled by some resistless force,
O'er seas and rocks shall urge their venturous course;
Rich fruits matured by glowing suns behold,
And China's groves of vegetable gold;
From every land the various harvest spoil,
And bear the tribute to their native soil;
But tell each land — while every toil they share,
Firm to sustain, and resolute to dare —
MAN is the nobler growth our realms supply,
And SOULS are ripened in our northern sky.

Some, pensive, creep along the shelly shore;
Unfold the silky texture of a flower;
With sharpened eyes inspect an hornet's sting,
And all the wonders of an insect's wing.
Some trace with curious search the hidden cause
Of Nature's changes, and her various laws;
Untwist her beauteous web, disrobe her charms,
And hunt her to her elemental forms;
Or prove what hidden powers in herbs are found,
To quench disease and cool the burning wound;
With cordial drops the fainting head sustain,
Call back the flitting soul, and still the throbs of pain.

The patriot passion this shall strongly feel;
Ardent, and glowing with undaunted zeal,

With lips of fire shall plead his country's cause,
And vindicate the majesty of laws;
This, clothed with Britain's thunder, spread alarms
Through the wide earth, and shake the pole with arms;
That, to the sounding lyre his deeds rehearse,
Enshrine his name in some immortal verse,
To long posterity his praise consign,
And pay a life of hardships by a line.
While others, consecrate to higher aims,
Whose hallowed bosoms glow with purer flames,
Love in their hearts, persuasion in their tongue,
With words of peace shall charm the listening throng,
Draw the dread veil that wraps the eternal throne,
And launch our souls into the bright unknown.

Here cease my song.   Such arduous themes require
A master's pencil and a poet's fire;
Unequal far such bright designs to paint,
Too weak her colors, and her lines too faint,
My drooping Muse folds up her fluttering wing,
And hides her head in the green lap of Spring.

THE GROANS OF THE TANKARD.

Dulci digne mero. — HORAT.

O F strange events I sing, and portents dire;
The wondrous themes a reverent ear require;
Though strange the tale, the faithful Muse believe,
And what she says with pious awe receive.

'T was at the solemn, silent, noontide hour,
When hunger rages with despotic power,
When the lean student quits his Hebrew roots
For the gross nourishment of English fruits,
And throws unfinished airy systems by
For solid pudding and substantial pie;
When hungry poets the glad summons own,
And leave spare Fast to dine with Gods alone:
Our sober meal despatched with silent haste,
The decent grace concludes the short repast:
Then, urged by thirst, we cast impatient eyes
Where deep, capacious, vast, of ample size,
The Tankard stood, replenished to the brink
With the cold beverage blue-eyed Naiads drink.
But lo! a sudden prodigy appears,
And our chilled hearts recoil with startling fears:

1 *

Its yawning mouth disclosed the deep profound,
And in low murmurs breathed a sullen sound;
Cold drops of dew did on the sides appear;
No finger touched it, and no hand was near.
At length the indignant vase its silence broke,
First heaved deep hollow groans, and then distinctly
    spoke.

"How changed the scene! — for what unpardoned
    crimes
Have I survived to these degenerate times?
I, who was wont the festal board to grace,
And 'midst the circle lift my honest face,
White o'er with froth, like Ætna crowned with snow,
Which mantled o'er the brown abyss below,
Where Ceres mingled with her golden store
The richer spoils of either India's shore,
The dulcet reed the Western islands boast,
And spicy fruits from Banda's fragrant coast.
At solemn feasts the nectared draught I poured,
And often journeyed round the ample board:
The portly Alderman, the stately Mayor,
And all the furry tribe my worth declare;
And the keen sportsman oft, his labors done,
To me retreating with the setting sun,
Deep draughts imbibed, and conquered land and sea,
And overthrew the pride of France, — by me.

" Let meaner clay contain the limpid wave,
The clay for such an office nature gave ;
Let China's earth enriched with colored stains,
Pencilled with gold, and streaked with azure veins,
The grateful flavor of the Indian leaf,
Or Mocha's sunburnt berry glad receive ;
The nobler metal claims more generous use,
And mine should flow with more exalted juice.
Did I for this my native bed resign
In the dark bowels of Potosi's mine ?
Was I for this with violence torn away
And dragged to regions of the upper day ?
For this the rage of torturing furnace bore,
From foreign dross to purge the brightening ore ?
For this have I endured the fiery test,
And was I stamped for this with Britain's lofty crest ?

" Unblest the day, and luckless was the hour,
Which doomed me to a Presbyterian's power ;
Fated to serve the Puritanic race,
Whose slender meal is shorter than their grace ;
Whose moping sons no jovial orgies keep ;
Where evening brings no summons — but to sleep ;
No Carnival is even Christmas here,
And one long Lent involves the meagre year.
Bear me, ye powers ! to some more genial scene,
Where on soft cushions lolls the gouty Dean,

Or rosy Prebend with cherubic face,
With double chin, and paunch of portly grace,
Who, lulled in downy slumbers, shall agree
To own no inspiration but from me.
Or to some spacious mansion, Gothic, old,
Where Comus' sprightly train their vigils hold;
There oft exhausted, and replenished oft,
O let me still supply the eternal draught,
Till care within the deep abyss be drowned,
And thought grows giddy at the vast profound!"

More had the goblet spoke, but lo! appears
'An ancient Sibyl, furrowed o'er with years.
Her aspect sour and stern ungracious look
With sudden damp the conscious vessel struck:
Chilled at her touch its mouth it slowly closed,
And in long silence all its griefs reposed;
Yet still low murmurs creep along the ground,
And the air vibrates with the silver sound.

ON THE BACKWARDNESS OF THE SPRING 1771.

Æstatem increpitans seram, Zephyrosque morantes. — VIRGIL.

IN vain the sprightly sun renews his course,
Climbs up the ascending signs and leads the day,
While long embattled clouds repel his force,
And lazy vapors choke the golden ray.

In vain the Spring proclaims the new-born year;
No flowers beneath her lingering footsteps spring,
No rosy garland binds her golden hair,
And in her train no feathered warblers sing;

Her opening breast is stained with frequent showers,
Her streaming tresses bathed in chilling dews;
And sad before her move the pensive hours,
Whose flagging wings no breathing sweets diffuse.

Like some lone pilgrim clad in mournful weed,
Whose wounded bosom drinks her falling tears,
On whose pale cheek relentless sorrows feed,
Whose dreary way no sprightly carol cheers.

Not thus she breathed on Arno's purple shore,
And called the Tuscan Muses to her bowers;

Not this the robe in Enna's vale she wore,
When Ceres' daughter filled her lap with flowers.

Clouds behind clouds in long succession rise,
And heavy snows oppress the springing green;
The dazzling waste fatigues the aching eyes,
And fancy droops beneath the unvaried scene.

Indulgent Nature, loose this frozen zone;
Through opening skies let genial sunbeams play;
Dissolving snows shall their glad impulse own,
And melt upon the bosom of the May.

VERSES WRITTEN IN AN ALCOVE.

Jam Cytherea choros ducit Venus, imminente Luna. — HORAT.

NOW the moonbeam's trembling lustre
    Silvers o'er the dewy green,
And in soft and shadowy colors
    Sweetly paints the checkered scene.

Here beneath the opening branches
    Streams a flood of softened light;
There the thick and twisted foliage
    Spreads the browner gloom of night.

This is sure the haunt of fairies ;
 In yon cool alcove they play ;
Care can never cross the threshold, —
 Care was only made for day.

Far from hence be noisy Clamor,
 Sick Disgust and anxious Fear ;
Pining Grief and wasting Anguish
 Never keep their vigils here.

Tell no tales of sheeted spectres
 Rising from the quiet tomb ;
Fairer forms this cell shall visit,
 Brighter visions gild the gloom.

Choral songs and sprightly voices
 Echo from her cell shall call,
Sweeter, sweeter than the murmur
 Of the distant waterfall.

Every ruder gust of passion
 Lulled with music dies away,
Till within the charmed bosom
 None but soft affections play.

Soft as when the evening breezes
 Gently stir the poplar grove ;

Brighter than the smile of Summer,
    Sweeter than the breath of Love.

Thee the enchanted Muse shall follow,
    Lissy! to the rustic cell;
And, each careless note repeating,
    Tune them to her charming shell.

Not the Muse who wreathed with laurel
    Solemn stalks with tragic gait,
And in clear and lofty vision
    Sees the future births of fate;

Not the maid who crowned with cypress
    Sweeps along in sceptred pall,
And in sad and solemn accents
    Mourns the crested hero's fall;

But that other smiling sister,
    With the blue and laughing eye,
Singing, in a lighter measure,
    Strains of woodland harmony:

All unknown to fame and glory,
    Easy, blithe, and debonair,
Crowned with flowers, her careless tresses
    Loosely floating on the air.

Then when next the star of evening
    Softly sheds the silent dew,
Let me in this rustic temple,
    Lissy! meet the Muse and you.

THE MOUSE'S PETITION.*

O HEAR a pensive prisoner's prayer,
    For liberty that sighs;
And never let thine heart be shut
    Against the wretch's cries!

For here forlorn and sad I sit,
    Within the wiry grate;
And tremble at the approaching morn,
    Which brings impending fate.

If e'er thy breast with freedom glowed,
    And spurned a tyrant's chain,
Let not thy strong oppressive force
    A free-born mouse detain!

* Found in the trap, where he had been confined all night by Dr. Priestley for the sake of making experiments with different kinds of air.

B

O do not stain with guiltless blood
   Thy hospitable hearth ;
Nor triumph that thy wiles betrayed
   A prize so little worth.

The scattered gleanings of a feast
   My frugal meals supply ;
But if thine unrelenting heart
   That slender boon deny, —

The cheerful light, the vital air,
   Are blessings widely given ;
Let nature's commoners enjoy
   The common gifts of heaven.

The well-taught philosophic mind
   To all compassion gives :
Casts round the world an equal eye,
   And feels for all that lives.

If mind, — as ancient sages taught, —
   A never-dying flame,
Still shifts through matter's varying forms,
   In every form the same ;

Beware, lest in the worm you crush
   A brother's soul you find ;

And tremble lest thy luckless hand
    Dislodge a kindred mind.

Or, if this transient gleam of day
    Be *all* of life we share,
Let pity plead within thy breast
    That little *all* to spare.

So may thy hospitable board
    With wealth and peace be crowned;
And every charm of heartfelt ease
    Beneath thy roof be found.

So when destruction lurks unseen,
    Which men, like mice, may share,
May some kind angel clear thy path,
    And break the hidden snare.

TO MRS. P********.

WITH SOME DRAWINGS OF BIRDS AND INSECTS.

> The kindred arts to please thee shall conspire ;
> One dip the pencil, and one string the lyre.
>
> POPE.

AMANDA bids ; — at her command again
I seize the pencil, or resume the pen ;
No other call my willing hand requires,
And Friendship, better than a Muse, inspires.

Painting and Poetry are near allied ;
The kindred arts two sister Muses guide :
This charms the eye, that steals upon the ear ;
There sounds are tuned, and colors blended here :
This with a silent touch enchants our eyes,
And bids a gayer, brighter world arise ;
That, less allied to sense, with deeper art
Can pierce the close recesses of the heart ;
By well-set syllables, and potent sound,
Can rouse, can chill the breath, can soothe, can wound ;
To life adds motion, and to beauty soul,
And breathes a spirit through the finished whole ;
Each perfects each, in friendly union joined, —
This gives Amanda's form, and that her mind.

But humbler themes my artless hand requires,
Nor higher than the feathered tribe aspires.
Yet who the various nations can declare
That plough with busy wings the peopled air?
These cleave the crumbling bark for insect food,
Those dip their crooked beak in kindred blood;
Some haunt the rushy moor, the lonely woods,
Some bathe their silver plumage in the floods;
Some fly to man, his household gods implore,
And gather round his hospitable door;
Wait the known call, and find protection there
From all the lesser tyrants of the air.

The tawny Eagle seats his callow brood
High on the cliff, and feasts his young with blood.
On Snowdon's rocks, or Orkney's wide domain,
Whose beetling cliffs o'erhang the Western main,
The royal bird his lonely kingdom forms
Amidst the gathering clouds and sullen storms;
Through the wide waste of air he darts his sight,
And holds his sounding pinions poised for flight;
With cruel eye premeditates the war,
And marks his destined victim from afar;
Descending in a whirlwind to the ground,
His pinions like the rush of water sound;
The fairest of the fold he bears away,
And to his nest compels the struggling prey;

He scorns the game by meaner hunters tore,
And dips his talons in no vulgar gore.

With lovelier pomp along the grassy plain
The Silver Pheasant draws his shining train;
On Asia's myrtle shores, by Phasis' stream,
He spreads his plumage to the sunny gleam;
But when the wiry net his flight confines,
He lowers his purple crest, and inly pines;
The beauteous captive hangs his ruffled wing,
Oppressed by bondage and our chilly spring.
To claim the verse unnumbered tribes appear,
That swell the music of the vernal year;
Seized with the spirit of the kindly May,
They sleek the glossy wing, and tune the lay;
With emulative strife the notes prolong,
And pour out all their little souls in song.
When Winter bites upon the naked plain,
Nor food nor shelter in the groves remain;
By instinct led, a firm united band,
As marshalled by some skilful general's hand,
The congregated nations wing their way
In dusky columns o'er the trackless sea;
In clouds unnumbered annual hover o'er
The craggy Bass, or Kilda's utmost shore;
Thence spread their sails to meet the Southern wind,
And leave the gathering tempest far behind;

Pursue the circling sun's indulgent ray,
Course the swift seasons, and o'ertake the day.

Not so the insect race, ordained to keep
The lazy sabbath of a half year's sleep:
Entombed beneath the filmy web they lie,
And wait the influence of a kinder sky.
When vernal sunbeams pierce their dark retreat,
The heaving tomb distends with vital heat;
The full-formed brood, impatient of their cell,
Start from their trance, and burst their silken shell;—
Trembling awhile they stand, and scarcely dare
To launch at once upon the untried air:
At length assured, they catch the favoring gale,
And leave their sordid spoils, and high in ether sail.
So when brave Tancred struck the conscious rind,
He found a nymph in every trunk confined;
The forest labors with convulsive throes,
The bursting trees the lovely births disclose,
And a gay troop of damsels round him stood,
Where late was rugged bark and lifeless wood.
Lo the bright train their radiant wings unfold!
With silver fringed, and freckled o'er with gold:
On the gay bosom of some fragrant flower
They idly fluttering live their little hour;
Their life all pleasure, and their talk all play,
All spring their age, and sunshine all their day.

Not so the child of sorrow, wretched Man;
His course with toil concludes, with pain began;
That his high destiny he might discern,
And in misfortune's school this lesson learn, —
Pleasure 's the portion of the inferior kind;
But glory, virtue, Heaven for Man designed.

What atom-forms of insect life appear!
And who can follow Nature's pencil here?
Their wings with azure, green, and purple glossed,
Studded with colored eyes, with gems embossed,
Inlaid with pearl, and marked with various stains
Of lively crimson through their dusky veins;
Some shoot like living stars athwart the night,
And scatter from their wings a vivid light,
To guide the Indian to his tawny loves,
As through the woods with cautious steps he moves.
See the proud giant of the beetle race!
What shining arms his polished limbs enchase!
Like some stern warrior formidably bright,
His steely sides reflect a gleaming light;
On his large forehead spreading horns he wears,
And high in air the branching antlers bears;
O'er many an inch extends his wide domain,
And his rich treasury swells with hoarded grain.

Thy friend thus strives to cheat the lonely hour
With song or paint, an insect or a flower;

With song or paint, an insect or a flower;
Yet if Amanda praise the flowing line,
And bend delighted o'er the gay design,
I envy not nor emulate the fame
Or of the painter's or the poet's name, —
Could I to both with equal claim pretend,—
Yet far, far dearer were the name of Friend.

TO SLEEP.*

COME, gentle god of soft repose,
    Come soothe this tortured breast;
Shed kind oblivion o'er my woes,
    And lull my cares to rest.

Come, gentle god, without thy aid
    I sink in dark despair;
O wrap me in thy silent shade,
    For peace is only there.

Let hope in some propitious dream
    Her bright illusions spread;
Once more let rays of comfort beam
    Around my drooping head.

* Dr. Aikin's Collection of Songs. — ED.

O quickly send thy kind relief;
　　These heartfelt pangs remove;
Let me forget myself, my grief,
　　And every care, — but love.

A DIRGE.*

BOW the head, thou lily fair,
　　Bow the head in mournful guise;
Sickly turn thy shining white,
　　Bend thy stalk, and never rise.

Shed thy leaves, thou lovely rose,
　　Shed thy leaves so sweet and gay;
Spread them wide on the cold earth,
　　Quickly let them fade away.

Fragrant woodbine all untwine,
　　All untwine from yonder bower;
Drag thy branches on the ground,
　　Stain with dust each tender flower.

For, woe is me! the gentle knot,
　　That did in willing durance bind

* Dr. Aikin's Collection of Songs. — ED.

My Emma and her happy swain,
  By cruel death is now untwined.

Her head with dim half-closed eyes,
  Is bowed upon her breast of snow ;
And cold and faded are those cheeks
  That wont with cheerful red to glow.

And mute is that harmonious voice
  That wont to breathe the sounds of love ;
And lifeless are those beauteous limbs,
  That with such ease and grace did move.

And I, of all my bliss bereft,
  Lonely and sad must ever moan ;
Dead to each joy the world can give,
  Alive to memory alone.

CHARACTERS.

O BORN to soothe distress and lighten care,
  Lively as soft, and innocent as fair !
Blest with that sweet simplicity of thought
So rarely found, and never to be taught ;

Of winning speech, endearing, artless, kind,
The loveliest pattern of a female mind;
Like some fair spirit from the realms of rest,
With all her native heaven within her breast;
So pure, so good, she scarce can guess at sin,
But thinks the world without like that within;
Such melting tenderness, so fond to bless,
Her charity almost becomes excess.
Wealth may be courted, Wisdom be revered,
And Beauty praised, and brutal Strength be feared;
But Goodness only can Affection move,
And Love must owe its origin to Love.

Illam quicquid agit, quoquo vestigia flectit
Componit furtim, subsequiturque decor.

TIBUL.

OF gentle manners, and of taste refined,
With all the graces of a polished mind;
Clear sense and truth still shone in all she spoke,
And from her lips no idle sentence broke.
Each nicer elegance of art she knew;
Correctly fair, and regularly true;
Her ready fingers plied with equal skill
The pencil's task, the needle, or the quill;
So poised her feelings, so composed her soul,
So subject all to reason's calm control, —

One only passion, strong and unconfined,
Disturbed the balance of her even mind :
One passion ruled despotic in her breast,
In every word, and look, and thought confest ; —
But that was love ; and love delights to bless
The generous transports of a fond excess.

HAPPY old man ! who, stretched beneath the shade
Of large grown trees, or in the rustic porch
With woodbine canopied, where linger yet
The hospitable virtues, calm enjoy'st
Nature's best blessings all, — a healthy age
Ruddy and vigorous, native cheerfulness,
Plain-hearted friendship, simple piety,
The rural manners and the rural joys,
Friendly to life.   O rude of speech, yet rich
In genuine worth, not unobserved shall pass
Thy bashful virtues ! for the Muse shall mark,
Detect thy charities, and call to light
Thy secret deeds of mercy ; while the poor,
The desolate and friendless, at thy gate,
A numerous family, with better praise
Shall hallow in their hearts thy spotless name.

SUCH were the dames of old heroic days,
Which faithful story yet delights to praise ;

Who, great in useful works, hung o'er the loom,—
The mighty mothers of immortal Rome :
Obscure, in sober dignity retired,
They more deserved than sought to be admired ;
The household virtues o'er their honored head
Their simple grace and modest lustre shed : —
Chaste their attire, their feet unused to roam,
They loved the sacred threshold of their home ;
Yet, true to glory, fanned the generous flame,
Bade lovers, brothers, sons, aspire to fame ;
In the young bosom cherished Virtue's seed,
The secret springs of many a godlike deed.
So the fair stream in some sequestered glade
With lowly state glides silent through the shade ;
Yet by the smiling meads her urn is blest,
With freshest flowers her rising banks are drest,
And groves of laurel, by her sweetness fed,
High o'er the forest lift their verdant head.

Is there whom genius and whom taste adorn
With rare but happy union ; in whose breast
Calm, philosophic, thoughtful, largely fraught
With stores of various knowledge, dwell the powers
That trace out secret causes, and unveil
Great Nature's awful face ?   Is there whose hours
Of still domestic leisure breathe the soul

Of friendship, peace, and elegant delight
Beneath poetic shades, where leads the Muse
Through walks of fragrance, and the fairy groves
Where young ideas blossom ? — Is there one
Whose tender hand, lenient of human woes,
Wards off the dart of death, and smooths the couch
Of torturing anguish ? On so dear a name
May blessings dwell, honor, and cordial praise ;
Nor need he be a brother to be loved.

CHAMPION of Truth, alike through Nature's field,
And where in sacred leaves she shines revealed, —
Alike in both, eccentric, piercing, bold,
Like his own lightnings, which no chains can hold,
Neglecting caution, and disdaining art,
He seeks no armor for a naked heart : —
Pursue the track thy ardent genius shows,
That like the sun illumines where it goes ;
Travel the various map of Science o'er,
Record past wonders, and discover more ;
Pour thy free spirit o'er the breathing page,
And wake the virtue of a careless age.
But O forgive, if touched with fond regret
Fancy recalls the scenes she can't forget ;
Recalls the vacant smile, the social hours
Which charmed us once, for once those scenes were ours!

And while thy praises through wide realms extend,
We sit in shades, and mourn the absent friend.
So when the impetuous river sweeps the plain,
Itself a sea, and rushes to the main;
While its firm banks repel conflicting tides,
And stately on its breast the vessel glides;
Admiring much the shepherd stands to gaze,
Awe-struck, and mingling wonder with his praise;
Yet more he loves its winding path to trace
Through beds of flowers, and Nature's rural face,
While yet a stream the silent vale it cheered,
By many a recollected scene endeared,
Where trembling first beneath the poplar shade
He tuned his pipe, to suit the wild cascade.

AN INVENTORY OF THE FURNITURE IN
DR. PRIESTLEY'S STUDY.

A MAP of every country known,
   With not a foot of land his own.
A list of folks that kicked the dust
On this poor globe, from Ptol. the First;
He hopes — indeed, it is but fair —
Some day to get a corner there.
A group of all the British kings —
Fair emblem! — on a pack-thread swings.

The Fathers, ranged in goodly row,
A decent, venerable show,
Writ a great while ago, they tell us,
And many an inch o'ertop their fellows.
A Juvenal to hunt for mottoes,
And Ovid's tales of nymphs and grottos.
The meek-robed lawyers, all in white,
Pure as the lamb, — at least to sight.
A shelf of bottles, jar, and phial,
By which the rogues he can defy all, —
All filled with lightning keen and genuine,
And many a little imp he 'll pen you in ;
Which, like Le Sage's sprite, let out,
Among the neighbors makes a rout ;
Brings down the lightning on their houses,
And kills their geese, and frights their spouses.
A rare thermometer, by which
He settles to the nicest pitch
The just degrees of heat, to raise
Sermons, or politics, or plays.
Papers and books, a strange mixed olio,
From shilling touch to pompous folio ;
Answer, remark, reply, rejoinder,
Fresh from the mint, all stamped and coined here ;
Like new-made glass, set by to cool,
Before it bears the workman's tool.
A blotted proof-sheet, wet from Bowling,—

" How can a man his anger hold in ? " —
Forgotten rhymes and college themes,
Worm-eaten plans and embryo schemes : —
A mass of heterogeneous matter,
A chaos dark, nor land nor water ;
New books, like new-born infants, stand,
Waiting the printer's clothing hand : —
Others, a motley ragged brood,
Their limbs unfashioned all, and nude,
Like Cadmus' half-formed men, appear ;
One rears a helm, one lifts a spear ;
And feet were lopped and fingers torn
Before their fellow limbs were born ;
A leg began to kick and sprawl
Before the head was seen at all,
Which quiet as a mushroom lay
Till crumbling hillocks gave it way ;
And all, like controversial writing,
Were born with teeth, and sprang up fighting.

" But what is this," I hear you say,
" Which saucily provokes my eye ? " —
A thing unknown, without a name,
Born of the air and doomed to flame.

HYMN TO CONTENT.

Natura beatis
Omnibus esse dedit, si quis cognoverit uti.
CLAUDIAN.

O THOU, the Nymph with placid eye!
O seldom found, yet ever nigh!
Receive my temperate vow;
Not all the storms that shake the pole
Can e'er disturb thy halcyon soul
    And smooth unaltered brow.

O come, in simple vest arrayed,
With all thy sober cheer displayed,
    To bless my longing sight;
Thy mien composed, thy even pace,
Thy meek regard, thy matron grace,
    And chaste subdued delight.

No more by varying passions beat,
O gently guide my pilgrim feet
    To find thy hermit cell;
Where in some pure and equal sky,
Beneath thy soft indulgent eye,
    The modest virtues dwell.

Simplicity in Attic vest,
And Innocence with candid breast,
  And clear undaunted eye ;
And Hope, who points to distant years,
Fair opening through this vale of tears
  A vista to the sky.

There Health, through whose calm bosom glide
The temperate joys in even tide,
  That rarely ebb or flow ;
And Patience there, thy sister meek,
Presents her mild unvarying cheek
  To meet the offered blow.

Her influence taught the Phrygian sage
A tyrant master's wanton rage
  With settled smiles to meet ;
Inured to toil and bitter bread,
He bowed his meek submitted head
  And kissed thy sainted feet.

But thou, O Nymph, retired and coy !
In what brown hamlet dost thou joy
  To tell thy tender tale ?
The lowliest children of the ground,
Moss-rose and violet, blossom round,
  And lily of the vale.

O say what soft propitious hour
I best may choose to hail thy power,
   And court thy gentle sway ?
When Autumn, friendly to the Muse,
Shall thy own modest tints diffuse,
   And shed thy milder day.

When Eve, her dewy star beneath,
Thy balmy spirit loves to breathe,
   And every storm is laid ; —
If such an hour was e'er thy choice,
Oft let me hear thy soothing voice
   Low whispering through the shade.

TO WISDOM.

Dona præsentis rape lætus horæ, ac
Linque severa.
HORAT.

O WISDOM ! if thy soft control
   Can soothe the sickness of the soul,
Can bid the warring passions cease,
And breathe the calm of tender peace ;
Wisdom ! I bless thy gentle sway,
And ever, ever will obey.

But if thou com'st with frown austere
To nurse the brood of Care and Fear;
To bid our sweetest passions die,
And leave us in their room a sigh;
Or if thine aspect stern have power
To wither each poor transient flower
That cheers their pilgrimage of woe,
And dry the springs whence hope should flow, —
Wisdom! thine empire I disclaim,
Thou empty boast of pompous name!
In gloomy shade of cloisters dwell,
But never haunt my cheerful cell.
Hail to Pleasure's frolic train!
Hail to Fancy's golden reign!
Festive Mirth, and Laughter wild,
Free and sportful as the child!
Hope with eager sparkling eyes,
And easy faith and fond surprise!
Let these, in fairy colors drest,
Forever share my careless breast;
Then, though wise I may not be,
The wise themselves shall envy me.

THE ORIGIN OF SONG-WRITING.*

Illic indocto primum se exercuit arcu;
Hei mihi quam doctas nunc habet ille manus !

TIBUL.

WHEN Cupid, wanton boy ! was young,
His wings unfledged, and rude his tongue,
He loitered in Arcadian bowers,
And hid his bow in wreaths of flowers ;
Or pierced some fond, unguarded heart
With now and then a random dart ;
But heroes scorned the idle boy,
And love was but a shepherd's toy.
When Venus, vexed to see her child
Amid the forests thus run wild,
Would point him out some nobler game, —
Gods and godlike men to tame.
She seized the boy's reluctant hand,
And led him to the virgin band,
Where the sister Muses round
Swell the deep, majestic sound ;
And in solemn strains unite,
Breathing chaste, severe delight ; —

* Addressed to the author of Essays on Song-Writing, Dr. Aikin. —
ED.

Songs of chiefs and heroes old,
In unsubmitting virtue bold;
Of even valor's temperate heat,
And toils to stubborn patience sweet;
Of nodding plumes and burnished arms,
And glory's bright, terrific charms.

The potent sounds like lightning dart
Resistless through the glowing heart;
Of power to lift the fixed soul
High over Fortune's proud control;
Thrilling deep prophetic musing;
Love of beauteous death infusing;
Scorn and unconquerable hate
Of tyrant pride's unhallowed state.
The boy, abashed and half afraid,
Beheld each chaste immortal maid, —
Pallas spread her Egis there;
Mars stood by with threatening air;
And stern Diana's icy look
With sudden chill his bosom struck.

"Daughters of Jove, receive the child,"
The queen of beauty said, and smiled;
Her rosy breath perfumed the air,
And scattered sweet contagion there;
Relenting Nature learned to languish,

And sickened with delightful anguish : —
" Receive him, artless yet and young ;
Refine his air and smooth his tongue ;
Conduct him through your favorite bowers,
Enriched with fair perennial flowers,
To solemn shades and springs that lie
Remote from each unhallowed eye ;
Teach him to spell those mystic names
That kindle bright immortal flames ;
And guide his young, unpractised feet
To reach coy Learning's lofty seat."

Ah, luckless hour ! mistaken maids,
When Cupid sought the Muse's shades !
Of their sweetest notes beguiled
By the sly, insidious child ;
Now of power his darts are found
Twice ten thousand times to wound.
Now no more the slackened strings
Breathe of high, immortal things,
But Cupid tunes the Muse's lyre
To languid notes of soft desire.
In every clime, in every tongue,
'T is love inspires the poet's song.
Hence Sappho's soft, infectious page ;
Monimia's woe ; Othello's rage ;
Abandoned Dido's fruitless prayer ;

And Eloisa's long despair ;
The garland, blest with many a vow,
For haughty Sacharissa's brow ;
And, washed with tears, the mournful verse
That Petrarch laid on Laura's hearse.

But more than all the sister quire,
Music confessed the pleasing fire.
Here sovereign Cupid reigned alone ;
Music and song were all his own.
Sweet as in old Arcadian plains,
The British pipe has caught the strains :
And where the Tweed's pure current glides,
Or Liffey rolls her limpid tides,
Or Thames his oozy waters leads
Through rural bowers or yellow meads, —
With many an old romantic tale
Has cheered the lone, sequestered vale ;
With many a sweet and tender lay
Deceived the tiresome summer day.

'T is yours to cull with happy art
Each meaning verse that speaks the heart ;
And, fair arrayed, in order meet,
To lay the wreath at Beauty's feet.

SONGS.

SONG.

COME here, fond youth, whoe'er thou be,
    That boasts to love as well as me.
And if thy breast have felt so wide a wound,
    Come hither, and thy flame approve ;
    I 'll teach thee what it is to love,
And by what marks true passion may be found.

    It is to be all bathed in tears ;
    To live upon a smile for years ;
To lie whole ages at a beauty's feet :
    To kneel, to languish, and implore ;
    And still, though she disdain, adore : —
It is to do all this, and think thy sufferings sweet.

    It is to gaze upon her eyes
    With eager joy and fond surprise ;
Yet tempered with such chaste and awful fear
    As wretches feel who wait their doom ;
    Nor must one ruder thought presume,
Though but in whispers breathed, to meet her ear.

It is to hope, though hope were lost;
 Though heaven and earth thy passion crossed;
Though she were bright as sainted queens above,
  And thou the least and meanest swain
  That folds his flock upon the plain, —
Yet, if thou dar'st not hope, thou dost not love.

It is to quench thy joy in tears,
 To nurse strange doubts and groundless fears;
If pangs of jealousy thou hast not proved, —
  Though she were fonder and more true
  Than any nymph old poets drew, —
O, never dream again that thou hast loved !

If, when the darling maid is gone,
 Thou dost not seek to be alone,
Wrapt in a pleasing trance of tender woe,
  And muse, and fold thy languid arms,
  Feeding thy fancy on her charms,
Thou dost not love, — for love is nourished so.

If any hopes thy bosom share
 But those which Love has planted there,
Or any cares but his thy breast inthrall, —
  Thou never yet his power hast known ;
  Love sits on a despotic throne,
And reigns a tyrant, if he reigns at all.

Now if thou art so lost a thing,
Here all thy tender sorrows bring,
And prove whose patience longest can endure :
　We 'll strive whose fancy shall be lost
　In dreams of fondest passion most ;
For if thou thus hast loved, O never hope a cure !

ADDRESS TO CUPID.

If ever thou didst joy to bind
Two hearts in equal passion joined,
O Son of Venus ! hear me now,
And bid Florella bless my vow.

If any bliss reserved for me
Thou in the leaves of fate shouldst see ;
If any white, propitious hour
Pregnant with hoarded joys in store ;

Now, now the mighty treasure give,
In her for whom alone I live ;
In sterling love pay all the sum,
And I 'll absolve the fates to come.

In all the pride of full-blown charms
Yield her, relenting, to my arms :

Her bosom touch with soft desires,
And let her feel what she inspires.

But Cupid, if thine aid be vain,
The dear reluctant maid to gain;
If still with cold, averted eyes
She dash my hopes and scorn my sighs;

O grant!—'t is all I ask of thee,—
That I no more may change than she,
But still with duteous zeal love on,
When every gleam of hope is gone.

Leave me then alone to languish;
Think not time can heal my anguish;
Pity the woes which I endure,—
But never, never grant a cure.

SONG.

When gentle Celia first I knew,
A breast so good, so kind, so true,
  Reason and taste approved;
Pleased to indulge so pure a flame,
I called it by too soft a name,
  And fondly thought I loved,

Till Chloris came : — with sad surprise
I felt the lightning of her eyes
    Through all my senses run ;
All glowing with resistless charms,
She filled my breast with new alarms, —
    I saw, and was undone.

O Celia ! dear, unhappy maid,
Forbear the weakness to upbraid
    Which ought your scorn to move ;
I know this beauty false and vain,
I know she triumphs in my pain,
    Yet still I feel I love.

Thy gentle smiles no more can please,
Nor can thy softest friendship ease
    The torments I endure :
Think what that wounded breast must feel
Which truth and kindness cannot heal,
    Nor e'en thy pity cure !

Oft shall I curse my iron chain,
And wish again thy milder reign
    With long and vain regret ;
All that I can, to thee I give ;
And could I still to reason live,
    I were thy captive yet.

But passion's wild, impetuous sea
Hurries me far from peace and thee;
   'T were vain to struggle more.
Thus the poor sailor slumbering lies,
While swelling tides around him rise,
   And push his bark from shore.

In vain he spreads his helpless arms,
His pitying friends with fond alarms
   In vain deplore his state;
Still far and farther from the coast,
On the high surge his bark is tost,
   And foundering yields to fate.

SONG.

As near a weeping spring reclined,
The beauteous Araminta pined,
And mourned a false, ungrateful youth;
While dying echoes caught the sound,
And spread the soft complaints around
Of broken vows and altered truth; —

An aged shepherd heard her moan,
And thus in pity's kindest tone
Addressed the lost, despairing maid:
" Cease, cease, unhappy fair, to grieve,

For sounds, though sweet, can ne'er relieve
A breaking heart by love betrayed.

"Why shouldst thou waste such precious showers,
That fall like dew on withered flowers,
But dying passion ne'er restored ?
In Beauty's empire is no mean, —
And woman, either slave or queen,
Is quickly scorned when not adored.

" Those liquid pearls from either eye,
Which might an Eastern empire buy,
Unvalued here and fruitless fall ;
No art the season can renew,
When love was young and Damon true ;
No tears a wandering heart recall.

" Cease, cease to grieve ; thy tears are vain,
Should those fair orbs in drops of rain
Vie with a weeping southern sky :
For hearts o'ercome with love and grief
All nature yields but one relief ; —
Die, hapless Araminta, die !"

SONG.

WHEN first upon your tender cheek
I saw the morn of beauty break
  With mild and cheering beam,
I bowed before your infant shrine;
The earliest sighs you had were mine,
  And you my darling theme.

I saw you in that opening morn
For Beauty's boundless empire born,
  And first confessed your sway;
And ere your thoughts, devoid of art,
Could learn the value of a heart,
  I gave my heart away.

I watched the dawn of every grace,
And gazed upon that angel face,
  While yet 't was safe to gaze;
And fondly blessed each rising charm,
Nor thought such innocence could harm
  The peace of future days.

But now despotic o'er the plains
The awful noon of beauty reigns,
  And kneeling crowds adore;

Its beams arise too fiercely bright,
Danger and death attend the sight,
   And I must hope no more.

Thus to the rising God of day
Their early vows the Persians pay,
   And bless the spreading fire;
Whose glowing chariot, mounting soon,
Pours on their heads the burning noon;
   They sicken and expire.

SONG.*

ASPASIA rolls her sparkling eyes,
   And every bosom feels her power;
The Indians thus view Phœbus rise,
   And gaze in rapture, and adore,
Quick to the soul the piercing splendors dart,
Fire every vein, and melt the coldest heart.

Aspasia speaks; the listening crowd
   Drink in the sound with greedy ears,
Mute are the giddy and the loud,
   And self-admiring Folly hears.

* Dr. Aikin's "Collection of Songs." — ED.

Her wit secures the conquests of her face,
Points every charm, and brightens every grace.

Aspasia moves; her well-turned limbs
Slide stately with harmonious ease;
Now through the mazy dance she swims,
　　Like a tall bark o'er summer seas;
'T was thus Æneas knew the queen of love,
Majestic moving through the golden grove.

But ah! how cruel is my lot,
　　To doat on one so heavenly fair!
For in my humble state forgot,
　　Each charm but adds to my despair.
The tuneful swan thus faintly warbling lies,
Looks on his mate, and while he sings he dies.

TO THE BARON DE STONNE.

WITH AIKIN'S ESSAY ON SONG-WRITING.

TO Gallia's gay and gallant coast
　　Haste, little volume, speed thy flight;
And proudly there go make thy boast
How Britons love — how Britons write.

Say, Love can hold his torch as high
Beneath our heaven deformed with showers,
As in her pure and brilliant sky,
By vine-clad hills or myrtle bowers.

Ask if her damsels bloom more fair;
Ask if her swains can love as true;
And urge her poets' tuneful care
To sing their praise in numbers due.

EDWIN AND ETHELINDE.*

" ONE parting kiss, my Ethelinde!"
        Young Edwin faltering cried,
" I hear thy father's hasty tread,
    Nor longer must I bide.

" To-morrow eve, in yonder wood,
    Beneath the well-known tree,
Say, wilt thou meet thy own true love,
    Whose only joy 's in thee?"

She clasped the dear, beloved youth,
    And sighed, and dropt a tear;

* This first appeared in the "Gentleman's Magazine," then in
Aikin's "Collection of Songs "(ed. 1810). — ED.

"Whate'er betide, my only love,
    I 'll surely meet thee there."

They kiss, they part; a listening page,
    To malice ever bent,
O'erheard their talk, and to his lord
    Revealed their fond intent.

The baron's brow grew dark with frowns,
    And rage distained his cheek.
"Heavens! shall a vassal shepherd dare
    My daughter's love to seek!

"But know, rash boy, thy bold attempt
    Full sorely shalt thou rue;
Nor e'er again, ignoble maid,
    Shalt thou thy lover view."

The dews of evening fast did fall,
    And darkness spread apace,
When Ethelinde with beating breast
    Flew to the appointed place.

With eager eye she looks around,
    No Edwin there was seen;
"He was not wont to break his faith,
    What can his absence mean!"

Her heart beat thick at every noise,
  Each rustling through the wood;
And now she traversed quick the ground,
  And now she listening stood.

Enlivening hope and chilling fear
  By turns her bosom share,
And now she calls upon his name,
  Now weeps in sad despair.

Meantime the day's last glimmerings fled,
  And, blackening all the sky,
A hideous tempest dreadful rose,
  And thunders rolled on high.

Poor Ethelinde aghast, dismayed,
  Beholds with wild affright
The threatening sky, the lonely wood,
  And horrors of the night.

" Where art thou now, my Edwin dear!
  Thy friendly aid I want;
Ah me ! my boding heart foretells
  That aid thou canst not grant."

Thus racked with pangs, and beat with storms,
  Confused and lost she roves ;

Now looks to Heaven with earnest prayer,
   Now calls on him she loves.

At length a distant taper's ray
   Struck beaming on her sight;
Through brakes she guides her fainting steps
   Towards the welcome light.

An aged hermit peaceful dwelt
   In this sequestered wild;
Calm goodness sat upon his brow,
   His words were soft and mild.

He oped his hospitable door,
   And much admiring viewed
The tender virgin's graceful form,
   Dashed by the tempest rude.

" Welcome, fair maid, whoe'er thou art,
   To this warm, sheltered cell;
Here rest secure thy wearied feet,
   Here peace and safety dwell."

He saw the heart-wrung starting tear,
   And gently sought to know,
With kindest pity's soothing looks,
   The story of her woe.

Scarce had she told her mournful tale,
   When, struck with dread, they hear
Voices confused with dying groans
   The cell approaching near.

"Help, father! help!" they loudly cry,
   "A wretch here bleeds to death;
Some cordial balsam quickly give
   To stay his parting breath."

All deadly pale they lay him down,
   And gashed with many a wound;
When, woful sight! 't was Edwin's self
   Lay bleeding on the ground.

With frantic grief poor Ethelinde
   Beside his body falls;
"Lift up thine eyes, my Edwin dear,
   'T is Ethelinde that calls!"

That much-loved sound recalls his life,
   He lifts his closing eyes,
Then, feebly murmuring out her name,
   He gasps, he faints, he dies.

Stupid awhile, in dumb despair
   She gazed on Edwin dead;
Dim grew her eyes, her lips turned pale,
   And life's warm spirit fled.

3 *

TO A LADY.

WITH SOME PAINTED FLOWERS.

> . . . . tibi lilia plenis
> Ecce ferunt nymphæ calathis.
>
> VIRGIL.

FLOWERS to the fair: To you these flowers I bring,
And strive to greet you with an earlier spring.
Flowers sweet and gay and delicate like you,
Emblems of innocence and beauty too.
With flowers the Graces bind their yellow hair,
And flowery wreaths consenting lovers wear.
Flowers, the sole luxury which Nature knew,
In Eden's pure and guiltless garden grew.
To loftier forms are rougher tasks assigned;
The sheltering oak resists the stormy wind,
The tougher yew repels invading foes,
And the tall pine for future navies grows;
But this soft family, to cares unknown,
Were born for pleasure and delight alone:
Gay without toil, and lovely without art,
They spring to cheer the sense, and glad the heart.
Nor blush, my fair, to own you copy these;
Your best, your sweetest empire is — to please.

ODE TO SPRING.

S WEET daughter of a rough and stormy sire,
Hoar Winter's blooming child; delightful Spring!
  Whose unshorn locks with leaves
  And swelling buds are crowned;

From the green islands of eternal youth, —
Crowned with fresh blooms and ever-springing shade,—
  Turn, hither turn thy step,
  O thou, whose powerful voice

More sweet than softest touch of Doric reed,
Or Lydian flute, can soothe the madding wind, —
  And through the stormy deep
  Breathe thine own tender calm.

Thee, best beloved! the virgin train await
With songs and festal rites, and joy to rove
  Thy blooming wilds among,
  And vales and dewy lawns,

With untired feet; and cull thy earliest sweets
To weave fresh garlands for the glowing brow
  Of him, the favored youth
  That prompts their whispered sigh.

Unlock thy copious stores, — those tender showers
That drop their sweetness on the infant buds;
　　　　And silent dews that swell
　　　　The milky ear's green stem,

And feed the flowering osier's early shoots;
And call those winds which through the whispering boughs
　　　　With warm and pleasant breath
　　　　Salute the blowing flowers.

Now let me sit beneath the whitening thorn,
And mark thy spreading tints steal o'er the dale;
　　　　And watch with patient eye
　　　　Thy fair, unfolding charms.

O nymph, approach! while yet the temperate sun
With bashful forehead through the cool, moist air
　　　　Throws his young, maiden beams,
　　　　And with chaste kisses wooes

The earth's fair bosom; while the streaming veil
Of lucid clouds with kind and frequent shade
　　　　Protects thy modest blooms
　　　　From his severer blaze.

Sweet is thy reign, but short: — The red dog-star
Shall scorch thy tresses, and the mower's scythe
　　　　Thy greens, thy flowerets all,
　　　　Remorseless shall destroy.

Reluctant shall I bid thee then farewell ;
For O, not all that Autumn's lap contains,
    Nor Summer's ruddiest fruits,
    Can aught for thee atone,

Fair Spring ! whose simplest promise more delights
Than all their largest wealth, and through the heart
    Each joy and new-born hope
    With softest influence breathes.

EPITHALAMIUM.*

VIRGIN, brighter than the morning,
    Haste and finish thy adorning !
Hymen claims his promised day, —
Come from thy chamber, come away !

Roses strew, and myrtles bring,
Till you drain the wasted Spring ;
The altars are already drest,
The bower is fitted for its guest,
The scattered rose begins to fade, —
Come away, reluctant maid !

* Designed for the opening of a tragedy.

See what a war of blushes breaks
O'er the pure whiteness of her cheeks;
The shifting colors prove by turns
The torch of Love unsteady burns.
Pleading now, now lingering, fainting,
Her soft heart with fear is panting; —
Cling not to thy mother so,
Thy mother smiles, and bids thee go.

Mind not what thy maidens say;
Though they chide the cruel day,
Though they weep, and strive to hold thee
From his arms that would infold thee;
Kiss, and take a short farewell, —
They wish the chance to them befell.

Mighty Love demands his crown
Now for all his sufferings done;
For all Love's tears, for all his sighs,
Thyself must be the sacrifice.
Virgin, brighter than the day,
Haste from thy chamber, come away!

TO A DOG.

DEAR, faithful object of my tender care,
   Whom but my partial eyes none fancy fair;
May I unblamed display thy social mirth,
Thy modest virtues and domestic worth:
Thou silent, humble flatterer, yet sincere,
More swayed by love than interest or fear;
Solely to please, thy most ambitious view,
As lovers fond, and more than lovers true.
Who can resist those dumb, beseeching eyes,
Where genuine eloquence persuasive lies?
Those eyes, where language fails, display the heart
Beyond the pomp of phrase and pride of art.
Thou safe companion, and almost a friend,
Whose kind attachment but with life shall end, —
Blest were mankind if many a prouder name
Could boast thy grateful truth and spotless fame!

AN ADDRESS TO THE DEITY.

GOD of my life! and author of my days!
  Permit my feeble voice to lisp thy praise;
And trembling take upon a mortal tongue
That hallowed name to harps of seraphs sung.
Yet here the brightest seraphs could no more
Than veil their faces, tremble, and adore.
Worms, angels, men in every different sphere
Are equal all, — for all are nothing here.
All nature faints beneath the mighty name,
Which nature's works through all their parts proclaim.
I feel that name my inmost thoughts control,
And breathe an awful stillness through my soul;
As by a charm the waves of grief subside;
Impetuous Passion stops her headlong tide:
At thy felt presence all emotions cease,
And my hushed spirit finds a sudden peace,
Till every worldly thought within me dies,
And earth's gay pageants vanish from my eyes;
Till all my sense is lost in infinite,
And one vast object fills my aching sight.

But soon alas! this holy calm is broke;
My soul submits to wear her wonted yoke;

With shackled pinions strives to soar in vain,
And mingles with the dross of earth again.
But he, our gracious Master, kind as just,
Knowing our frame, remembers man is dust.
His spirit, ever brooding o'er our mind,
Sees the first wish to better hopes inclined;
Marks the young dawn of every virtuous aim,
And fans the smoking flax into a flame.
His ears are open to the softest cry,
His grace descends to meet the lifted eye;
He reads the language of a silent tear,
And sighs are incense from a heart sincere.
Such are the vows, the sacrifice I give;
Accept the vow, and bid the suppliant live:
From each terrestial bondage set me free;
Still every wish that centres not in thee;
Bid my fond hopes, my vain disquiets cease,
And point my path to everlasting peace.

If the soft hand of winning Pleasure leads
By living waters and through flowery meads,
When all is smiling, tranquil, and serene,
And vernal beauty paints the flattering scene,
O, teach me to elude each latent snare,
And whisper to my sliding heart — Beware!
With caution let me hear the siren's voice,
And doubtful, with a trembling heart, rejoice.

If friendless in a vale of tears I stray,
Where briers wound, and thorns perplex my way,
Still let my steady soul thy goodness see,
And with strong confidence lay hold on thee;
With equal eye my various lot receive,
Resigned to die, or resolute to live;
Prepared to kiss the sceptre or the rod,
While God is seen in all, and all in God.

I read his awful name, emblazoned high
With golden letters on the illumined sky;
Nor less the mystic characters I see
Wrought in each flower, inscribed on every tree;
In every leaf that trembles to the breeze
I hear the voice of God among the trees;
With thee in shady solitudes I walk,
With thee in busy, crowded cities talk,
In every creature own thy forming power,
In each event thy providence adore.
Thy hopes shall animate my drooping soul,
Thy precepts guide me, and thy fear control:
Thus shall I rest, unmoved by all alarms,
Secure within the temple of thine arms;
From anxious cares, from gloomy terrors free,
And feel myself omnipotent in thee.

Then when the last, the closing hour draws nigh,
And earth recedes before my swimming eye;

When trembling on the doubtful edge of fate
I stand and stretch my view to either state :
Teach me to quit this transitory scene
With decent triumph and a look serene ;
Teach me to fix my ardent hopes on high,
And, having lived to thee, in thee to die.

A SUMMER EVENING'S MEDITATION.

'TIS past ! The sultry tyrant of the south
   Has spent his short-lived rage; more grateful hours
Move silent on ; the skies no more repel
The dazzled sight, but with mild, maiden beams
Of tempered lustre court the cherished eye
To wander o'er their sphere ; where hung aloft
Dian's bright crescent, like a silver bow
New strung in heaven, lifts high its beamy horns
Impatient for the night, and seems to push
Her brother down the sky.   Fair Venus shines
Even in the eye of day ; with sweetest beam
Propitious shines, and shakes a trembling flood
Of softened radiance from her dewy locks.
The shadows spread apace ; while meekened Eve,
Her cheek yet warm with blushes, slow retires
Through the Hesperian gardens of the west,

And shuts the gates of day. 'T is now the hour
When Contemplation, from her sunless haunts,
The cool damp grotto, or the lonely depth
Of unpierced woods, where wrapt in solid shade
She mused away the gaudy hours of noon,
And fed on thoughts unripened by the sun,
Moves forward ; and with radiant finger points
To yon blue concave swelled by breath divine,
When, one by one, the living eyes of heaven
Awake, quick kindling o'er the face of ether
One boundless blaze ; ten thousand trembling fires,
And dancing lustres, where the unsteady eye,
Restless and dazzled, wanders unconfined
O'er all this field of glories ; spacious field,
And worthy of the Master : he whose hand
With hieroglyphics elder than the Nile
Inscribed the mystic tablet, hung on high
To public gaze, and said, " Adore, O man !
The finger of thy God."   From what pure wells
Of milky light, what soft o'erflowing urn,
Are all these lamps so fill'd ? these friendly lamps,
Forever streaming o'er the azure deep
To point our path, and light us to our home.
How soft they slide along their lucid spheres !
And silent as the foot of Time, fulfil
Their destined courses : Nature's self is hushed,
And, but a scattered leaf, which rustles through

The thick-wove foliage, not a sound is heard
To break the midnight air; though the raised ear,
Intensely listening, drinks in every breath.
How deep the silence, yet how loud the praise !
But are they silent all ? or is there not
A tongue in every star that talks with man,
And wooes him to be wise ? nor wooes in vain :
This dead of midnight is the noon of thought,
And Wisdom mounts her zenith with the stars.
At this still hour the self-collected soul
Turns inward, and behold a stranger there
Of high descent, and more than mortal rank ;
An embryo God ; a spark of fire divine
Which must burn on for ages, when the sun, —
Fair transitory creature of a day ! —
Has closed his golden eye, and wrapt in shades
Forgets his wonted journey through the east.

Ye citadels of light, and seats of gods !
Perhaps my future home, from whence the soul,
Revolving periods past, may oft look back,
With recollected tenderness, on all
The various busy scenes she left below,
Its deep-laid projects and its strange events,
As on some fond and doting tale that soothed
Her infant hours, — O be it lawful now
To tread the hallowed circle of your courts,

And with mute wonder and delighted awe
Approach your burning confines. Seized in thought,
On Fancy's wild and roving wing I sail
From the green borders of the peopled Earth,
And the pale Moon, her duteous fair attendant ;
From solitary Mars ; from the vast orb
Of Jupiter, whose huge gigantic bulk
Dances in ether like the lightest leaf ;
To the dim verge, the suburbs of the system,
Where cheerless Saturn 'midst his watery moons,
Girt with a lucid zone, in gloomy pomp,   •
Sits like an exiled monarch : fearless thence
I launch into the trackless deeps of space,
When, burning round, ten thousand suns appear,
Of elder beam, which ask no leave to shine
Of our terrestial star, nor borrow light
From the proud regent of our scanty day ;
Sons of the morning, first-born of creation,
And only less than him who marks their track,
And guides their fiery wheels.   Here must I stop,
Or is there aught beyond ?   What hand unseen
Impels me onward through the glowing orbs
Of habitable nature, far remote,
To the dread confines of eternal night,
To solitudes of vast unpeopled space,
The deserts of creation, wide and wild ;
Where embryo systems and unkindled suns

Sleep in the womb of chaos ? fancy droops,
And thought astonished stops her bold career.
But O thou mighty mind ! whose powerful word
Said, thus let all things be, and thus they were,
Where shall I seek thy presence ? how unblamed
Invoke thy dread perfection ?
Have the broad eyelids of the morn beheld thee ?
Or does the beamy shoulder of Orion
Support thy throne ? O, look with pity down
On erring, guilty man ! not in thy names
Of terror clad ; not with those thunders armed
That conscious Sinai felt, when fear appalled
The scattered tribes ; — thou hast a gentler voice,
That whispers comfort to the swelling heart,
Abashed, yet longing to behold her Maker.

But now my soul, unused to stretch her powers
In flight so daring, drops her weary wing,
And seeks again the known, accustomed spot,
Drest up with sun, and shade, and lawns, and streams,
A mansion fair, and spacious for its guest,
And full replete with wonders. Let me here,
Content and grateful, wait the appointed time,
And ripen for the skies : the hour will come
When all these splendors bursting on my sight
Shall stand unveiled, and to my ravished sense
Unlock the glories of the world unknown.

THE EPIPHANY.

DEEP in Sabea's fragrant groves retired,
 Long had the Eastern Sages studious dwelt,
By love sublime of sacred science fired :
 Long had they trained the inquiring youth,
With liberal hand the bread of wisdom dealt,
And sung in solemn verse mysterious truth.
The sacred characters they knew to trace
 Derived from Egypt's elder race ;
And all that Greece, with copious learning fraught,
Through different schools by various masters taught ;
 And all Arabia's glowing store
Of fabled truths and rich poetic lore :
Stars, plants, and gems, and talismans they knew,
And far was spread their fame and wide their praises
  grew.
The admiring East their praises spread ;
But with uncheated eyes themselves they viewed ;
Mourning they sat with dust upon their head,
 And oft in melancholy strain
  The fond complaint renewed,
How little yet they knew, how much was learned in vain.
 For human guilt and mortal woe
 Their sympathizing sorrows flow ;

Their hallowed prayers ascend in incense pure ;
　　They mourned the narrow bounds assigned
To the keen glances of the searching mind,
　　They mourned the ills they could not cure,
　　They mourned the doubts they could not clear,
　　They mourned that prophet yet, nor seer,
　　The great Eternal had made known,
Or reached the lowest step of that immortal throne.

　　And oft the starry cope of heaven beneath,
　　When day's tumultuous sounds had ceased to breathe,
　　　　With fixed feet, as rooted there,
　　Through the long night they drew the chilly air ;
　　　　While sliding o'er their head,
　　　　In solemn silence dread,
　　The ethereal orbs their shining course pursued,
　　In holy trance enwrapt the sages stood,
　　With folded arms laid on their reverend breast,
And to that Heaven they knew, their orisons addrest.

　　A Star appears ; they marked its kindling beam
　　O'er night's dark breast unusual splendors stream ;
　　　　The lesser lights that deck the sky,
　　In wondering silence softly gliding by,
　　　　At the fair stranger seemed to gaze,
Or veiled their trembling fires and half withdrew their
　　　　rays.

4

The blameless men the wonder saw,
And hailed the joyful sign with pious awe ;
 They knew 't was none of all the train
With which in shadowy forms and shapes uncouth,
  Monsters of earth and of the main,
   Remote from nature as from truth,
  Their learned pens the sky had figured o'er ;
 No star with such kind aspect shone before ;
 Nor e'er did wandering planet stoop so low
To guide benighted pilgrims through this vale of woe.

  The heavenly impulse they obey,
   The new-born light directs their way ;
 Through deserts never marked by human tread,
 And billowy waves of loose, unfaithful sand,
 O'er many an unknown hill and foreign strand,
  The silver clew unerring led,
 And peopled towns they pass, and glittering spires ;
No cloud could veil its light, no sun could quench its fires.

 Thus passed the venerable pilgrims on,
 Till Salem's stately towers before them shone,
 And soon their feet her hallowed pavements prest ;
  Not in her marble courts to rest, —
 From pomp and royal state aloof,
 Their shining guide its beams withdrew ;
 And points their path, and points their view,

To Bethlehem's rustic cots, to Mary's lowly roof.
 There the bright sentinel kept watch,
 While other stars arose and set ;
 For there, within its humble thatch,
 Weakness and power, and heaven and earth were met.
 Now, sages, now your search give o'er,
 Believe, fall prostrate, and adore !
Here spread your spicy gifts, your golden offerings here ;
 No more the fond complaint renew,
 Of human guilt and mortal woe,
 Of knowledge checked by doubt, and hope with fear ;
 What angels wished to see, ye view ;
 What angels wished to learn, ye know ; —
Peace is proclaimed to man, and heaven begun below.

TO MR. BARBAULD,

WITH A MAP OF THE LAND OF MATRIMONY.*

THE sailor, worn by toil and wet with storms,
 As in the wished-for port secure he rides,
With transport numbers o'er the dangers past
From threatening quicksands and from adverse tides.

---

* The map, published under this title, was a *jeu-d'esprit* of Mrs. Barbauld's. — ED.

Joyous he tells among his jocund mates
Of loud alarms that chased his broken sleep,
And blesses every kinder star that led
His favored vessel through the raging deep.

Thus canst thou, Rochemont, view this pictured chart,
And trace thy voyage to the promised shore ;
Thus does thy faithful bosom beat with joy,
To think the tempest past, the wanderings o'er ?

Canst thou recall the days when jealous Doubt,
When boding Fears thy anxious heart opprest,
When Hope, our star, shone faintly through the gloom,
And the pale check betrayed the tortured breast ?

And say ; — the land through Fancy's glass descried,
The bright Elysian fields her pencil drew, —
Has time the dear ideas realized ?
Or are her optics false, her tints untrue ?

O, say they are not ! — Though life's ceaseless cares,
Life's ceaseless toils, demand thy golden hours,
Tell her glad heart whose hand these lines confess,
That Peace resides in Hymen's happy bowers.

But soon the restless seaman longs to change
His bounded view and tempt the deeps again ;

Careless he breaks from weeping Susan's arms,
To fight with billows and to plough the main.

So shalt not thou, for no returning prow
E'er cut the ocean which thy bark has past;
For strong, relentless Fate has fixed her bars,
And I my destined captive hold too fast.

LOVE AND TIME.

TO MRS. MULSO.

ON Stella's brow as lately envious Time
His crooked lines with iron pencil traced,
That brow, erewhile like ivory tablets smooth,
With Love's high trophies hung, and victories graced,
Digging him little caves in every cell,
And every dimple, once where Love was wont to dwell;

He spied the God: and wondered still to spy,
Who higher held his torch in Time's despite;
Nor seemed to care for aught that he could do.
Then sternly thus he sought him thence to affright:
The sovereign boy, entrenched in a smile,
At his sour, crabbed speech sat mocking all the while.

" What dost thou here, fond boy ? Away, for shame!
Mine is this field, by conquest fairly won ;
Love cannot reap his joys where Time has ploughed,
Thou and thy light-winged troop should now be gone.
Go revel with fresh youth in scenes of folly,
Sage Thought I bring, and Care, and pale-eyed Melancholy.

" Thy streams are froze, that once so briskly ran,
Thy bough is shaken by the mellow year;
Boreas and Zephyr dwell not in one cave,
And swallows spread their wings when winter 's near;
See where Florella's cheeks soft bloom disclose,
Go seek the springing bud, and leave the faded rose."

Thus spake old Time, of Love the deadliest foe, —
Ah me, that gentle Love such foes should meet !
But nothing daunted he returned again,
Tempering with looks austere his native sweet;
And, " Fool !" said he, " to think I e'er shall fly
From that rich palace where my choicest treasures lie !

" Dost thou not see — or art thou blind with age —
How many Graces on her eyelids sit,
Linking those viewless chains that bind the soul,
And sharpening smooth discourse with pointed wit;
How many, where she moves, attendant wait,
The slow smooth step inspire, or high commanding gait ?

" Each one a several charm around her throws,
Some to attract, some powerful to repel,
Some mix the honeyed speech with winning smiles,
Or call wild Laughter from his antic cell,
Severer some, to strike with awful fear
Each rude licentious tongue that wounds the virtuous ear.

" Not one of them is of thy scythe in dread,
Or for thy cankered malice careth aught ;
Thy shaking fingers never can untwist
The magic cestus by their cunning wrought ;
And I, their knight, their bidding must obey,
For where the Graces are will Love forever stay.

" In my rich fields now boast the ravage done
Those lesser spoils, — her brow, her cheek, her hair,
All that the touches of decay can feel, —
Take these, she has enough to spare ;
I cannot thee dislodge, nor shalt thou me,
So thou and I, old Time, perforce must once agree.

"Nor is the boasted ravage all thine own,
Nor was the field by conquest fairly gained ;
For, leagued with Sickness, Life, and Nature's foe,
That fiend accurst thy savage wars maintained ;
His hand the furrows sunk where thou didst plough,
·He undermined the tree, where thou didst shake the
    bough.

"But both unite, for both I here defy;
Spoils ye have made, but have no triumphs won;
And though the daffodil more freshly blooms,
Spreading her gay leaves to the morning sun;
Yet never will I leave the faded rose,
Whilst the pale lovely flower such sweetness still be-
          stows."

This said, exulting Cupid clapped his wings.
The sullen power, who found his rage restrained,
And felt the strong control of higher charms,
Shaking his glass, vowed while the sands would run
For many a year the strife should be maintained;
But Jove decreed no force should Love destroy,
Nor Time should quell the might of that immortal boy.

TO MISS F. B.,

ON HER ASKING FOR MRS. B.'S "LOVE AND TIME."

OF Love and Time say what would Fanny know?
    That time is precious, and that love is sweet?
That both, the choicest blessings lent below,
With gay sixteen in envied union meet?

Time without Love is tasteless, dull, and cold,
Love out of Time will fond and doting prove;
To bright sixteen are all their treasures told,
Love suits the Time, and Time then favors Love.

No longer then of matron brows inquire
For sprightly Love, or swiftly wasting Time;
Look but at home, you have what you require, —
With gay sixteen they both are in their prime.

TO-MORROW.

SEE where the falling day
In silence steals away
Behind the western hills withdrawn:
Her fires are quenched, her beauty fled,
While blushes all her face o'erspread,
As conscious she had ill fulfilled
The promise of the dawn.

Another morning soon shall rise,
Another day salute our eyes,
As smiling and as fair as she,
And make as many promises:

4 *   F

But do not thou
The tale believe,
They 're sisters all,
And all deceive.

WRITTEN ON A MARBLE.

THE world 's something bigger,
    But just of this figure,
And speckled with mountains and seas;
Your heroes are overgrown school-boys
Who scuffle for empires and toys,
And kick the poor ball as they please.
Now Cæsar, now Pompey, gives law;
    And Pharsalia's plain,
    Though heaped with the slain,
    Was only a game at *taw*.

LINES

PLACED OVER A CHIMNEY-PIECE.

SURLY Winter, come not here;
    Bluster in thy proper sphere;
Howl along the naked plain,
There exert thy joyless reign;

Triumph o'er the withered flower,
The leafless shrub, the ruined bower,
But our cottage come not near ; —
Other springs inhabit here,
Other sunshine decks our board,
Than the niggard skies afford.
Gloomy Winter, hence ! away !
Love and Fancy scorn thy sway ;
Love and Joy, and friendly Mirth,
Shall bless this roof, these walls, this hearth ;
The rigor of the year control,
And thaw the winter in the soul.

WHAT DO THE FUTURES SPEAK OF ?

IN ANSWER TO A QUESTION IN THE GREEK GRAMMAR.

THEY speak of never-withering shades,
  And bowers of opening joy ;
They promise mines of fairy gold,
  And bliss without alloy.

They whisper strange, enchanting things
  Within Hope's greedy ears ;
And sure this tuneful voice exceeds
  The music of the spheres.

They speak of pleasure to the gay,
  And wisdom to the wise ;
And soothe the poet's beating heart
  With fame that never dies.

To virgins languishing in love
  They speak the minute nigh ;
And warm, consenting hearts they join,
  And paint the rapture high.

In every language, every tongue,
  The same kind things they say ;
In gentle slumbers speak by night,
  In waking dreams by day.

Cassandra's fate reversed is theirs ;
  She true, no faith could gain,
They every passing hour deceive,
  Yet are believed again.

AUTUMN.

A FRAGMENT.

FAREWELL the softer hours, spring's opening blush
And summer's deeper glow, the shepherd's pipe
Tuned to the murmurs of a weeping spring,
And song of birds, and gay, enamelled fields, —
Farewell! 'T is now the sickness of the year,
Not to be medicined by the skilful hand.
Pale suns arise that like weak kings behold
Their predecessor's empire moulder from them ;
While swift-increasing spreads the black domain
Of melancholy Night ; — no more content
With equal sway, her stretching shadows gain
On the bright morn, and cloud the evening sky.
Farewell the careless, lingering walk at eve,
Sweet with the breath of kine and new-spread hay ;
And slumber on a bank, where the lulled youth,
His head on flowers, delicious languor feels
Creep in the blood.   A different season now
Invites a different song.   The naked trees
Admit the tempest ; rent is Nature's robe ;
Fast, fast the blush of summer fades away
From her wan cheek, and scarce a flower remains
To deck her bosom ; winter follows close,

Pressing impatient on, and with rude breath
Fans her discolored tresses.   Yet not all
Of grace and beauty from the falling year
Is torn ungenial.   Still the taper fir
Lifts its green spire, and the dark holly edged
With gold, and many a strong perennial plant,
Yet cheer the waste: nor does yon knot of oaks
Resign its honors to the infant blast.
This is the time, and these the solemn walks,
When inspiration rushes o'er the soul
Sudden, as through the grove the rustling breeze.

ON A LADY'S WRITING.

HER even lines her steady temper show,
   Neat as her dress, and polished as her brow ;
Strong as her judgment, easy as her air ;
Correct though free, and regular though fair :
And the same graces o'er her pen preside,
That form her manners and her footsteps guide.

AN AUTUMNAL THOUGHT.

1795.

'TIS past ! we breathe ! assuaged at length
    The flames that drank our vital strength !
Smote with intolerable heat
No more our throbbing temples beat.
How clear the sky, how pure the air,
The heavens how bright, the earth how fair !
The bosom cool, the spirits light,
Active the day, and calm the night !

But O, the swiftly shortening day !
Low in the west the sinking ray !
With rapid pace advancing still
" The morning hoar, the evening chill,"
The falling leaf, the fading year,
And Winter ambushed in the rear !

Thus, when the fervid Passions cool,
And Judgment, late, begins to rule ;
When Reason mounts her throne serene,
And social Friendship gilds the scene ;
When man, of ripened powers possest,
Broods o'er the treasures of his breast ;
Exults, in conscious worth elate,

Lord of himself, — almost of fate;
Then, then declines the unsteady flame,
Disease, slow mining, saps the frame;
Cold damps of age around are shed
That chill the heart and cloud the head.
The failing spirits prompt no more,
The curtain drops, life's day is o'er.

ON THE DESERTED VILLAGE.

IN vain fair Auburn weeps her desert plains,
    She moves our envy who so well complains;
In vain has proud oppression laid her low,
So sweet a garland on her faded brow.
Now, Auburn, now absolve impartial fate,
Which if it made thee wretched, makes thee great;
So, unobserved, some humble plant may bloom,
Till crushed it fills the air with sweet perfume.
So had thy swains in ease and plenty slept,
Thy Poet had not sung, nor Britain wept.
Nor let Britannia mourn her drooping bay,
Unhonored genius, and her swift decay;
O Patron of the poor! it cannot be,
While one — one Poet yet remains like thee!
Nor can the Muse desert our favored isle,
Till thou desert the Muse and scorn her smile.

HYMN.

"Ye are the salt of the earth."

SALT of the earth, ye virtuous few,
   Who season human-kind ;
Light of the world, whose cheering ray
   Illumes the realms of mind :

Where Misery spreads her deepest shade,
   Your strong compassion glows ;
From your blest lips the balm distils,
   That softens mortal woes.

By dying-beds, in prison glooms,
   Your frequent steps are found ;
Angels of love ! you hover near,
   To bind the stranger's wound.

You wash with tears the bloody page
   Which human crimes deform ;
When vengeance threats, your prayers ascend
   And break the gathering storm.

As down the summer stream of vice
   The thoughtless many glide ;

Upward you steer your steady bark,
   And stem the rushing tide.

Where guilt her foul contagion breathes,
   And golden spoils allure ;
Unspotted still your garments shine, —
   .Your hands are ever pure.

Whene'er you touch the poet's lyre,
   A loftier strain is heard ;
Each ardent thought is yours alone,
   And every burning word.

Yours is the large, expansive thought,
   The high, heroic deed ;
Exile and chains to you are dear, —
   To you 't is sweet to bleed.

You lift on high the warning voice,
   When public ills prevail ;
Yours is the writing on the wall
   That turns the tyrant pale.

The dogs of hell your steps pursue,
   With scoff, and shame, and loss.
The hemlock bowl 't is yours to drain,
   To taste the bitter cross.

E'en yet the steaming scaffolds smoke
   By Seine's polluted stream ;
With your rich blood the fields are drenched
   Where Polish sabres gleam.

E'en now, through those accursed bars
   In vain we send our sighs ;
Where, deep in Olmutz' dungeon glooms,
   The patriot martyr lies.

Yet yours is all through History's rolls
   The kindling bosom feels ;
And at your tomb, with throbbing heart,
   The fond enthusiast kneels.

In every faith, through every clime,
   Your pilgrim steps we trace ;
And shrines are dressed, and temples rise,
   Each hallowed spot to grace ;

And pæans loud, in every tongue,
   And choral hymns resound ;
And lengthening honors hand your name
   To time's remotest bound.

Proceed ! your race of glory run,
   Your virtuous toils endure !
You come, commissioned from on high,
   And your reward is sure.

WASHING-DAY.

> " . . . . And their voice,
> Turning again towards childish treble, pipes
> And whistles in its sound."

THE Muses are turned gossips ; they have lost
   The buskined step, and clear, high-sounding phrase,
Language of gods.   Come, then, domestic Muse,
In slipshod measure loosely prattling on
Of farm or orchard, pleasant curds and cream,
Or drowning flies, or shoe lost in the mire
By little whimpering boy, with rueful face ;
Come, Muse, and sing the dreaded Washing-day.
Ye who beneath the yoke of wedlock bend,
With bowed soul, full well ye ken the day
Which week, smooth sliding after week, brings on
Too soon ; — for to that day nor peace belongs,
Nor comfort ; ere the first gray streak of dawn,
The red-armed washers come and chase repose.
Nor pleasant smile, nor quaint device of mirth,
E'er visited that day : the very cat,
From the wet kitchen's scared and reeking hearth,
Visits the parlor, — an unwonted guest.
The silent breakfast-meal is soon despatched ;
Uninterrupted, save by anxious looks

Cast at the lowering sky, if sky should lower.
From that last evil, O preserve us, heavens !
For should the skies pour down, adieu to all
Remains of quiet : then expect to hear
Of sad disasters, — dirt and gravel stains
Hard to efface, and loaded lines at once
Snapped short, — and linen-horse by dog thrown down,
And all the petty miseries of life.
Saints have been calm while stretched upon the rack,
And Guatimozin smiled on burning coals ;
But never yet did housewife notable
Greet with a smile a rainy washing-day.
But grant the welkin fair, require not thou
Who call'st thyself perchance the master there,
Or study swept, or nicely dusted coat,
Or usual 'tendance, — ask not, indiscreet,
Thy stockings mended, though the yawning rents
Gape wide as Erebus ; nor hope to find
Some snug recess impervious : shouldst thou try
The 'customed garden-walks, thine eyes shall rue
The budding fragrance of thy tender shrubs,
Myrtle or rose, all crushed beneath the weight
Of coarse checked apron, — with impatient hand
Twitched off when showers impend : or crossing lines
Shall mar thy musings, as the wet, cold sheet
Flaps in thy face abrupt.   Woe to the friend
Whose evil stars have urged him forth to claim

On such a day the hospitable rites!
Looks, blank at best, and stinted courtesy,
Shall he receive.   Vainly he feeds his hopes
With dinner of roast chicken, savory pie,
Or tart, or pudding : — pudding he nor tart
That day shall eat ; nor, though the husband try,
Mending what can't be helped, to kindle mirth
From cheer deficient, shall his consort's brow
Clear up propitious : the unlucky guest
In silence dines, and early slinks away.
I well remember, when a child, the awe
This day struck into me; for then the maids,
I scarce knew why, looked cross, and drove me from
          them :
Nor soft caress could I obtain ; nor hope
Usual indulgences ; jelly or creams,
Relic of costly suppers, and set by
For me their petted one, or buttered toast,
When butter was forbid ; or thrilling tale
Of ghost or witch or murder, — so I went
And sheltered me beside the parlor fire :
There my dear grandmother, eldest of forms,
Tended the little ones, and watched from harm,
Anxiously fond, though oft her spectacles
With elfin cunning hid, and oft the pins
Drawn from her ravelled stockings, might have soured
One less indulgent. —

At intervals my mother's voice was heard,
Urging despatch : briskly the work went on,
All hands employed to wash, to rinse, to wring,
To fold, and starch, and clap, and iron, and plait.
Then would I sit me down, and ponder much
Why washings were.   Sometimes through hollow bowl
Of pipe amused we blew, and sent aloft
The floating bubbles; little dreaming then
To see, Montgolfier, thy silken ball
Ride buoyant through the clouds, — so near approach
The sports of children and the toils of men.
Earth, air, and sky, and ocean hath its bubbles,
And verse is one of them, — this most of all.

TO MR. S. T. COLERIDGE.

1797.

MIDWAY the hill of science, after steep
And rugged paths that tire the unpractised feet,
A grove extends; in tangled mazes wrought,
And filled with strange enchantment : — dubious shapes
Flit through dim glades, and lure the eager foot
Of youthful ardor to eternal chase.
Dreams hang on every leaf : unearthly forms
Glide through the gloom ; and mystic visions swim

Before the cheated sense. Athwart the mists,
Far into vacant space, huge shadows stretch,
And seem realities; while things of life,
Obvious to sight and touch, all glowing round,
Fade to the hue of shadows. — Scruples here,
With filmy net, most like the autumnal webs
Of floating gossamer, arrest the foot
Of generous enterprise; and palsy hope
And fair ambition with the chilling touch
Of sickly hesitation and blank fear.
Nor seldom Indolence these lawns among
Fixes her turf-built seat; and wears the garb
Of deep philosophy, and museful sits,
In dreamy twilight of the vacant mind,
Soothed by the whispering shade; for soothing soft
The shades; and vistas lengthening into air,
With moonbeam rainbows tinted. Here each mind
Of finer mould, acute and delicate,
In its high progress to eternal truth
Rests for a space, in fairy bowers entranced;
And loves the softened light and tender gloom;
And, pampered with most unsubstantial food,
Looks down indignant on the grosser world,
And matter's cumbrous shapings. Youth beloved
Of Science, — of the Muse beloved, — not here,
Not in the maze of metaphysic lore,
Build thou thy place of resting! lightly tread

The dangerous ground, on noble aims intent;
And be this Circe of the studious cell
Enjoyed, but still subservient.   Active scenes
Shall soon with healthful spirit brace thy mind;
And fair exertion, for bright fame sustained;
For friends, for country, close each spleen-fed fog
That blots the wide creation. —
Now Heaven conduct thee with a parent's love!

PEACE AND SHEPHERD.

L OW in a deep, sequestered vale,
        Whence Alpine heights ascend,
A beauteous nymph, in pilgrim garb,
    Is seen her steps to bend.

Her olive garland drops with gore;
    Her scattered tresses torn,
Her bleeding breast, her bruised feet,
    Bespeak a maid forlorn.

" From bower, and hall, and palace driven,
    To these lone wilds I flee;
My name is Peace, — I love the cot;
    O Shepherd, shelter me!"

"O beauteous pilgrim, why dost thou
   From bower and palace flee ?
So soft thy voice, so sweet thy look,
   Sure all would shelter thee !'

" Like Noah's dove, no rest I find;
   The din of battle roars
Where once my steps I loved to print
   Along the myrtle shores :

"Forever in my frighted ears
   The savage war-whoop sounds ;
And like a panting hare I fly
   Before the opening hounds."

" Pilgrim, those spiry groves among,
   The mansions thou mayst see,
Where cloistered saints chant holy hymns, —
   Sure such would shelter thee !"

".Those roofs with trophied banners stream,
   There martial hymns resound ; —
And, Shephard, oft from crosiered hands
   This breast has felt a wound."

" Ah ! gentle pilgrim, glad would I
   Those tones forever hear !

With thee to share my scanty lot,
　　That lot to me were dear."

" But lo, along the vine-clad steep,
　　The gleam of armor shines ;
His scattered flock, his straw-roofed hut,
　　The helpless swain resigns.

" And now the smouldering flames aspire';
　　Their lurid light I see ;
I hear the human wolves approach,
　　I *cannot* shelter thee."

WEST END FAIR.

D AME Charity one day was tired
　　With nursing of her children three, —
　　　　So might you be
If you had nursed and nursed so long
　　　　A little squalling throng ; —
So she, like any earthly lady,
Resolved for once she 'd have a play-day.

" I cannot always go about
To hospitals and prisons trudging,

Or fag from morn to night
  Teaching to spell and write
    A barefoot rout,
Swept from the streets by poor Lancaster,
  My sub-master.

"That Howard ran me out of breath,
And Thornton and a hundred more
    Will be my death ;
The air is sweet, the month is gay,
"And I," said she, "must have a holiday."

So said, she doffed her robes of brown,
In which she commonly is seen, —
    Like French Béguine, —
And sent for ornaments to town :
And Taste in Flavia's form stood by,
Pencilled her eyebrows, curled her hair,
Disposed each ornament with care,
And hung her round with trinkets rare, —
She scarcely, looking in the glass,
    Knew her own face.

So forth she sallied blithe and gay,
And met Dame Fashion by the way ;
And many a kind and friendly greeting
  Passed on their meeting ;

Nor let the fact your wonder move,
    Abroad and on a gala-day
Fashion and she are hand and glove.

    So on they walked together,
    Bright was the weather;
Dame Charity was frank and warm,
But being rather apt to tire
    She leant on Fashion's arm.

And now away for West End Fair,
Where whiskey, chariot, coach, and chair
    Are all in requisition.
    In neat attire the Graces
Behind the counters take their places,
    And humbly do petition
To dress the booths with flowers and sweets,
    As fine as any May-day,
Where Charity with Fashion meets,
    And keeps her play-day.

.

DIRGE.

WRITTEN NOVEMBER, 1808.

PURE spirit! O, where art thou now?
　　O, whisper to my soul!
O, let some soothing thought of thee
　　This bitter grief control!

'T is not for thee the tears I shed,
　　Thy sufferings now are o'er;
The sea is calm, the tempest past,
　　On that eternal shore.

No more the storms that wrecked thy peace
　　Shall tear that gentle breast;
Nor Summer's rage, nor Winter's cold,
　　Thy poor, poor frame molest.

Thy peace is sealed, thy rest is sure,
　　My sorrows are to come;
Awhile I weep and linger here,
　　Then follow to the tomb.

And is the awful veil withdrawn,
　　That shrouds from mortal eyes,

In deep, impenetrable gloom,
    The secrets of the skies ?

O, in some dream of visioned bliss,
    Some trance of rapture, show
Where, on the bosom of thy God,
    Thou rest'st from human woe !

Hence may thy pure devotion's flame
    On me, on me descend ;
To me thy strong aspiring hopes,
    Thy faith, thy fervors, lend.

Let these my lonely path illume,
    And teach my weakened mind
To welcome all that 's left of good,
    To all that 's lost resigned.

Farewell ! with honor, peace, and love,
    Be thy dear memory blest ;
Thou hast no tears for me to shed
    When I too am at rest.

THE UNKNOWN GOD.

TO learned Athens, led by fame,
  As once the man of Tarsus came,
    With pity and surprise,
'Midst idol altars as he stood,
O'er sculptured marble, brass, and wood
    He rolled his awful eyes.

But one, apart, his notice caught,
That seemed with higher meaning fraught,
    Graved on the wounded stone;
Nor form nor name was there expressed;
Deep reverence filled the musing breast,
    Perusing, "To the God Unknown."

Age after age has rolled away,
Altars and thrones have felt decay,
    Sages and saints have risen;
And, like a giant roused from sleep,
Man has explored the pathless deep,
    And lightnings snatched from heaven.

And many a shrine in dust is laid,
Where kneeling nations homage paid,

By rock, or fount, or grove :
Ephesian Dian sees no more
    Her workmen fuse the silver ore,
        Nor Capitolian Jove.

E'en Salem's hallowed courts have ceased
With solemn pomps her tribes to feast,
    No more the victim bleeds ;
To censers filled with rare perfumes,
And vestments from Egyptian looms, —
    A purer rite succeeds.

Yet still where'er presumptuous man
His Maker's essence strives to scan,
    And lifts his feeble hands,
Though saint and sage their powers unite
To fathom that abyss of light,
    Ah ! still *that altar* stands.

ODE TO REMORSE.

DREAD offspring of the holy light within,
    Offspring of Conscience and of Sin,
Stern as thine awful sire, and fraught with woe
From bitter springs thy mother taught to flow, —

Remorse!   To man alone 't is given
Of all on earth, or all in heaven,
To wretched man thy bitter cup to drain,
Feel thy awakening stings, and taste thy wholesome pain.

'Midst Eden's blissful bowers,
And amaranthine flowers,
Thy birth portentous dimmed the orient day,
What time our hapless sire,
O'ercome by fond desire,
The high command presumed to disobey;
Then didst thou rear thy snaky crest,
And raise thy scorpion lash to tear the guilty breast :
And never, since that fatal hour,
May man, of woman born, expect to escape thy power.

Thy goading stings the branded Cain
'Cross the untrodden desert drove,
Ere from his cradling home and native plain
Domestic man had learnt to rove.
By gloomy shade or lonely flood
Of vast primeval solitude,
Thy step his hurried steps pursued,
Thy voice awoke his conscious fears,
Forever sounding in his ears
A father's curse, a brother's blood ;
Till life was misery too great to bear,
And torturing thought was lost in sullen, dumb despair.

The king who sat on Judah's throne,

By guilty love to murder wrought,

Was taught thy searching power to own,

When, sent of Heaven, the seer his royal presence sought.

As, wrapt in artful phrase, with sorrow feigned

He told of helpless, meek distress,

And wrongs that sought from power redress,

The pity-moving tale his ear obtained,

And bade his better feelings wake ;

Then, sudden as the trodden snake

On the scared traveller darts his fangs,

The prophet's bold rebuke aroused thy keenest pangs.

And O that look, that soft, upbraiding look !

A thousand cutting, tender things it spoke, —

The sword so lately drawn was not so keen, —

Which, as the injured Master turned him round

In the strange, solemn scene,

And the shrill clarion gave the appointed sound,

Pierced sudden through the reins

Awakening all thy pains,

And drew a silent shower of bitter tears

Down Peter's blushing cheek, late pale with coward fears.

Cruel Remorse ! where Youth and Pleasure sport,

And thoughtless Folly keeps her court, —

Crouching 'midst rosy bowers thou lurk'st unseen ;

Slumbering the festal hours away,

While Youth disports in that enchanting scene ;
  Till on some fated day
Thou with a tiger-spring dost leap upon thy prey,
And tear his helpless breast, o'erwhelmed with wild
  dismay.

  Mark that poor wretch with clasped hands !
  Pale o'er his parents' grave he stands, —
  The grave by his ingratitude prepared ;
  Ah, then, where'er he rests his head,
  On roses pillowed or the softest down,
  Though festal wreaths his temples crown,
  He well might envy Guatimozin's bed,
  With·burning coals and sulphur spread,
And with less agony his torturing hour have shared.

For Thou art by to point the keen reproach ;
Thou draw'st the curtains of his nightly couch,
Bring'st back the reverend face with tears bedewed,
  That o'er his follies yearned ;
  The warnings oft in vain renewed,
  The looks of anguish and of love,
  His stubborn breast that failed to move,
When in the scorner's chair he sat, and wholesome
  counsel spurned.

  Lives there a man whose laboring breast
  Is with some dark and guilty secret prest,

Who hides within its inmost fold
Strange crimes to mortal ear untold ?
In vain to sad Chartreuse he flies,
'Midst savage rocks and cloisters dim and drear,
And there to shun thee tries :
In vain untold his crime to mortal ear,
Silence and whispered sounds but make thy voice more
clear.

Lo where the cowled monk with frantic rage
Lifts high the sounding scourge, his bleeding shoulders
smites !
Penance and fasts his anxious thoughts engage,
Weary his days and joyless are his nights,
His naked feet the flinty pavement tears,
His knee at every shrine the marble wears ; —
Why does he lift the cruel scourge ?
The restless pilgrimage why urge ?
'T is all to quell thy fiercer rage,
'T is all to soothe thy deep despair,
He courts the body's pangs, for thine he cannot bear.

See, o'er the bleeding corse of her he loved
The jealous murderer bends unmoved,
Trembling with rage, his livid lips express
His frantic passion's wild and rash excess.
O God, she 's innocent ! transfixt he stands,

Pierced through with shafts from thine avenging hands;
   Down his pale cheek no tear will flow,
Nor can he shun, nor can he bear, his woe.

'T was phantoms summoned by thy power,
Round Richard's couch at midnight hour,
That scared the tyrant from unblest repose;
With frantic haste, " To horse ! to horse !" he cries,
While on his crowned brow cold sweat-drops rise,
   And fancied spears his spear oppose;
But not the swiftest steed can bear away
From thy firm grasp thine agonizing prey.

Thou wast the fiend, and thou alone,
   That stood'st by Beaufort's mitred head,
With upright hair and visage ghastly pale:
   Thy terrors shook his dying bed,
Past crimes and blood his sinking heart assail,
His hands are clasped, — hark to that hollow groan !
See how his glazed, dim eyeballs wildly roll,
'T is not dissolving nature's pains; that pang is of the
      soul.

   Where guilty souls are doomed to dwell,
   'T is thou that mak'st their fiercest hell,
The vulture thou that on their liver feeds,
As rise to view their past unhallowed deeds:

With thee condemned to stay
Till time has rolled away
Long æras of uncounted years,
And every stain is washed in soft, repentant tears.

Servant of God, — but unbeloved, — proceed,
For thou must live and ply thy scorpion-scourge ;
Thy sharp upbraidings urge
Against the unrighteous deed,
Till thine accursed mother shall expire,
And a new world spring forth from renovating fire.

O ! when the glare of day is fled,
And calm, beneath the evening-star,
Reflection leans her pensive head,
And calls the passions to her solemn bar ;
Reviews the censure rash, the hasty word,
The purposed act too long deferred,
Of time the wasted treasures lent,
And fair occasions lost and golden hours misspent ;

When anxious Memory numbers o'er
Each offered prize we failed to seize ;
Or friends laid low, whom now no more
Our fondest love can serve or please,
And thou, dread power, bring'st back in terror drest
The irrevocable past, to sting the careless breast ; —

O ! in that hour be mine to know,
While fast the silent sorrows flow,
And wisdom cherishes the wholesome pain,
No heavier guilt, no deeper stain,
Than tears of meek contrition may atone,
Shed at the mercy-seat of Heaven's eternal throne.

ETERNITY.

. . . . The year has run
Its round of seasons, has fulfilled its course,
Absolved its destined period, and is borne,
Silent and swift, to that devouring gulf,
Their womb the grave, where seasons, months, and years,
Revolving periods of uncounted time,
All merge and are forgotten. — Thou alone,
In thy deep bosom burying all the past,
Still art ; and still from thine exhaustless store
New periods spring, Eternity. — Thy name,
Or glad, or fearful, we pronounce, as thoughts
Wandering in darkness shape thee.   Thou strange being,
Which art and must be, yet which contradict'st
All sense, all reasoning, — thou who never wast
Less than thyself, and who art still thyself
Entire, though the deep draught which Time has taken

Equals thy present store. — No line can reach
To thy unfathomed depths. The reasoning sage
Who can dissect a sunbeam, count the stars,
And measure distant worlds, is here a child,
And, humbled, drops his calculating pen.
And wrecks of empire and of world are borne
Like atoms on its bosom. Still *thou art*,
And he who does inhabit thee. .

EIGHTEEN HUNDRED AND ELEVEN.

STILL the loud death-drum, thundering from afar,
 O'er the vext nations pours the storm of war:
To the stern call still Britain leads her ear,
Feeds the fierce strife, the alternate hope and fear;
Bravely, though vainly, dares to strive with Fate,
And seeks by turns to prop each sinking state.
Colossal power with overwhelming force
Bears down each foot of Freedom in its course;
Prostrate she lies beneath the despot's sway,
While the hushed nations curse him — and obey.

Bounteous in vain, with frantic man at strife,
Glad Nature pours the means — the joys of life;

In vain with orange-blossoms scents the gale,
The hills with olives clothes, with corn the vale;
Man calls to Famine, nor invokes in vain,
Disease and Rapine follow in her train;
The tramp of marching hosts disturbs the plough,
The sword, not sickle, reaps the harvest now,
And where the soldier gleans the scant supply,
The helpless peasant but retires to die;
No laws his hut from licensed outrage shield,
And war's least horror is the ensanguined field.

Fruitful in vain, the matron counts with pride
The blooming youths that grace her honored side;
No son returns to press her widowed hand,
Her fallen blossoms strew a foreign strand.
— Fruitful in vain, she boasts her virgin race,
Whom cultured arts adorn and gentlest grace;
Defrauded of its homage, Beauty mourns
And the rose withers on its virgin thorns.
Frequent, some stream obscure, some uncouth name,
By deeds of blood is lifted into fame;
Oft o'er the daily page some soft one bends
To learn the fate of husband, brothers, friends,
Or the spread map with anxious eye explores,
Its dotted boundaries and pencilled shores,
Asks where the spot that wrecked her bliss is found,
And learns its name but to detest the sound.

And think'st thou, Britain, still to sit at ease,
An island queen amidst thy subject seas,
While the vext billows, in their distant roar,
But soothe thy slumbers, and but kiss thy shore?
To sport in wars, while danger keeps aloof,
Thy grassy turf unbruised by hostile hoof?
So sing thy flatterers; — but, Britain, know,
Thou who hast shared the guilt must share the woe.
Nor distant is the hour; low murmurs spread,
And whispered fears, creating what they dread;
Ruin, as with an earthquake shock, is here,
There, the heart-witherings of unuttered fear,
And that sad death, whence most affection bleeds,
Which sickness, only of the soul, precedes.
Thy baseless wealth dissolves in air away,
Like mists that melt before the morning ray:
No more on crowded mart or busy street
Friends, meeting friends, with cheerful hurry greet;
Sad, on the ground thy princely merchants bend
Their altered looks, and evil days portend,
And fold their arms, and watch with anxious breast
The tempest blackening in the distant West.

Yes, thou must droop; thy Midas dream is o'er;
The golden tide of Commerce leaves thy shore,
Leaves thee to prove the alternate ills that haunt
Enfeebling Luxury and ghastly Want;

Leaves thee, perhaps, to visit distant lands,
And deal the gifts of Heaven with equal hands.

Yet, O my Country, name beloved, revered,
By every tie that binds the soul endeared,
Whose image to my infant senses came
Mixt with Religion's light and Freedom's holy flame!
If prayers may not avert, if 't is thy fate
To rank amongst the names that once were great,
Not like the dim, cold Crescent shalt thou fade,
Thy debt to Science and the Muse unpaid;
Thine are the laws surrounding states revere,
Thine the full harvest of the mental year,
Thine the bright stars in Glory's sky that shine,
And arts that make it life to live are thine.
If westward streams the light that leaves thy shores,
Still from thy lamp the streaming radiance pours.
Wide spreads thy race from Ganges to the pole,
O'er half the Western world thy accents roll:
Nations beyond the Apalachian hills
Thy hand has planted and thy spirit fills:
Soon as their gradual progress shall impart
The finer sense of morals and of art,
Thy stores of knowledge the new states shall know,
And think thy thoughts, and with thy fancy glow;
Thy Lockes, thy Paleys, shall instruct their youth,
Thy leading star direct their search for truth;

Beneath the spreading platane's tent-like shade, ·
Or by Missouri's rushing waters laid,
" Old Father Thames " shall be the poet's theme,
Of Hagley's woods the enamored virgin dream,
And Milton's tones the raptured ear enthrall,
Mixt with the roaring of Niagara's fall;
In Thomson's glass the ingenuous youth shall learn
A fairer face of Nature to discern ;
Nor of the bards that swept the British lyre
Shall fade one laurel, or one note expire.
Then, loved Joanna, to admiring eyes
Thy storied groups in scenic pomp shall rise ;
Their high-souled strains and Shakespeare's noble rage
Shall with alternate passion shake the stage.
Some youthful Basil from thy moral lay
With stricter hand his fond desires shall sway ;
Some Ethwald, as the fleeting shadows pass,
Start at his likeness in the mystic glass ;
The tragic Muse resume her just control,
With pity and with terror purge the soul,
While wide o'er transatlantic realms thy name
Shall live in light and gather all its fame.

Where wanders Fancy down the lapse of years,
Shedding o'er imaged woes untimely tears ?
Fond, moody power ! as hopes — as fears prevail,
She longs, or dreads, to lift the awful veil,

On visions of delight now loves to dwell,
Now hears the shriek of woe or Freedom's knell:
Perhaps, she says, long ages past away,
And set in western wave our closing day,
Night, Gothic night, again may shade the plains
Where Power is seated, and where Science reigns;
England, the seat of arts, be only known
By the gray ruin and the mouldering stone;
That Time may tear the garland from her brow,
And Europe sit in dust, as Asia now.

Yet then the ingenuous youth whom Fancy fires
With pictured glories of illustrious sires,
With duteous zeal their pilgrimage shall take
From the Blue Mountains, or Ontario's lake,
With fond, adoring steps to press the sod
By statesmen, sages, poets, heroes, trod;
On Isis' banks to draw inspiring air,
From Runnymede to send the patriot's prayer;
In pensive thought, where Cam's slow waters wind,
To meet those shades that ruled the realms of mind;
In silent halls to sculptured marbles bow,
And hang fresh wreaths round Newton's awful brow.
Oft shall they seek some peasant's homely shed,
Who toils, unconscious of the mighty dead,
To ask where Avon's winding waters stray,
And thence a knot of wild flowers bear away;

Anxious inquire where Clarkson, friend of man,
Or all-accomplished Jones his race began;
If of the modest mansion aught remains
Where Heaven and Nature prompted Cowper's strains;
Where Roscoe, to whose patriot breast belong
The Roman virtue and the Tuscan song,
Led Ceres to the black and barren moor
Where Ceres never gained a wreath before: *
With curious search their pilgrim steps shall rove
By many a ruined tower and proud alcove,
Shall listen for those strains that soothed of yore
Thy rock, stern Skiddaw, and thy fall, Lodore;
Feast with Dun Edin's classic brow their sight,
And "visit Melross by the pale moonlight."

But who their mingled feelings shall pursue
When London's faded glories rise to view?
The mighty city, which by every road,
In floods of people poured itself abroad
Ungirt by walls, irregularly great,
No jealous drawbridge, and no closing gate;
Whose merchants (such the state which commerce brings)
Sent forth their mandates to dependent kings;
Streets, where the turbaned Moslem, bearded Jew,
And woolly Afric, met the brown Hindu;

---

* The historian of the age of Leo brought into cultivation the extensive tract of Chatmoss. — Ed.

Where through each vein spontaneous plenty flowed,
Where Wealth enjoyed, and Charity bestowed.
Pensive and thoughtful shall the wanderers greet
Each splendid square, and still, untrodden street ;
Or of some crumbling turret, mined by time,
The broken stairs with perilous step shall climb,
Thence stretch their view the wide horizon round,
By scattered hamlets trace its ancient bound,
And, choked no more with fleets, fair Thames survey
Through reeds and sedge pursue his idle way.

With throbbing bosoms shall the wanderers tread
The hallowed mansions of the silent dead.
Shall enter the long aisle and vaulted dome
Where Genius and where Valor find a home ;
Awe-struck 'midst chill sepulchral marbles breathe,
Where all above is still, as all beneath ;
Bend at each antique shrine, and frequent turn
To clasp with fond delight some sculptured urn,
The ponderous mass of Johnson's form to greet,
Or breathe the prayer at Howard's sainted feet.

Perhaps some Briton, in whose musing mind
Those ages live which Time has cast behind,
To every spot shall lead his wondering guests
On whose known site the beam of glory rests ;
Here Chatham's eloquence in thunder broke,

Here Fox persuaded, or here Garrick spoke;
Shall boast how Nelson, fame and death in view,
To wonted victory led his ardent crew,
In England's name enforced, with loftiest tone,[*]
Their duty, — and too well fulfilled his own:
How gallant Moore,[†] as ebbing life dissolved,
But hoped his country had his fame absolved.
Or call up sages whose capacious mind
Left in its course a track of light behind;
Point where mute crowds on Davy's lips reposed,
And Nature's coyest secrets were disclosed;
Join with their Franklin, Priestley's injured name,
Whom, then, each continent shall proudly claim.

Oft shall the strangers turn their eager feet
The rich remains of ancient art to greet,
The pictured walls with critic eye explore,
And Reynolds be what Raphael was before.
On spoils from every clime their eyes shall gaze,
Egyptian granites and the Etruscan vase;
And when 'midst fallen London they survey
The stone where Alexander's ashes lay,
Shall own with humbled pride the lesson just

---

[*] Every reader will recollect the sublime telegraphic despatch, "England expects every man to do his duty."

[†] "I hope England will be satisfied," were the last words of General Moore. — ED.

By Time's slow finger written in the dust.
There walks a Spirit o'er the peopled earth,
Secret his progress is, unknown his birth;
Moody and viewless as the changing wind,
No force arrests his foot, no chains can bind;
Where'er he turns, the human brute awakes,
And, roused to better life, his sordid hut forsakes:
He thinks, he reasons, glows with purer fires,
Feels finer wants, and burns with new desires:
Obedient Nature follows where he leads;
The steaming marsh is changed to fruitful meads;
The beasts retire from man's asserted reign,
And prove his kingdom was not given in vain.
Then from its bed is drawn the ponderous ore,
Then Commerce pours her gifts on every shore,
Then Babel's towers and terraced gardens rise,
And pointed obelisks invade the skies;
The prince commands, in Tyrian purple drest,
And Egypt's virgins weave the linen vest.
Then spans the graceful arch the roaring tide,
And stricter bounds the cultured fields divide.
Then kindles Fancy, then expands the heart,
Then blow the flowers of Genius and of Art;
Saints, heroes, sages, who the land adorn,
Seems rather to descend than to be born;
While History, 'midst the rolls consigned to fame,
With pen of adamant inscribes their name.

The Genius now forsakes the favored shore,
And hates, capricious, what he loved before;
Then empires fall to dust, then arts decay,
And wasted realms enfeebled despots sway;
Even Nature's changed; without his fostering smile
Ophir no gold, no plenty yields the Nile;
The thirsty sand absorbs the useless rill,
And spotted plagues from putrid fens distil.
In desert solitudes then Tadmor sleeps,
Stern Marius then o'er fallen Carthage weeps;
Then with enthusiast love the pilgrim roves
To seek his footsteps in forsaken groves,
Explores the fractured arch, the ruined tower,
Those limbs disjointed of gigantic power;
Still at each step he dreads the adder's sting,
The Arab's javelin, or the tiger's spring;
With doubtful caution treads the echoing ground,
And asks where Troy or Babylon is found.

And now the vagrant Power no more detains
The vale of Tempe or Ausonian plains;
Northward he throws the animating ray,
O'er Celtic nations bursts the mental day;
And, as some playful child the mirror turns,
Now here, now there, the moving lustre burns;
Now o'er his changeful fancy more prevail
Batavia's dykes than Arno's purple vale;

And stinted suns, and rivers bound with frost,
Than Enna's plains or Baia's viny coast;
Venice the Adriatic weds in vain,
And Death sits brooding o'er Campania's plain;
O'er Baltic shores and through Hercynian groves,
Stirring the soul, the mighty impulse moves;
Art plies his tools, and Commerce spreads her sail,
And wealth is wafted in each shifting gale.
The sons of Odin tread on Persian looms,
And Odin's daughters breathe distilled perfumes;
Loud minstrel bards, in Gothic halls, rehearse
The Runic rhyme, and "build the lofty verse":
The Muse, whose liquid notes were wont to swell
To the soft breathings of the Æolian shell,
Submits, reluctant, to the harsher tone,
And scarce believes the altered voice her own.
And now, where Cæsar saw with proud disdain
The wattled hut and skin of azure stain,
Corinthian columns rear their graceful forms,
And light verandas brave the wintry storms,
While British tongues the fading fame prolong
Of Tully's eloquence and Maro's song.
Where once Bonduca whirled the scythed car,
And the fierce matrons raised the shriek of war,
Light forms beneath transparent muslins float,
And tutored voices swell the artful note.
Light-leaved acacias and the shady plane

And spreading cedar grace the woodland reign ;
While crystal walls the tenderer plants confine,
The fragrant orange and the nectared pine ;
The Syrian grape there hangs her rich festoons,
Nor asks for purer air or brighter noons :
Science and Art urge on the useful toil,
New mould a climate and create the soil,
Subdue the rigor of the Northern Bear,
O'er polar climes shed aromatic air,
On yielding Nature urge their new demands,
And ask not gifts, but tribute, at her hands.

London exults : — on London Art bestows
Her summer ices and her winter rose ;
Gems of the East her mural crown adorn,
And Plenty at her feet pours forth her horn.
While even the exiles her just laws disclaim,
People a continent, and build a name :
August she sits, and with extended hands
Holds forth the book of life to distant lands.

But fairest flowers expand but to decay ;
The worm is in thy core, thy glories pass away ;
Arts, arms, and wealth destroy the fruits they bring ;
Commerce, like beauty, knows no second spring.
Crime walks thy streets, Fraud earns her unblest bread,
O'er want and woe thy gorgeous robe is spread,

And angel charities in vain oppose :
With grandeur's growth the mass of misery grows.
For, see, — to other climes the Genius soars,
He turns from Europe's desolated shores ;
And lo ! even now, 'midst mountains wrapt in storm,
On Andes' heights he shrouds his awful form ;
On Chimborazo's summits treads sublime,
Measuring in lofty thought the march of Time ;
Sudden he calls : " 'T is now the hour ! " he cries,
Spreads his broad hand, and bids the nation rise.
La Plata hears amidst her torrents' roar ;
Potosi hears it, as she digs the ore :
Ardent, the Genius fans the noble strife,
And pours through feeble souls a higher life,
Shouts to the mingled tribes from sea to sea,
And swears — Thy world, Columbus, shall be free.

LIFE.

" Animula, vagula, blandula."

LIFE ! I know not what thou art,
But know that thou and I must part ;
And when, or how, or where we met
I own to me 's a secret yet.
But this I know, when thou art fled,

Where'er they lay these limbs, this head,
No clod so valueless shall be,
As all that then remains of me.
O whither, whither dost thou fly,
Where bend unseen thy trackless course,
    And in this strange divorce,
Ah, tell where I must seek this compound I ?

To the vast ocean of empyreal flame,
    From whence thy essence came,
    Dost thou thy flight pursue, when freed
    From matter's base encumbering weed ?
        Or dost thou, hid from sight,
        Wait, like some spell-bound knight,
Through blank, oblivious years the appointed hours
To break thy trance and reassume thy power ?
Yet canst thou, without thought or feeling be ?
O say what art thou, when no more thou 'rt thee ?

Life ! we 've been long together
Through pleasant and through cloudy weather ;
    'T is hard to part when friends are dear, —
    Perhaps 't will cost a sigh, a tear ;
    Then steal away, give little warning,
        Choose thine own time ;
Say not Good Night, — but in some brighter clime
    Bid me Good Morning.

ON THE KING'S ILLNESS.

1811.

REST, rest, afflicted spirit, quickly pass
     Thine hour of bitter suffering! Rest awaits thee,
There, where, the load of weary life laid down,
The peasant and the king repose together:
There peaceful sleep, thy quiet grave bedewed
With tears of those who loved thee. Not for thee,
In the dark chambers of the nether world,
Shall spectre kings rise from their burning thrones
And point the vacant seat, and scoffing say,
Art thou become like us? — O not for thee!
For thou hadst human feelings, and hast lived
A man with men; and kindly charities,
Even such as warm the cottage hearth, were thine.
And therefore falls the tear from eyes not used
To gaze on kings with admiration fond.
And thou hast knelt at meek Religion's shrine
With no mock homage, and hast owned her rights
Sacred in every breast; and therefore rise,
Affectionate, for thee, the orisons
And mingled prayers, alike from vaulted domes
Whence the loud organ peals, and raftered roofs
Of humbler worship. — Still remembering this,

A nation's pity and a nation's love
Linger beside thy couch, in this the day
Of thy sad visitation, veiling faults
Of erring judgment, and not will perverse.
Yet, O that thou hadst closed the wounds of war!
That had been praise to suit a higher strain.

Farewell the years rolled down the gulf of time!
Thy name has chronicled a long, bright page
Of England's story; and perhaps the babe
Who opens, as thou closest thine, his eyes
On this eventful world, when aged grown,
Musing on times gone by, shall sigh, and say,
Shaking his thin gray hairs, whitened with grief,
Our father's days were happy. Fare thee well!
My thread of life has even run with thine
For many a lustre; and thy closing day
I contemplate, not mindless of my own,
Nor to its call reluctant.

A THOUGHT ON DEATH:

NOVEMBER, 1814.

WHEN life as opening buds is sweet,
And golden hopes the fancy greet,
And Youth prepares his joys to meet, —
Alas, how hard it is to die!

When just is seized some valued prize,
And duties press, and tender ties
Forbid the soul from earth to rise, —
How awful then it is to die!

When, one by one, those ties are torn,
And friend from friend is snatched forlorn,
And man is left alone to mourn, —
Ah, then how easy 't is to die!

When faith is firm and conscience clear,
And words of peace the spirit cheer,
And visioned glories half appear, —
'T is joy, 't is triumph, then, to die.

When trembling limbs refuse their weight,
And films, slow gathering, dim the sight,
And clouds obscure the mental light, —
'T is nature's precious boon to die.

STANZAS;

IN THE MANNER OF SPENSER.

SO long estranged from every Muse's lyre,
   And grovelling in the tangled net of Care;
What powerful breath shall kindle up that fire
Smothered with damps of most unkindly air?
Ah, how is quenched the lamp that burnt so fair!
Come, sweet seducers, late too far away,
Once more to my deserted cell repair,
Your rebel courts again your gentle sway;—
Come, soothe the winter's night, and charm the sum-
      mer's day.

Come, dear companions of my youthful hour,
Fill my fond breast with your majestic themes;
Meet me again on hill, by stream, or bower,
And bathe my fancy in the bliss of dreams.
Vain wish! no more the star of Fancy gleams;
They with becoming scorn reject thy prayer;
Nor will they haunt thy bower, or bless thy streams,
No more to thy deserted cell repair:—
"Go, court the world," they cry, "thou art not worth
      our care."

Bustle and hurry, noise and thrall they hate,
And plodding Method with her leaden rule;

And all that swells the unwieldy pomp of state ;
And all that binds to earth the golden fool ;
And creeping Labor with his patient tool ;
Free like the birds they wander unconfined,
Nor dip their wings in Lucre's muddy pool ;
Business they hate, in crowded nooks enshrined,
That spins her dirty web, and clouds the ethereal mind.

Ah, why should man, in hard, unsocial strife,
And withering care whose vigils never cease,
Fretting away this little thread of life,
Of his sad birthright reap such large increase !
Why should he toil for aught but bread and peace ?
Why rear to heaven his day-built pyramids ?
Nor from his tasks himself, poor slave ! release ;
With anxious thought, which wholesome rest forbids,
Drying the balm of sleep from Sorrow's swollen lids.

Despising cheap delights, he loves to scoop
His marble palace from the rock's hard breast,
And in close dungeon walls himself to coop,
On golden couches wooing pale unrest ;
With foreign looms his stately halls are drest,
And grim-wrought tapestry clothes the darkened room ;
While in the flowery vale Peace builds her nest,
Amidst the purple heath or yellow broom,
Or where 'midst rustling corn the nodding poppies
        bloom.

THE FIRST FIRE.

OCTOBER 1st, 1815.

HA, old acquaintance! many a month has past
    Since last I viewed thy ruddy face; and I,
Shame on me! had meantime wellnigh forgot
That such a friend existed. Welcome now!—
When summer suns ride high, and tepid airs
Dissolve in pleasing languor, then indeed
We think thee needless, and in wanton pride
Mock at thy grim attire and sooty jaws,
And breath sulphureous, generating spleen,—
As Frenchmen say; Frenchmen, who never knew
The sober comforts of a good coal fire.

  —Let me imbibe thy warmth, and spread **myself**
Before thy shrine adoring:—magnet thou
Of strong attraction, daily gathering in
Friends, brethren, kinsmen, variously dispersed,
All the dear charities of social life,
To thy close circle. Here a man might stand,
And say, This is my world! who would not bleed
Rather than see thy violated hearth
Prest by a hostile foot? The winds sing shrill;
Heap on the fuel! Not the costly board,
Nor sparkling glass, nor wit, nor music, cheer
Without thy aid. If thrifty thou dispense

Thy gladdening influence, in the chill saloon
The silent shrug declares the unpleased guest.

— How grateful to belated traveller,
Homeward returning, to behold the blaze
From cottage window, rendering visible
The cheerful scene within! There sits the sire,
Whose wicker chair, in sunniest nook enshrined,
His age's privilege, — a privilege for which
Age gladly yields up all precedence else
In gay and bustling scenes, — supports his limbs.
Cherished by thee, he feels the grateful warmth
Creep through his feeble frame and thaw the ice
Of fourscore years, and thoughts of youth arise.

— Nor less the young ones press within, to see
Thy face delighted, and with husk of nuts,
Or crackling holly, or the gummy pine,
Feed thy immortal hunger: cheaply pleased,
They gaze delighted while the leaping flames
Dart like an adder's tongue upon their prey;
Or touch with lighted reed thy wreaths of smoke;
Or listen, while the matron sage remarks
Thy bright blue scorching flame and aspect clear,
Denoting frosty skies. Thus pass the hours,
While Winter spends without his idle rage.

— Companion of the solitary man,
From gayer scenes withheld! With thee he sits,

Converses, moralizes ; musing asks
How many æras of uncounted time
Have rolled away since thy black, unctuous food
Was green with vegetative life, and what
This planet then : or marks, in sprightlier mood,
Thy flickering smiles play round the illumined room,
And fancies gay discourse, life, motion, mirth,
And half forgets he is a lonely creature.

— Nor less the bashful poet loves to sit
Snug, at the midnight hour, with only thee
Of his lone musings conscious. Oft he writes,
And blots, and writes again ; and oft, by fits,
Gazes intent with eyes of vacancy
On thy bright face ; and still at intervals,
Dreading the critic's scorn, to thee commits,
Sole confidant and safe, his fancies crude.

— O wretched he, with bolts and massy bars
In narrow cell immured, whose green, damp walls,
That weep unwholesome dews, have never felt
Thy purifying influence ! Sad he sits
Day after day till in his youthful limbs
Life stagnates, and the hue of hope is fled
From his wan cheek. And scarce less wretched he, —
When wintry winds blow loud and frosts bite keen, —
The dweller of the clay-built tenement,

Poverty-struck, who, heartless, strives to raise
From sullen turf, or stick plucked from the hedge,
The short-lived blaze ; while chill around him' spreads
The dreary fen, and Ague, sallow-faced,
Stares through the broken pane ; — assist him, ye
On whose warm roofs the sun of plenty shines,
And feel a glow beyond material fire !

THE CATERPILLAR.

NO, helpless thing, I cannot harm thee now ;
   Depart in peace, thy little life is safe,
For I have scanned thy form with curious eye,
Noted the silver line that streaks thy back,
The azure and the orange that divide
Thy velvet sides ; thee, houseless wanderer,
My garment has enfolded, and my arm
Felt the light pressure of thy hairy feet ;
Thou hast curled around my finger ; from its tip,
Precipitous descent ! with stretched-out neck,
Bending thy head in airy vacancy
This way and that, inquiring, thou hast seemed
To ask protection ; now, I cannot kill thee.
Yet I have sworn perdition to thy race,
And recent from the slaughter am I come

Of tribes and embryo nations: I have sought
With sharpened eye and persecuting zeal,
Where, folded in their silken webs they lay
Thriving and happy; swept them from the tree
And crushed whole families beneath my foot; .
Or, sudden, poured on their devoted heads
The vials of destruction. This I've done,
Nor felt the touch of pity: but when thou —
A single wretch, escaped the general doom,
Making me feel and clearly recognize
Thine individual existence, life,
And fellowship of sense with all that breathes —
Present'st thyself before me, I relent,
And cannot hurt thy weakness. So the storm
Of horrid war, o'erwhelming cities, fields,
And peaceful villages, rolls dreadful on:
The victor shouts triumphant; he enjoys
The roar of cannon and the clang of arms,
And urges, by no soft relentings stopped,
The work of death and carnage. Yet should one,
A single sufferer from the field escaped,
Panting and pale, and bleeding at his feet,
Lift his imploring eyes, — the hero weeps;
He is grown human, and capricious Pity,
Which would not stir for thousands, melts for one
With sympathy spontaneous: — 'T is not Virtue,
Yet 't is the weakness of a virtuous mind.

ON THE DEATH OF THE PRINCESS CHARLOTTE.

YES, Britain mourns, as with electric touch,
    For youth, for love, for happiness destroyed;
Her universal population melts
In grief spontaneous, and hard hearts are moved,
And rough, unpolished natures learn to feel
For those they envied, levelled in the dust
By Fate's impartial stroke; and pulpits sound
With vanity and woe to earthly goods,
And urge and dry the tear. — Yet one there is
Who 'midst this general burst of grief remains
In strange tranquillity; whom not the stir
And long-drawn murmurs of the gathering crowd,
That by his very windows trail the pomp
Of hearse and blazoned arms, and long array
Of sad funereal rites, nor the loud groans
And deep-felt anguish of a husband's heart,
Can move to mingle with this flood one tear:
In careless apathy, perhaps in mirth,
He wears the day.   Yet is he near in blood,
The very stem on which this blossom grew,
And at his knees she fondled in the charm
And grace spontaneous which alone belongs
To untaught infancy.   Yet, O forbear!

Nor deem him hard of heart ; for awful, struck
By Heaven's severest visitation, sad,
Like a scathed oak amidst the forest trees,
Lonely he stands ; — leaves, bud, and shoot, and fall ;
He holds no sympathy with living nature
Or time's incessant change. Then in this hour,
While pensive thought is busy with the woes
And restless change of poor humanity,
Think then, O think of him, and breathe one prayer,
From the full tide of sorrows spare one tear
For him who does not weep !

THE WAKE OF THE KING OF SPAIN.*

ARRAYED in robes of regal state,
But stiff and cold, the monarch sate ;
In gorgeous vests, his chair beside,
Stood prince and peer, the nation's pride ;
And paladin and high-born dame
Their place amid the circle claim ;
And wands of office lifted high,
And arms and blazoned heraldry, —

* The kings of Spain for nine days after death are placed sitting in
robes of state with their attendants around them, and solemnly summoned by the proper officers to their meals and their amusements as
if living. — ED.

All mute like marble statues stand,
Nor raise the eye, nor move the hand :
No voice, no sound to stir the air,
The silence of the grave is there.

The portal opens, — hark, a voice !
" Come forth, O king ! O king, rejoice !
The bowl is filled, the feast is spread,
Come forth, O king !"   The king is dead.
The bowl, the feast, he tastes no more,
The feast of life for him is o'er.

Again the sounding portals shake,
And speaks again the voice that spake :
" The sun is high, the sun is warm,
Forth to the field the gallants swarm,
The foaming bit the courser champs,
His hoof the turf impatient stamps ;
Light on their steeds the hunters spring ;
The sun is high, — Come forth, O king !"

Along these melancholy walls
In vain the voice of pleasure calls :
The horse may neigh, and bay the hound, —
He hears no more ; his sleep is sound.
Retire ; — once more the portals close ;
Leave, leave him to his dread repose.

THE BABY-HOUSE.

DEAR Agatha, I give you joy,
And much admire your pretty toy,
A mansion in itself complete,
And fitted to give guests a treat;
With couch and table, chest and chair,
The bed or supper to prepare;
We almost wish to change ourselves
To fairy forms of tripping elves,
To press the velvet couch, and eat
From tiny cups the sugared meat.
I much suspect that many a sprite
Inhabits it at dead of night;
That, as they dance, the listening ear
The pat of fairy feet might hear;
That, just as you have said your prayers,
They hurry-scurry down the stairs:
And you 'll do well to try to find
Tester or ring they 've left behind.

But think not, Agatha, you own
That toy, a Baby-house, alone;
For many a sumptuous one is found
To press an ampler space of ground.

The broad-based Pyramid that stands
Casting its shade in distant lands,
Which asked some mighty nation's toil
With mountain-weight to press the soil,
And there has raised its head sublime
Through æras of uncounted time,—
Its use, if asked, 't is only said,
A Baby-house to lodge the dead.
Nor less beneath more genial skies
The domes of pomp and folly rise,
Whose sun through diamond windows streams,
While gems and gold reflect his beams;
Where tapestry clothès the storied wall,
And fountains spout and waters fall;
The peasant faints beneath his load,
Nor tastes the grain his hands have sowed,
While scarce a nation's wealth avails
To raise thy Baby-house, Versailles.
And Baby-houses oft appear
On British ground, of prince or peer;
Awhile their stately heads they raise,
The admiring traveller stops to gaze;
He looks again — where are they now?
Gone to the hammer or the plough:
Then trees, the pride of ages, fall,
And naked stands the pictured wall;
And treasured coins from distant lands

Must feel the touch of sordid hands ;
And gems, of classic stores the boast,
Fall to the cry of — Who bids most ?
Then do not, Agatha, repine
That cheaper Baby-house is thine.

RIDDLE.

THIS creature, though extremely thin,
  In shape is almost square ;
Has many heads, on which ne'er grew
  One single lock of hair.

Yet several of their tribe there are
  Whose case you must bewail,
Of whom in truth it may be said
  They 've neither head nor tail.

In purer times, ere vice prevailed,
  They met with due regard,
The wholesome counsels that they gave
  With reverence were heard.

To marriages and funerals
  Their presence added grace,

And though the king himself were by,
    They took the highest place.

Their business is to stir up men
    A constant watch to keep;
Instead of which, — O sad reverse! —
    They make them fall asleep.

Not so in former times it was,
    Howe'er it came to pass;
Though they their company ne'er left
    Till empty was the glass.

The moderns can't be charged with this,
    But may their foes defy,
To prove such practices on them,
    Though they 're extremely dry.

LINES

WRITTEN IN A YOUNG LADY'S ALBUM OF DIFFERENT COLORED PAPER.

LIFE'S checkered scenes these varied leaves display,
   Pure white, and tenderest blush, and fading gray;—
The rosy tints of morning will not last,
And youth's gay, flattering season soon is past.
O may thy gentle breast no changes know,
But such as from time's smoothest currents flow;
No cares, but those whose mellowing influence steals
Mild o'er the expansive heart that thinks and feels!
And with affection tried, experienced truth
Tint the white page of innocence and youth!
May Love for thee exert his fullest power,
And gild with sunniest gleams life's latest hour!
And friendship, health, and pleasure long be thine,
When cold the heart that pens this feeble line!

TO A FRIEND.

MAY never more of pensive melancholy
    Within thy heart, beneath thy roof appear,
Than just to break the charm of idle folly,
And prompt for others' woes the melting tear;
No more than just that tender gloom to spread
Where thy beloved Muses wont to stray,
To lift the thought from this low earthy bed,
Or bid hope languish from a brighter day;
And deeper sink within thy feeling heart
Love's pleasing wounds, or friendship's polished dart!

DEJECTION.

WHEN sickness clouds the languid eye,
    And seeds of sharp diseases fly
  Swift through the vital frame;
Rich drugs are torn from earth and sea,
And balsam drops from every tree,
  To quench the parching flame.

But oh! what opiate can assuage
The throbbing breast's tumultuous rage,
  Which mingling passions tear!
What art the wounds of grief can bind,
Or soothe the sick, impatient mind
  Beneath corroding care!

Not all the potent herbs that grow
On purple heath or mountain's brow
  Can banished peace restore;
In vain the spring of tears to dry,
For purer air or softer sky
  We quit our native shore.

Friendship, the richest balm that flows,
Was meant to heal our sharpest woes,
  But runs not always pure;
And Love — has sorrows of his own,
Which not an herb beneath the moon
  Is found of power to cure.

Soft Pity, mild, dejected maid,
With tenderest hand applies her aid
  To dry the frequent tear;
But her own griefs, of finer kind,
Too deeply wound the feeling mind
  With anguish more severe.

TO MR. BOWRING,

ON HIS POETICAL TRANSLATIONS FROM VARIOUS LANGUAGES.

BOWRING, the music of thy polished strains
Through every tongue its equal power sustains.
To the rude Russ it gives a softer touch,
It melts to mellower sounds the homely Dutch,
With bloodless conquest from each land it bears
The precious spoil of long-recorded years ;
And, pleased its holy ardor to diffuse,
With thy own spirit sanctifies the Muse.
Thus, in some window's deep recesses laid,
The soft Æolian harp its power displayed,
From the shrill east-wind and the stormy north
It drew soft airs and gentle breathings forth ;
Subdued to harmony each passing sound,
Waked with unusual notes the echoes round,
With happy magic softened, as it past,
The hollow whistling of the keenest blast ;
And each rude gust that swept the changing sky
Dissolved to strains of liquid harmony.

FRAGMENT.

A S the poor school-boy, when the slow-paced months
Have brought vacation times, and one by one
His playmates and companions all are fled
Or ready ; and to him — to him alone
No summons comes ; he left of all the train
Paces with lingering steps the vacant halls,
No longer murmuring with the Muse's song,
And silent playground scattered wide around
With implements of sports, resounding once
With cheerful shouts ; and hears no sound of wheels
To bear him to his father's bosom home ;
For, conscious though he be of time misspent,
And heedless faults and much amiss, yet hopes
A father's pardon and a father's smile
Blessing his glad return . . . . Thus I
Look to the hour when I shall follow those
That are at rest before me.

OCTOGENARY REFLECTIONS.

SAY, ye who through this round of eighty years
Have proved its joys and sorrows, hopes and fears,
Say, what is life, ye veterans, who have trod,
Step following steps, its flowery, thorny road ?
Enough of good to kindle strong desire,
Enough of ill to damp the rising fire,
Enough of love and fancy, joy and hope,
To fan desire and give the passions scope.
Enough of disappointment, sorrow, pain,
To seal the wise man's sentence, All is vain, —
And quench the wish to live those years again.
Science for man unlocks her various store,
And gives enough to urge the wish for more ;
Systems and suns lie open to his gaze,
Nature invites his love, and God his praise ;
Yet doubt and ignorance with his feelings sport,
And Jacob's ladder is some rounds too short.
Yet still to humble hope enough is given
Of light from reason's lamp and light from Heaven,
To teach us what to follow, what to shun,
To bow the head and say, " Thy will be done ! "

THE DEATH OF THE VIRTUOUS.

SWEET is the scene when Virtue dies !
　　When sinks a righteous soul to rest,
How mildly beam the closing eyes,
　　How gently heaves the expiring breast :

So fades a summer cloud away ;
　　So sinks the gale when storms are o'er ;
So gently shuts the eye of day ;
　　So dies a wave along the shore.

Triumphant smiles the victor's brow,
　　Fanned by some angel's purple wing ;
Where is, O Grave ! thy victory now ?
　　And where, insidious Death ! thy sting ?

Farewell, conflicting joys and fears,
　　Where light and shade alternate dwell ;
How bright the unchanging morn appears !
　　Farewell, inconstant world, farewell !

Its duty done, — as sinks the clay,
　　Light from its load the spirit flies ;
While heaven and earth combine to say,
　　"Sweet is the scene when Virtue dies !"

HYMNS.

JEHOVAH reigns: let every nation hear,
  And at his footstool bow with holy fear;
  Let heaven's high arches echo with his name,
  And the wide-peopled earth his praise proclaim;
Then send it down to hell's deep glooms resounding,
Through all her caves in dreadful murmurs sounding.

  He rules with wide and absolute command
  O'er the broad ocean and the steadfast land:
  Jehovah reigns, unbounded and alone,
  And all creation hangs beneath his throne:
He reigns alone; let no inferior nature
Usurp or share the throne of the Creator.

  He saw the struggling beams of infant light
  Shoot through the massy gloom of ancient night;
  His spirit hushed the elemental strife,
  And brooded o'er the kindling seeds of life;
Seasons and months began their long procession,
And measured o'er the year in bright succession.

  The joyful sun sprung up the ethereal way,
  Strong as a giant, as a bridegroom gay;

And the pale moon diffused her shadowy light,
  Superior o'er the dusky brow of night;
Ten thousand glittering lamps the skies adorning,
Numerous as dew-drops from the womb of morning.

  Earth's blooming face with rising flowers he drest,
  And spread a verdant mantle o'er her breast;
  Then from the hollow of his hand he pours
  The circling water round her winding shores,
The new-born world in their cool arms embracing
And with soft murmurs still her banks caressing.

  At length she rose complete in finished pride,
  All fair and spotless as a virgin bride;
  Fresh with untarnished lustre as she stood,
  Her Maker blessed his work, and called it good;
The morning-stars with joyful acclamation
Exulting sang, and hailed the new creation.

  Yet this fair world, the creature of a day,
  Though built by God's right hand, must pass away;
  And long oblivion creep o'er mortal things,
  The fate of empires, and the pride of kings;
External night shall veil their proudest story,
And drop the curtain o'er all human glory.

  The sun himself, with weary clouds opprest,
  Shall in his silent, dark pavilion rest;

7 *

His golden urn shall broke and useless lie,
Amidst the common ruins of the sky;
The stars rush headlong in the wild commotion,
And bathe their glittering foreheads in the ocean.

But fixed, O God! forever stands thy throne;
Jehovah reigns, a universe alone;
The eternal fire that feeds each vital flame,
Collected or diffused, is still the same.
He dwells within his own unfathomed essence,
And fills all space with his unbounded presence.

But, oh! our highest notes the theme debase,
And silence is our least injurious praise:
Cease, cease your songs, the daring flight control,
Revere him in the stillness of the soul;
With silent duty meekly bend before him,
And deep within your inmost hearts adore him.

HYMN II.

PRAISE to God, immortal praise,*
For the love that crowns our days;

* "Although the fig-tree shall not blossom, neither shall fruit be in
the vines; the labor of the olive shall fail, and the fields shall yield
no meat; the flocks shall be cut off from the fold, and there shall be
no herd in the stalls: yet I will rejoice in the Lord, I will joy in
the God of my salvation."—HABAKKUK iii. 17, 18.

Bounteous source of every joy,
Let thy praise our tongues employ;

For the blessings of the field,
For the stores the gardens yield,
For the vine's exalted juice,
For the generous olive's use;

Flocks that whiten all the plain,
Yellow sheaves of ripened grain;
Clouds that drop their fattening dews,
Suns that temperate warmth diffuse:

All that Spring with bounteous hand
Scatters o'er the smiling land:
All that liberal Autumn pours
From her rich, o'erflowing stores:

These to thee, my God, we owe;
Source whence all our blessings flow;
And for these my soul shall raise
Grateful vows and solemn praise.

Yet should rising whirlwinds tear
From its stem the ripening ear;
Should the fig-tree's blasted shoot
Drop her green, untimely fruit;

Should the vine put forth no more,
Nor the olive yield her store ;
Though the sickening flocks should fall,
And the herds desert the stall ;

Should thine altered hand restrain
The early and the latter rain ;
Blast each opening bud of joy,
And the rising year destroy :

Yet to thee my soul should raise
Grateful vows and solemn praise ;
And, when every blessing 's flown,
Love thee — for thyself alone.

HYMN III.

FOR EASTER SUNDAY.

AGAIN the Lord of life and light
  Awakes the kindling ray ;
Unseals the eyelids of the morn,
  And pours increasing day.

O what a night was that, which wrapt
  The heathen world in gloom !

O what a sun which broke this day,
  Triumphant from the tomb !

This day be grateful homage paid,
  And loud hosannas sung ;
Let gladness dwell in every heart,
  And praise on every tongue.

Ten thousand differing lips shall join
  To hail this welcome morn,
Which scatters blessings from its wings
  To nations yet unborn.

Jesus, the friend of human-kind,
  With strong compassion moved,
Descended like a pitying God,
  To save the souls he loved.

The powers of darkness leagued in vain
  To bind his soul in death ;
He shook their kingdom, when he fell,
  With his expiring breath.

Not long the toils of hell could keep
  The hope of Judah's line ;
Corruption never could take hold
  On aught so much divine.

And now his conquering chariot-wheels
 Ascend the lofty skies;
While broke beneath his powerful cross
 Death's iron sceptre lies.

Exalted high at God's right hand,
 The Lord of all below,
Through him is pardoning love dispensed,
 And boundless blessings flow.

And still for erring, guilty man
 A brother's pity flows;
And still his bleeding heart is touched
 With memory of our woes.

To thee, my Saviour and my King,
 Glad homage let me give;
And stand prepared like thee to die,
 With thee that I may live.

HYMN IV.

BEHOLD, where, breathing love divine,
 Our dying Master stands!
His weeping followers, gathering round,
 Receive his last commands.

From that mild teacher's parting lips
   What tender accents fell!
The gentle precept which he gave
   Became its author well.

"Blest is the man whose softening heart
   Feels all another's pain ;
To whom the supplicating eye
   Was never raised in vain.

"Whose breast expands with generous warmth
   A stranger's woes to feel;
And bleeds in pity o'er the wound
   He wants the power to heal.

"He spreads his kind, supporting arms
   To every child of grief;
His secret bounty largely flows,
   And brings unasked relief.

"To gentle offices of love
   His feet are never slow ;
He views through mercy's melting eye
   A brother in a foe.

"Peace from the bosom of his God,
   My peace to him I give ;

And when he kneels before the throne,
  His trembling soul shall live.

"To him protection shall be shown,
  And mercy from above
Descend on those who thus fulfil
  The perfect law of love."

HYMN V.

AWAKE, my soul! lift up thine eyes,
See where thy foes against thee rise,
In long array, a numerous host;
Awake, my soul! or thou art lost.

Here giant Danger threatening stands
Mustering his pale, terrific bands;
There Pleasure's silken banners spread,
And willing souls are captive led.

See where rebellious passions rage,
And fierce desires and lusts engage;
The meanest foe of all the train
Has thousands and ten thousands slain.

Thou tread'st upon enchanted ground,
Perils and snares beset thee round;

Beware of all, guard every part,
But most, the traitor in thy heart.

"Come then, my soul, now learn to wield
The weight of thine immortal shield";
Put on the armor from above,
Of heavenly truth and heavenly love.

The terror and the charm repel,
And powers of earth, and powers of hell;
The Man of Calvary triumphed here;
Why should his faithful followers fear?

HYMN VI.

PIOUS FRIENDSHIP.

How blest the sacred tie that binds,
In union sweet, according minds!
How swift the heavenly course they run,
Whose hearts, whose faith, whose hopes, are one!

To each the soul of each how dear!
What jealous love, what holy fear!
How doth the generous flame within
Refine from earth and cleanse from sin!

K

Their streaming tears together flow
For human guilt and mortal woe;
Their ardent prayers together rise
Like mingled flames in sacrifice.

Together both they seek the place
Where God reveals his awful face:
How high, how strong, their raptures swell,
There 's none but kindred souls can tell.

Nor shall the glowing flame expire
When nature droops her sickening fire;
Then shall they meet in realms above,
A heaven of joy — because of love.

HYMN VII.

" Come unto me, all that are weary and heavy laden, and I will give you rest."

COME, said Jesus' sacred voice,
Come and make my paths your choice;
I will guide you to your home;
Weary pilgrim, hither come!

Thou who houseless, sole, forlorn,
Long hast borne the proud world's scorn,

Long hast roamed the barren waste, —
Weary pilgrim, hither haste !

Ye, who tossed on beds of pain,
Seek for ease, but seek in vain,
Ye, whose swollen and sleepless eyes
Watch to see the morning rise ;

Ye, by fiercer anguish torn,
In remorse for guilt who mourn ;
Here repose your heavy care,
A wounded spirit who can bear !

Sinner, come ! for here is found
Balm that flows for every wound ;
Peace that ever shall endure,
Rest eternal, sacred, sure.

HYMN VIII.

"The world is not their friend, nor the world's law."

Lo, where a crowd of pilgrims toil
  Yon craggy steeps among !
Strange their attire, and strange their mien,
  As wild they press along.

Their eyes with bitter streaming tears
  Now bend towards the ground,

Now rapt, to heaven their looks they raise;
   And bursts of song resound.

And hark! a voice from midst the throng
   Cries, "Stranger, wouldst thou know
Our name, our race, our destined home,
   Our cause of joy or woe, —

"Our country is Emanuel's land,
   We seek that promised soil;
The songs of Zion cheer our hearts,
   While strangers here we toil.

"Oft do our eyes with joy o'erflow,
   And oft are bathed in tears;
Yet naught but heaven our hopes can raise,
   And naught but sin our fears.

"The flowers that spring along the road
   We scarcely stoop to pluck;
We walk o'er beds of shining ore,
   Nor waste one wistful look;

"We tread the path our Master trod,
   We bear the cross he bore;
And every thorn that wounds our feet
   His temples pierced before:

" Our powers arc oft dissolved away
    In ecstasies of love ;
And while our bodies wander here,
    Our souls are fixed above ;

" We purge our mortal dross away,
    Refining as we run ;
But while we die to earth and sense,
    Our heaven is begun."

HYMN IX.

Joy to the followers of the Lord !
Thus saith the sure, the eternal word.
Not of earth the joy it brings,
Tempered in celestial springs :

'T is the joy of pardoned sin,
When conscience cries, 'T is well within ;
'T is the joy that fills the breast
When the passions sink to rest :

'T is a joy that, seated deep,
Leaves not when we sigh and weep ;
It spreads itself in virtuous deeds,
With sorrow sighs, in pity bleeds.

Stern and awful are its tones
When the patriot martyr groans,
And the throbbing pulse beats high
To rapture, mixed with agony.

A tenderer, softer form it wears,
Dissolved in love, dissolved in tears,
When humble souls a Saviour greet,
And sinners clasp the mercy-seat.

'T is joy e'en here! a budding flower,
Struggling with snows and storm and shower,
And waits the moment to expand,
Transplanted to its native land.

HYMN X.

A PASTORAL HYMN.

"GENTLE pilgrim, tell me why
Dost thou fold thine arms and sigh,
And wistful cast thine eyes around, —
Whither, pilgrim, art thou bound?"
"The road to Zion's gates I seek;
If thou canst inform me, speak."
"Keep yon right-hand path with care,

Though crags obstruct, and brambles tear;
You just discern a narrow track, —
Enter there and turn not back."
" Say where that pleasant pathway leads,
Winding down yon flowery meads ?
Songs and dance the way beguiles,
Every face is drest in smiles."
" Shun with care that flowery way ;
'T will lead thee, pilgrim, far astray."
" Guide or counsel do I need ? "
" Pilgrim, he who runs may read."
" Is the way that I must keep
Crossed by waters wide and deep ? "
" Did it lead through flood and fire,
Thou must not stop, — thou must not tire."
" Till I have my journey past,
Tell me, will the daylight last ?
Will the sky be bright and clear
Till the evening shades appear ? "
" Though the sun now rides so high,
Clouds may veil the evening sky ;
Fast sinks the sun, fast wears the day,
Thou must not stop — thou must not stay :
God speed thee, pilgrim, on thy way ! "

SABBATH HYMNS.

HYMN XI.

SLEEP, sleep to-day, tormenting cares,
   Of earth and folly born!
Ye shall not dim the light that streams
   From this celestial morn.

To-morrow will be time enough
   To feel your harsh control;
Ye shall not violate this day,
   The sabbath of my soul.

Sleep, sleep forever, guilty thoughts!
   Let fires of vengeance die;
And, purged from sin, may I behold
   A God of purity.

HYMN XII.

WHEN, as returns this solemn day,
Man comes to meet his maker, God,
What rites, what honors shall he pay?
How spread his sovereign's praise abroad?

From marble domes and gilded spires
Shall curling clouds of incense rise ?
And gems, and gold, and garlands deck
The costly pomp of sacrifice ?

Vain sinful man ! Creation's lord
Thy golden offerings well may spare ;
But give thy heart, and thou shalt find
Here dwells a God who heareth prayer.

PROSE WORKS.

PROSE WORKS.

THE HILL OF SCIENCE:

A VISION.

IN that season of the year when the serenity of the
sky, the various fruits which cover the ground, the
discolored foliage of the trees, and all the sweet but
fading graces of inspiring autumn open the mind to
benevolence, and dispose it for contemplation, I was
wandering in a beautiful and romantic country, till
curiosity began to give way to weariness; and I sat me
down on the fragment of a rock overgrown with moss,
where the rustling of the falling leaves, the dashing of
waters, and the hum of the distant city soothed my
mind into the most perfect tranquillity; and sleep
insensibly stole upon me as I was indulging the
agreeable reveries which the objects around me naturally inspired.

I immediately found myself in a vast extended plain,
in the middle of which arose a mountain higher than I

had before any conception of. It was covered with a multitude of people, chiefly youth; many of whom pressed forwards with the liveliest expression of ardor in their countenance, though the way was in many places steep and difficult. I observed that those who had but just begun to climb the hill thought themselves not far from the top; but as they proceeded, new hills were continually rising to their view; and the summit of the highest they could before discern seemed but the foot of another, till the mountain at length appeared to lose itself in the clouds. As I was gazing on these things with astonishment, my good genius suddenly appeared. "The mountain before thee," said he, "is the hill of Science. On the top is the temple of Truth, whose head is above the clouds, and whose face is covered with a veil of pure light. Observe the progress of her votaries; be silent and attentive."

I saw that the only regular approach to the mountain was by a gate called the gate of languages. It was kept by a woman of a pensive and thoughtful appearance, whose lips were continually moving, as though she repeated something to herself. Her name was Memory. On entering this first enclosure I was stunned with a confused murmur of jarring voices and dissonant sounds, which increased upon me to such a degree that I was utterly confounded, and could compare the noise to nothing but the confusion of tongues at Babel. The road was also rough and stony, and rendered more difficult by heaps of rubbish continually tumbled down from the higher parts of the mountain, and by broken ruins of ancient buildings, which the travellers were obliged to climb over at every step; insomuch that many, disgusted with so rough a beginning, turned back, and attempted the mountain no more: while others, having conquered this difficulty, had no spirits to ascend further, and, sitting down on some fragment of the rubbish, harangued the multitude below with the greatest marks of importance and self-complacency.

About half-way up the hill, I observed on each side of the path a thick forest covered with continual fogs, and cut out into labyrinths, cross alleys, and serpentine walks, entangled with thorns and briers. This was called the wood of Error: and I heard the voices of many who were lost up and down in it, calling to one another, and endeavoring in vain to extricate themselves. The trees in many places shot their boughs over the path, and a thick mist often rested on it; yet never so much but that it was discernible by the light which beamed from the countenance of Truth.

In the pleasantest part of the mountain were placed the bowers of the Muses, whose office it was to cheer the spirits of the travellers, and encourage their fainting steps with songs from their divine harps. Not far from hence were the fields of Fiction, filled with a variety of wild flowers springing up in the greatest luxuriance, of richer scents and brighter colors than I had observed in any other climate. And near them was the dark walk of Allegory, so artificially shaded that the light at noonday was never stronger than that of a bright moonshine. This gave it a pleasingly romantic air for those who delighted in contemplation. The paths and alleys were perplexed with intricate windings, and were all terminated with the statue of a Grace, a Virtue, or a Muse.

After I had observed these things I turned my eyes towards the multitudes who were climbing the steep ascent, and observed amongst them a youth of a lively look, a piercing eye, and something fiery and irregular in all his motions. His name was Genius. He darted like an eagle up the mountain, and left his companions gazing after him with envy and admiration: but his progress was unequal, and interrupted by a thousand caprices. When Pleasure warbled in the valley, he mingled in her train. When Pride beckoned towards the precipice, he ventured to the tottering edge. He delighted in devious and untried paths; and made so many excursions from the road that his feebler companions often outstripped him. I observed that the Muses beheld him with partiality; but Truth often frowned and turned aside her face. While Genius was thus wasting his strength in eccentric flights, I saw a person of a very different appearance, named Application. He crept along with a slow and unremitting pace, his eyes fixed on the top of the mountain, patiently removing every stone that obstructed his way, till he saw most of those below him who had at first derided his slow and toilsome progress. Indeed, there were few who ascended the hill with equal and uninterrupted steadiness; for, besides the difficulties of the way, they were continually solicited to turn aside by a numerous crowd of Appetites, Passions, and Pleasures, whose importunity, when they had once complied with, they became less and less able to resist; and, though they often returned to the path, the asperities of the road were more severely felt, the hill appeared more steep and rugged, the fruits which were wholesome and refreshing seemed harsh and ill-tasted, their sight grew dim, and their feet tripped at every little obstruction.

I saw, with some surprise, that the Muses, whose business was to cheer and encourage those who were toiling up the ascent, would often sing in the bowers of Pleasure, and accompany those who were enticed away at the call of the Passions. They accompanied them, however, but a little way, and always forsook them when they lost sight of the hill. Their tyrants then doubled their chains upon the unhappy captives, and led them away without resistance to the cells of

8 *   L

Ignorance or the mansions of Misery. Amongst the innumerable seducers who were endeavoring to draw away the votaries of Truth from the path of Science, there was one so little formidable in her appearance, and so gentle and languid in her attempts, that I should scarcely have taken notice of her, but for the numbers she had imperceptibly loaded with her chains. Indolence (for so she was called), far from proceeding to open hostilities, did not attempt to turn their feet out of the path, but contented herself with retarding their progress; and the purpose she could not force them to abandon, she persuaded them to delay. Her touch had a power like that of the torpedo, which withered the strength of those who came within its influence. Her unhappy captives still turned their faces towards the temple, and always hoped to arrive there; but the ground seemed to slide from beneath their feet, and they found themselves at the bottom before they suspected that they had changed their place. The placid serenity which at first appeared in their countenance changed by degrees into a melancholy languor, which was tinged with deeper and deeper gloom as they glided down the stream of Insignificance; a dark and sluggish water, which is curled by no breeze and enlivened by no murmur, till it falls into a dead sea, where the startled passengers are awakened by the shock, and the next moment buried in the gulf of Oblivion.

Of all the unhappy deserters from the paths of
Science, none seemed less able to return than the
followers of Indolence. The captives of Appetite and
Passion could often seize the moment when their
tyrants were languid or asleep, to escape from their
enchantment; but the dominion of Indolence was constant and unremitted, and seldom resisted till resistance
was in vain.

After contemplating these things I turned my eyes
towards the top of the mountain, where the air was
always pure and exhilarating, the path shaded with
laurels and other evergreens, and the effulgence which
beamed from the face of the goddess seemed to shed a
glory round her votaries. "Happy," said I, "are they
who are permitted to ascend the mountain!"—but while
I was pronouncing this exclamation with uncommon
ardor, I saw standing beside me a form of diviner
features and a more benign radiance. "Happier," said
she, "are those whom Virtue conducts to the mansions
of Content!"—"What," said I, "does Virtue then reside
in the vale?"—"I am found," said she, "in the vale,
and I illuminate the mountain. I cheer the cottager at
his toil, and inspire the sage at his meditation. I
mingle in the crowd of cities, and bless the hermit in
his cell. I have a temple in every heart that owns my
influence; and to him that wishes for me I am already
present. Science may raise you to eminence, but I alone

can guide you to felicity!" While the goddess was thus speaking, I stretched out my arms towards her with a vehemence which broke my slumbers. The chill dews were falling around me, and the shades of evening stretched over the landscape. I hastened homeward, and resigned the night to silence and meditation.

ON ROMANCES.

ON ROMANCES.

AN IMITATION.

O F all the multifarious productions which the efforts of superior genius or the labors of scholastic industry have crowded upon the world, none are perused with more insatiable avidity, or disseminated with more universal applause, than the narrations of feigned events, descriptions of imaginary scenes, and delineations of ideal characters. The celebrity of other authors is confined within very narrow limits. The geometrician and divine, the antiquary and the critic, however distinguished by uncontested excellence, can only hope to please those whom a conformity of disposition has engaged in similar pursuits; and must be content to be regarded by the rest of the world with the smile of frigid indifference, or the contemptuous sneer of self-sufficient folly. The collector of shells and the anatomist of insects is little inclined to enter into theological disputes: the divine is not apt to regard with veneration the uncouth diagrams and tedious calculations of the astronomer: the man whose life has been consumed in adjusting the disputes of lexicographers, or elucidating the learning of antiquity, cannot easily bend his thoughts to recent transactions, or readily interest himself in the unimportant history of his contemporaries: and the cit, who knows no business but acquiring wealth, and no pleasure but displaying it, has a heart equally shut up to argument and fancy, to the batteries of syllogism and the arrows of wit. To the writer of fiction alone every ear is open and every tongue lavish of applause: curiosity sparkles in every eye, and every bosom is throbbing with concern.

It is, however, easy to account for this enchantment. To follow the chain of perplexed ratiocination, to review with critical skill the airy architecture of systems, to unravel the web of sophistry, or weigh the merits of opposite hypotheses, requires perspicacity, and pre-supposes learning. Works of this kind, therefore, are not so well adapted to the generality of readers as familiar and colloquial composition; for few can reason, but all can feel; and many who cannot enter into any argument may yet listen to a tale. The writer of romance has even an advantage over those who endeavor to amuse by the play of fancy; who, from the fortuitous collision of dissimilar ideas, produce the scintillations of wit, or by the vivid glow of poetical imagery delight the imagination with colors of ideal radiance. The attraction of the magnet is only exerted upon similar particles; and to taste the beauties of Homer it is requi-

site to partake his fire; but every one can relish the
author who represents common life, because every one
can refer to the originals from whence his ideas were
taken. He relates events to which all are liable, and
applies to passions which all have felt. The gloom of
solitude, the languor of inaction, the corrosions of disappointment, and the toil of thought, induce men to
step aside from the rugged road of life, and wander in
the fairy land of fiction, where every bank is sprinkled
with flowers, and every gale loaded with perfume; where
every event introduces a hero, and every cottage is in-
habited by a Grace. Invited by these flattering scenes,
the student quits the investigation of truth, in which he
perhaps meets with no less fallacy, to exhilarate his
mind with new ideas, more agreeable, and more easily
attained: the busy relax their attention by desultory
reading, and smooth the agitation of a ruffled mind with
images of peace, tranquillity, and pleasure: the idle and
the gay relieve the listlessness of leisure, and diversify
the round of life by a rapid series of events pregnant
with rapture and astonishment; and the pensive solitary
fills up the vacuities of his heart by interesting himself
in the fortunes of imaginary beings, and forming connections with ideal excellence.

It is, indeed, no ways extraordinary that the mind
should be charmed by fancy and attracted by pleasure;
but that we should listen with complacence to the

groans of misery and delight to view the exacerbations
of complicated anguish, that we should choose to chill
the bosom with imaginary fears and dim the eyes with
fictitious sorrow, seems a kind of paradox of the heart,
and can only be credited because it is universally felt.
Various are the hypotheses which have been found to
account for the disposition of the mind to riot in this
species of intellectual luxury. Some have imagined
that we are induced to acquiesce with greater patience
in our own lot by beholding pictures of life tinged with
deeper horrors, and loaded with more excruciating calamities ; as to a person suddenly emerging out of a dark
room the faintest glimmering of twilight assumes a lustre from the contrasted gloom. Others, with yet deeper
refinement, suppose that we take upon ourselves this
burden of adscititious sorrows, in order to feast upon
the consciousness of our own virtue. We commiserate
others, say they, that we may applaud ourselves ; and
the sigh of compassionate sympathy is always followed
by the gratulations of self-complacent esteem. But
surely they who would thus reduce the sympathetic
emotions of pity to a system of refined selfishness have
but ill attended to the genuine feelings of humanity.
It would, however, exceed the limits of this paper
should I attempt an accurate investigation of these sentiments. But let it be remembered that we are more
attracted by those scenes which interest our passions,

or gratify our curiosity, than those which delight our
fancy ; and, so far from being indifferent to the miseries
of others, we are, at the time, totally regardless of our
own. And let not those on whom the hand of Time
has impressed the characters of oracular wisdom censure with too much acrimony productions which are
thus calculated to please the imagination and interest
the heart. They teach us to think, by inuring us to
feel: they ventilate the mind by sudden gusts of passion, and prevent the stagnation of thought by a fresh
infusion of dissimilar ideas.

AN INQUIRY INTO THOSE KINDS OF DISTRESS WHICH EXCITE AGREEABLE SENSATIONS.

WITH A TALE.

IT is undoubtedly true, though a phenomenon of the human mind difficult to account for, that the representation of distress frequently gives pleasure; from which general observation many of our modern writers of tragedy and romance seem to have drawn this inference,— that, in order to please, they have nothing more to do than to paint distress in natural and striking colors. With this view, they heap together all the afflicting events and dismal accidents their imagination can furnish; and when they have half broke the reader's heart, they expect he should thank them for his agreeable entertainment. An author of this class sits down, pretty much like an inquisitor, to compute how much suffering he can inflict upon the hero of his tale before he makes an end of him; with this difference, indeed, that the inquisitor only tortures those who are at least reputed criminals, whereas the writer generally chooses the most excellent character in his piece for the subject of his persecution. The great

criterion of excellence is placed in being able to draw
tears plentifully; and concluding we shall weep the
more, the more the picture is loaded with doleful events,
they go on, telling

> " . . . . of sorrows upon sorrows
> Even to a lamentable length of woe."

A monarch once proposed a reward for the discovery
of a new pleasure; but if any one could find out a new
torture, or nondescript calamity, he would be more
entitled to the applause of those who fabricate books
of entertainment.

But the springs of pity require to be touched with a
more delicate hand; and it is far from being true that
we are agreeably affected by everything that excites
our sympathy. It shall therefore be the business of
this essay to distinguish those kinds of distress which
are pleasing in the representation from those which are
really painful and disgusting.

The view or relation of mere misery can never be
pleasing. We have, indeed, a strong sympathy with
all kinds of misery; but it is a feeling of pure, unmixed
pain, similar in kind, though not equal in degree, to
what we feel for ourselves on the like occasions; and
never produces that melting sorrow, that thrill of
tenderness, to which we give the name of pity. They
are two distinct sensations, marked by very different
external expression. One causes the nerves to tingle,

the flesh to shudder, and the whole countenance to be
thrown into strong contractions : the other relaxes the
frame, opens the features, and produces tears. When
we crush a noxious or loathsome animal, we may sym-
pathize strongly with the pain it suffers, but with far
different emotions from the tender sentiment we feel
for the dog of Ulysses, who crawled to meet his long-
lost master, looked up, and died at his feet. Extreme
bodily pain is perhaps the most intense suffering we are
capable of, and if the fellow-feeling with misery alone
was grateful to the mind, the exhibition of a man in a
fit of the toothache, or under a chirurgical operation,
would have a fine effect in a tragedy.   But there must
be some other sentiment combined with this kind of instinctive sympathy before it becomes in any degree
pleasing, or produces the sweet emotion of pity.   This
sentiment is love, esteem, the complacency we take in
the contemplation of beauty, of mental or moral excellence, called forth and rendered more interesting by
circumstances of pain and danger.   Tenderness is, much
more properly than sorrow, the spring of tears ; for it
affects us in that manner, whether combined with joy or
grief ; perhaps more in the former case than the latter.
And I believe we may venture to assert, that no distress
which produces tears is wholly without a mixture of
pleasure.   When Joseph's brethren were sent to buy
corn, if they had perished in the desert by wild beasts,

or been reduced (as in the horrid adventures of a Pierre de Vaud) to eat one another, we might have shuddered, but we should not have wept for them. The gush of tears breaks forth when Joseph made himself known to his brethren, and fell on their neck, and kissed them. When Hubert prepares to burn out Prince Arthur's eyes, the shocking circumstance, of itself, would only affect us with horror: it is the amiable simplicity of the young prince, and his innocent affection to his intended murderer, that draws our tears, and excites that tender sorrow which we love to feel, and which refines the heart while we do feel it.

We see, therefore, from this view of our internal feelings, that no scenes of misery ought to be exhibited which are not connected with the display of some moral excellence or agreeable quality. If fortitude, power, and strength of mind are called forth, they produce the sublime feelings of wonder and admiration: if the softer qualities of gentleness, grace, and beauty, they inspire love and pity. The management of these latter emotions is our present object.

And let it be remembered, in the first place, that the misfortunes which excite pity must not be too horrid and overwhelming. The mind is rather stunned than softened by great calamities. They are little circumstances that work most sensibly upon the tender feelings. For this reason a well-written novel generally draws more tears than a tragedy. The distresses of tragedy are more calculated to amaze and terrify than to move compassion. Battles, torture, and death are in every page. The dignity of the characters, the importance of the events, the pomp of verse and imagery, interest the grander passions, and raise the mind to an enthusiasm little favorable to the weak and languid notes of pity. The tragedies of Young are in a fine strain of poetry, and the situations are worked up with great energy; but the pictures are in too deep a shade: all his pieces are full of violent and gloomy passions, and so overwrought with horror, that, instead of awakening any pleasing sensibility, they leave on the mind an impression of sadness mixed with terror. Shakespeare is sometimes guilty of presenting scenes too shocking. Such is the trampling out of Gloster's eyes, and such is the whole play of Titus Andronicus. But Lee, beyond all others, abounds with this kind of images. He delighted in painting the most daring crimes and cruel massacres; and though he has shown himself extremely capable of raising tenderness, he continually checks its course by shocking and disagreeable expressions. His pieces are in the same taste with the pictures of Spagnolet, and there are many scenes in his tragedies which no one can relish who would not look with pleasure on the flaying of St. Bartholomew. The following speech of Marguerite, in the Massacre of

Paris, was, I suppose, intended to express the utmost tenderness of affection.

> "Die for him ! that's too little ; I could burn
> Piecemeal away, or bleed to death by drops,
> Be flayed alive, then broke upon the wheel,
> Yet with a smile endure it all for Guise :
> And when let loose from torments, all one wound,
> Run with my mangled arms and crush him dead."

Images like these will never excite the softer passions. We are less moved at the description of an Indian tortured with all the dreadful ingenuity of that savage people, than with the fatal mistake of the lover in the Spectator, who pierced an artery in the arm of his mistress as he was letting her blood. Tragedy and romance writers are likewise apt to make too free with the more violent expressions of passion and distress, by which means they lose their effect. Thus an ordinary author does not know how to express any strong emotion otherwise than by swoonings or death ; so that a person experienced in this kind of reading, when a girl faints away at parting with her lover, or a hero kills himself for the loss of his mistress, considers it as the established etiquette upon such occasions, and turns over the pages with the utmost coolness and unconcern; whereas real sensibility, and a more intimate knowledge of human nature, would have suggested a thousand little touches of grief, which, though slight, are irresistible.

We are too gloomy a people. Some of the French novels
are remarkable for little affecting incidents, imagined
with delicacy and told with grace. Perhaps they have
a better turn than we have for this kind of writing.

A judicious author will never attempt to raise pity
by anything mean or disgusting. As we have already
observed, there must be a degree of complacence mixed
with our sorrows to produce an agreeable sympathy;
nothing, therefore, must be admitted which destroys
the grace and dignity of suffering; the imagination
must have an amiable figure to dwell upon; there are
circumstances so ludicrous and disgusting, that no
character can preserve a proper decorum under them,
or appear in an agreeable light. Who can read the
following description of Polypheme without finding
his compassion entirely destroyed by aversion and
loathing?

> " . . . . His bloody hand
> Snatched two unhappy of my martial band,
> And dashed like dogs against the stony floor,
> The pavement swims with brains and mingled gore ;
> Torn limb from limb, he spreads his horrid feast,
> And fierce devours it like a mountain beast ;
> He sucks the marrow, and the blood he drains,
> Nor entrails, flesh, nor solid bone remains."

Or that of Scylla, —

> " In the wide dungeon she devours her food,
> And the flesh trembles while she churns the blood."

Deformity is always disgusting, and the imagination cannot reconcile it with the idea of a favorite character; therefore the poet and romance-writer are fully justified in giving a larger share of beauty to their principal figures than is usually met with in common life. A late genius, indeed, in a whimsical mood, gave us a lady with her nose crushed for the heroine of his story; but the circumstance spoils the picture; and though in the course of the story it is kept a good deal out of sight, whenever it does occur to the imagination we are hurt and disgusted. It was an heroic instance of virtue in the nuns of a certain abbey, who cut off their noses and lips to avoid violation; yet this would make a very bad subject for a poem or a play. Something akin to this is the representation of anything unnatural, of which kind is the famous story of the Roman charity; and for this reason I cannot but think it an unpleasing subject for either the pen or the pencil.

Poverty, if truly represented, shocks our nicer feelings; therefore, whenever it is made use of to awaken our compassion, the rags and dirt, the squalid appearance and mean employments incident to that state, must be kept out of sight, and the distress must arise from the idea of depression, and the shock of falling from higher fortunes. We do not pity Belisarius as a poor, blind beggar; and a painter would succeed very ill who should sink him to the meanness of that condi-

tion. He must let us still discover the conqueror of the
Vandals, the general of the imperial armies, or we shall
be little interested. Let us look at the picture of the
old woman of Otway : —

> " . . . . A wrinkled hag with age grown double,
> Picking dry sticks, and muttering to herself ;
> Her eyes with scalding rheum were galled and red ;
> Cold palsy shook her head ; her hands seemed withered ;
> And on her crooked shoulder had she wrapt
> The tattered remnant of an old striped hanging,
> Which served to keep her carcass from the cold ;
> So there was nothing of a piece about her."

Here is the extreme of wretchedness, and instead of
melting into pity, we should turn away with disgust, if
we were not pleased with it, as we are with a Dutch
painting, from the exact imitation of nature. Indeed,
the author only intended it to strike horror. But how
different are the sentiments we feel for the lovely Belvidera ! We see none of those circumstances which render poverty an unamiable thing. When the goods are
seized by an execution, our attention is turned to *the
piles of massy plate, and all the ancient, most domestic
ornaments*, which imply grandeur and consequence ; or
to such instances of their hard fortune as will lead us to
pity them as lovers. We are struck and affected with the
general face of ruin ; but we are not brought near enough
to discern the ugliness of its features. Belvidera ruined,
Belvidera deprived of friends, without a home, aban-

doned to the wide world, — we can contemplate with
all the pleasing sympathy of pity; but had she been
represented as really sunk into low life, had we seen
her employed in the most servile offices of poverty, our
compassion would have given way to contempt and disgust. Indeed, we may observe in real life that poverty
is only pitied so long as people can keep themselves
from the effects of it. When in common language we
say *a miserable object*, we mean an object of distress
which, if we relieve, we turn away from at the same
time. To make pity pleasing, the object of it must not
in any view be disagreeable to the imagination. How
admirably has the author of "Clarissa" managed this
point! Amidst scenes of suffering which rend the heart,
in poverty, in a prison, under the most shocking outrages,
the grace and delicacy of her character never suffers
even for a moment: there seems to be a charm about
her which prevents her receiving a stain from anything
which happens; and Clarissa, abandoned and undone,
is the object not only of complacence but veneration.

I would likewise observe, that if an author would
have us feel a strong degree of compassion, his characters must not be too perfect. The stern fortitude and
inflexible resolution of a Cato may command esteem,
but does not excite tenderness; and faultless rectitude
of conduct, though no rigor be mixed with it, is of too
sublime a nature to inspire compassion. Virtue has a

kind of self-sufficiency; it stands upon its own basis,
and cannot be injured by any violence. It must therefore be mixed with something of helplessness and im-
perfection, with an excessive sensibility or a simplicity
bordering upon weakness, before it raises, in any great
degree, either tenderness or familiar love. If there be a
fault in the masterly performance just now mentioned,
it is that the character of Clarissa is so inflexibly right,
her passions are under such perfect command, and her
prudence is so equal to every occasion, that she seems
not to need that sympathy we should bestow upon one
of a less elevated character; and perhaps we should feel
a livelier emotion of tenderness for the innocent girl
whom Lovelace calls his Rose-bud, but that the story
of Clarissa is so worked up by the strength of coloring,
and the force of repeated impressions, as to command
all our sorrow.

Pity seems too degrading a sentiment to be offered at
the shrine of faultless excellence. The sufferings of
martyrs are rather beheld with admiration and sympathetic triumph than with tears; and we never feel
much for those whom we consider as themselves raised
above common feelings.

The last rule I shall insist upon is, that scenes of
distress should not be too long continued. All our
finer feelings are in a manner momentary, and no art
can carry them beyond a certain point, either in intense-

ness or duration. Constant suffering deadens the heart
to tender impressions; as we may observe in sailors and
others who are grown callous by a life of continual
hardships. It is therefore highly necessary, in a long
work, to relieve the mind by scenes of pleasure and
gayety; and I cannot think it so absurd a practice as
our modern delicacy has represented it, to intermix wit
and fancy with the pathetic, provided care be taken not
to check the passions while they are flowing. The
transition from a pleasurable state of mind to tender
sorrow is not so difficult as we imagine. When the
mind is opened by gay and agreeable scenes, every impression is felt more sensibly. Persons of a lively temper are much more susceptible of that sudden swell of
sensibility which occasions tears, than those of a grave
and saturnine cast; for this reason women are more
easily moved to weeping than men. Those who have
touched the springs of pity with the finest hand, have
mingled light strokes of pleasantry and mirth in their
most pathetic passages. Very different is the conduct
of many novel-writers, who, by plunging us into scenes
of distress without end or limit, exhaust the powers,
and before the conclusion either render us insensible to
everything, or fix a real sadness upon the mind. The
uniform style of tragedies is one reason why they affect
so little. In our old plays all the force of language is
reserved for the more interesting parts; and in scenes

of common life there is no attempt to rise above common language; whereas we, by that pompous manner and affected solemnity which we think it necessary to preserve through the whole piece, lose the force of an elevated or passionate expression where the occasion really suggests it.

Having thus considered the manner in which fictitious distress must be managed to render it pleasing, let us reflect a little upon the moral tendency of such representations. Much has been said in favor of them, and they are generally thought to improve the tender and humane feelings; but this, I own, appears to me very dubious. That they exercise sensibility is true; but sensibility does not increase with exercise. By the constitution of our frame our habits increase, our emotions decrease, by repeated acts; and thus a wise provision is made, that, as our compassion grows weaker, its place should be supplied by habitual benevolence. But in these writings our sensibility is strongly called forth without any possibility of exerting itself in virtuous action, and those emotions which we shall never feel again with equal force are wasted without advantage. Nothing is more dangerous than to let virtuous impressions of any kind pass through the mind without producing their proper effect. The awakenings of remorse, virtuous shame and indignation, the glow of moral approbation, — if they do not lead to action, grow

less and less vivid every time they recur, till at length
the mind grows absolutely callous. The being affected
with a pathetic story is undoubtedly a sign of an amiable disposition, but perhaps no means of increasing it.
On the contrary, young people, by a course of this kind
of reading, often acquire something of that apathy and
indifference which the experience of real life would have
given them, without its advantages.

Another reason why plays and romances do not improve our humanity is, that they lead us to require a
certain elegance of manners and delicacy of virtue which
is not often found with poverty, ignorance, and meanness. The objects of pity in romance are as different
from those in real life as our husbandmen from the
shepherds of Arcadia; and a girl who will sit weeping
the whole night at the delicate distresses of a lady
Charlotte, or lady Julia, shall be little moved at the
complaint of her neighbor, who, in a homely phrase and
vulgar accent, laments to her that she is not able to get
bread for her family. Romance-writers likewise make
great misfortunes so familiar to our ears, that we have
hardly any pity to spare for the common accidents of
life; but we ought to remember that misery has a claim
to relief, however we may be disgusted with its appearance; and that we must not fancy ourselves charitable,
when we are only pleasing our imagination.

It would perhaps be better if our romances were

more like those of the old stamp, which tended to raise
human nature, and inspire a certain grace and dignity
of manners of which we have hardly the idea. The
high notions of honor, the wild and fanciful spirit of
adventure and romantic love, elevated the mind: our
novels tend to depress and enfeeble it. Yet there is a
species of this kind of writing which must ever afford
an exquisite pleasure to persons of taste and sensibility;
where noble sentiments are mixed with well-fancied
incidents, pathetic touches with dignity and grace, and
invention with chaste correctness. Such will ever interest our sweetest passions. I shall conclude this paper
with the following tale.

In the happy period of the Golden Age, when all the
celestial inhabitants descended to the earth and con-
versed familiarly with mortals, among the most cherished of the heavenly powers were twins, the offspring
of Jupiter, Love and Joy. Where they appeared, the
flowers sprung up beneath their feet, the sun shone
with a brighter radiance, and all nature seemed embel-
lished by their presence. They were inseparable companions, and their growing attachment was favored by
Jupiter, who had decreed that a lasting union should
be solemnized between them as soon as they were
arrived at maturer years. But in the mean time the

sons of men deviated from their native innocence; vice
and ruin overran the earth with giant strides; and
Astrea, with her train of celestial visitants, forsook
their polluted abodes. Love alone remained, having
been stolen away by Hope, who was his nurse, and
conveyed by her to the forest of Arcadia, where he was
brought up among the shepherds. But Jupiter assigned
him a different partner, and commanded him to espouse
Sorrow, the daughter of Ate. He complied with reluctance; for her features were harsh and disagreeable,
her eyes sunk, her forehead contracted into perpetual
wrinkles, and her temples were covered with a wreath
of cypress and wormwood. From this union sprung a
virgin in whom might be traced a strong resemblance
to both her parents; but the sullen and unamiable
features of her mother were so mixed and blended with
the sweetness of her father, that her countenance,
though mournful, was highly pleasing. The maids and
shepherds of the neighboring plains gathered round,
and called her Pity. A redbreast was observed to build
in the cabin where she was born; and while she was
yet an infant, a dove pursued by a hawk flew into her
bosom. This nymph had a dejected appearance, but
so soft and gentle a mien that she was beloved to a
degree of enthusiasm. Her voice was low and plaintive,
but inexpressibly sweet; and she loved to lie for hours
together on the banks of some wild and melancholy

9 *

stream, singing to her lute. She taught men to weep, for she took a strange delight in tears; and often, when the virgins of the hamlet were assembled at their evening sports, she would steal in amongst them, and captivate their hearts by her tales full of a charming sadness. She wore on her head a garland composed of her father's myrtles twisted with her mother's cypress.

One day, as she sat musing by the waters of Helicon, her tears by chance fell into the fountain; and ever since the Muse's spring has retained a strong taste of the infusion. Pity was commanded by Jupiter to follow the steps of her mother through the world, dropping balm into the wounds she made, and binding up the hearts she had broken. She follows with her hair loose, her bosom bare and throbbing, her garments torn by the briers, and her feet bleeding with the roughness of the path. The nymph is mortal, for her mother is so; and when she has fulfilled her destined course upon the earth, they shall both expire together, and Love be again united to Joy, his immortal and long-betrothed bride.

THE CURÉ OF THE BANKS OF THE RHONE.

WRITTEN IN 1791.

A FRIEND of mine, who pretends to have very good information from the Continent, communicated to me the following account: I confess it comes in a shape a little questionable; however, I send it to you, Mr. Editor, exactly as my friend read it to me from a private letter which he said he had just received.

"A few days after the bishop of Paris and his vicars had set the example of renouncing their clerical character, a curé from a village on the banks of the Rhone, followed by some of his parishioners with an offering of gold and silver saints, chalices, rich vestments, etc., presented himself at the bar of the House. The sight of the gold put the Convention in very good humor, and the curé, a thin, venerable-looking man with gray hairs, was ordered to speak. 'I come,' said he, 'from the village of ——, where the only good building standing (for the château has been pulled down) is a very fine church; my parishioners beg you will take it to make a hospital for the sick and wounded of both parties, — they are both equally our countrymen: the gold and silver, part of which we have brought you, they entreat you will devote to the service of the state, and that you will cast the bells into cannon to drive away its foreign invaders: for myself, I come with great pleasure to resign my letters of ordination, of induction, and every deed and title by which I have been constituted a member of your ecclesiastical polity. Here are the papers; you may burn them, if you please, in the same fire with the genealogical trees and patents of the nobility. I desire likewise that you will discontinue my salary. I am still able to support myself by the labor of my hands, and I beg of you to believe that I never felt sincerer joy than I now do in making this renunciation. I have longed to see this day: I see it, and am glad.'

"When the old man had done speaking, the applauses were immoderate. 'You are an honest man,' said they all at once; 'you are a brave fellow; you do not believe in God'; — and the president advanced to give him the fraternal embrace. The curé did not seem greatly elated with these tokens of approbation; he retired back a few steps, and thus resumed his discourse. 'Before you applaud my sentiments, it is fit you should understand them; perhaps they may not entirely coincide with your own. I rejoice in this day, not because I wish to see religion degraded, but because I wish to see it exalted and purified. By dissolving its alliance with the state, you have given it dignity and independence. You have done it a piece of service which its well-wishers would, perhaps, never have had courage to render it, but which is the only thing wanted to make it appear in its genuine beauty and lustre. Nobody will now say of me that I am performing the offices of my religion as a trade; he is paid for telling the people such and such things; he is hired to keep up a useless piece of mummery. They cannot now say this, and therefore I feel myself raised in my own esteem, and shall speak to them with a confidence and frankness which, before this, I never durst venture to assume. We resign without reluctance our gold and silver images and embroidered vestments, because we have never found that gold and silver made the heart more pure or the affections more heavenly; we can also spare our churches, for the heart that wishes to lift itself up to God will never be at a loss for room to do it in; but we cannot spare our religion, because, to tell you the truth, we never had so much occasion for it. I understand that you accuse us priests of having told the people a great many falsehoods. I suspect this may have been the case; but till this day we have never been allowed to inquire whether the things which we taught them were true or not. You required us formerly to receive them all without proof, and you would have us now reject them all without discrimination; neither of these modes of conduct become philosophers, such as you would be thought to be. I am going to employ myself diligently along with my parishioners to sift the wheat from the chaff, the true from the false; if we are not successful, we shall be at least sincere. I do fear, indeed, that while I wore these vestments which we have brought you, and spoke in that gloomy building which we have given up to you, I told my flock a great many idle stories. I cannot but hope, however, that the errors we have fallen into have not been very material, since the village has been in general sober and good, the peasants are honest, docile, and laborious, the husbands love their wives and the wives their husbands; they are fortunately not too rich to be compassionate, and they have constantly relieved the sick and fugitives of all parties whenever it has lain in their way. I think, therefore, what I have taught them cannot be so very much amiss. You want to extirpate priests; but will you hinder the ignorant from applying for instruction, the unhappy for comfort and hope, the unlearned from looking up to the learned? If you do not, you will have priests, by whatever name you may order them to be called; but it certainly is not necessary they should wear a particular dress, or be appointed by state-letters of ordination. My letters of ordination are my

zeal, my charity, my ardent love for my dear children
of the village; if I were more learned, I would add
my knowledge, but alas! we all know very little; to
man every error is pardonable but want of humility.
We have a public walk with a spreading elm at the
end of it, and a circle of green round it, with a convenient bench. Here I shall draw together the children
as they are playing around me. I shall point to the
vines laden with fruit, to the orchards, to the herds of
cattle lowing around us, to the distant hills stretching
one behind another; and they will ask me, How came
all these things? I shall tell them all I know or have
heard from wise men who have lived before me; they
will be penetrated with love and veneration; they will
kneel, — I shall kneel with them; they will not be at
my feet, but all of us at the feet of that good Being
whom we shall worship together; and thus they will
receive within their tender minds a religion. The old
men will come sometimes from having deposited under
the green sod one of their companions, and place themselves by my side; they will look wistfully at the turf,
and anxiously inquire, Is he gone forever? Shall we
soon be like him? Will no morning break over the
tomb? When the wicked cease from troubling, will
the good cease from doing good? We will talk of these
things: I will comfort them. I will tell them of the
goodness of God; I will speak to them of a life to

come; I will bid them hope for a state of retribution. In a clear night, when the stars slide over our heads, they will ask what these bright bodies are, and by what rules they rise and set. And we will converse about different forms of being, and distant worlds in the immensity of space, governed by the same laws, till we feel our minds raised from what is grovelling, and refined from what is sordid. You talk of Nature,— this is Nature; and if you could at this moment extinguish religion in the minds of the world, thus would it be kindled again, and thus again excite the curiosity and interest the feelings of mankind. You have changed our holidays; you have an undoubted right, as our civil governors, so to do; it is very immaterial whether they are kept once in seven days, or once in ten; some, however, you will leave us, and when they occur, I shall tell those who choose to hear me, of the beauty and utility of virtue, of the dignity of right conduct. We shall talk of good men who have lived in the world, and of the doctrines they taught; and if any of them have been persecuted and put to death for their virtue, we shall reverence their memories the more. — I hope in all this there is no harm. There is a book out of which I have sometimes taught my people; it says we are to love those who do us hurt, and to pour oil and wine into the wounds of the stranger. It has enabled my children to bear patiently the spoiling

of their goods, and to give up their own interest for the
general welfare. I think it cannot be a very bad book.
I wish more of it had been read in your town; perhaps
you would not have had quite so many assassinations
and massacres. In this book we hear of a person called
Jesus. Some worship him as a God; others, as I am
told, say it is wrong to do so. — Some teach that he
existed from the beginning of ages; others, that he was
born of Joseph and Mary. I cannot tell whether these
controversies will ever be decided; but in the mean
time I think we cannot do otherwise than well in imi-
tating him; for I learn that he loved the poor, and went
about doing good.

"'Fellow-citizens, as I travelled hither from my own
village, I saw peasants sitting among the smoking ruins
of their cottages, — rich men and women reduced to
miserable poverty; fathers lamenting their children in
the bloom and pride of youth; and I said to myself,
these people cannot afford to part with their religion.
But indeed you cannot take it away; if, contrary to
your first declaration, you choose to try the experiment
of persecuting it, you will only make us prize it more
and love it better. Religion, true or false, is so necessary to the mind of man, that even you have begun to
make yourselves a new one. You are sowing the seeds
of superstition; and in two or three generations your
posterity will be worshipping some clumsy idol, with

N

the rites, perhaps, of a bloody Moloch or a lascivious Thammuz.   It was not worth while to have been philosophers and destroyed the images of our saints for this; but let every one choose the religion that pleases him; I and my parishioners are content with ours, — it teaches us to bear the evils your childish or sanguinary decrees have helped to bring upon the country.'"

The curé turned his footsteps homeward, and the Convention looked for some minutes on one another before they resumed their work of blood.

ON EVIL.

A RHAPSODY.

O EVIL, creature abhorred of God and man! whence is thy origin? how did so deformed and monstrous a birth gain entrance into the fair creation? Canst thou be from God, — since thou art so opposite to his nature? And if from man, — why was he suffered to produce thee? Weak, unexperienced, unsuspecting man, — why was he permitted to bring such enormous ruin on his own head, and that of all his posterity? Was there no warning voice, no sheltering hand, to save him from such a fall, — to save thy image, O God, from pollution? Let us sit down in sad shades, and join the moral poet, —

" Who mourns for virtue lost, and ruined man."

What fair, what amiable creatures were our first parents when they came from the hands of their Maker! They knew neither Pain, nor Sin, the sire of Pain; nor Shame, the daughter of Sin. Innocent, happy, and immortal : — so far from practising evil that they had not even the knowledge of it. Their passions, nicely balanced, admitted no internal war. A milky innocence

in their veins, their eyes beaming with smiles, — the
smiles of candor and simplicity, — they were the head
of the happy.creation, till one fatal moment ruined all.
The Garden of Paradise is shut forever; and man,
(unhappy outcast!) exposed to the war of elements
without and passions within, his peace broken, his
heart torn by the conflict of jarring emotions, his life
worn away by perplexing doubts and heart-withering
care, moistens his daily bread with tears; and, after
struggling a few years in the hard, unequal warfare, he
returns to the dust from whence he was taken.

Such is the dark side of the picture. — But let us
change the view, and see whether in reality the human
race have such great reason to lament the fall of their
first progenitor. Whether *virtuous* man now is not a
nobler creature than *sinless* man then ? the pupil of reason, than the child of nature ? the follower of the second,
than the offspring of the first Adam ?   Man in his first
state had a mind untainted with crimes; but unformed,
uncultivated, void of moral ideas, he could not rise
but by his fall; he could not attain to more perfection
but by moral discipline; he could not know the joys
of self-approbation, without being subject to remorse,
— of sympathy, without feeling distress.   Had he
been always innocent, he had been nothing more than
innocent; had he never known his weakness, he had
never acquired strength.   Behold him now, fashioned

by the hand of culture, and shining through the dark cloud of ruin, guilt, and pain that is spread over him. What a different creature from the former man! He now knows vice, but abhors it; temptation, but resists it; error, but he laments it. His passions were once balanced, they are now subdued; he has tasted good and evil, and he knows to choose the one and refuse the other. Intellectual ideas crowd upon him, and a new world opens within his breast. His nature is raised, refined, exalted: he lives by faith, by devotion, by spiritual communion, by repentance, — he, weeping beneath the bitter cross, washes off the stain of sin. The world is beneath his feet; for behold he prayeth, and things unseen become present to his soul. Meek resignation blunts the edge of suffering; and triumphant hope looks beyond all suffering to glory and to joy. Thus advancing through life, he learns some new lesson at every step; till by receiving, but still more by conferring benefits, by bearing, and still further by forgiving injuries, his mind is disciplined, his moral sense awakened, his taste for beauty, order, and rectitude unfolded. He becomes endeared to those he has wept and prayed and struggled with through this vale of sin and suffering; he learns to pity and to love his fellow-partners of mortality; till at length the divine flame of universal charity begins to kindle in his breast. Then is the era of a new birth; then does he become

partaker of a divine nature : sense is mortified, passion
is subdued, self is annihilated. And is not this a noble
creature ? a being worth forming by so expensive and
painful a process ? a being God may delight in ? a
faithful, well-disciplined soldier, fit to co-operate in any
plan, or mingle with any order of rational and moral
beings throughout the wide creation? Place him where
you will, he has learned to follow, to trust in, the
Supreme Being; he has learned humility from his
errors, steadiness and watchfulness from his weakness;
his virtues depend not now on constitution, but on firm
principles and established habits. Is this the feeble
being whose infant mind was unable to resist the
allurements of forbidden fruit ? who so easily listened
to the seduction of the tempter? See him now resisting unto blood, superior to principalities and powers,
to wicked men and bad angels: neither terrors nor
pleasures can move him. He once believed not the
living voice of his Maker; having not seen, he now
believes. His gratitude once was faint and languid,
though he was surrounded with pleasant things. He
now loves God, though overwhelmed with sorrow and
pain ; trusts in him, though surrounded with difficulties; hopes even against hope, and prays without
ceasing. His hopes now are superior to his joys then.
Glorious exchange ! from reposing on flowers, to tread
upon stars, — from naked purity, to a robe of glory,

— from the food which cometh out of the earth to the bread which cometh down from heaven. For ignorance of ill he hath knowledge of good; for smiles of innocence, tears of rapture; for the bowers of paradise, the gates of heaven. Hadst thou, Adam, never fallen, shepherds and husbandmen only would have sprung from thee; now patriots, martyrs, confessors, apostles !

ON MONASTIC INSTITUTIONS.

I HAPPENED the other day to take a solitary walk amongst the venerable ruins of an old abbey. The stillness and solemnity of the place were favorable to thought, and naturally led me to a train of ideas relative to the scene; when, like a good Protestant, I began to indulge a secret triumph in the ruin of so many structures which I had always considered as the haunts of ignorance and superstition.

Ye are fallen, said I, ye dark and gloomy mansions of mistaken zeal, where the proud priest and lazy monk fattened upon the riches of the land, and crept like vermin from their cells, to spread their poisonous doctrines through the nation, and disturb the peace of kings. Obscure in their origin, but daring and ambitious in their guilt! See how the pure light of heaven is clouded by the dim glass of the arched window, stained with the gaudy colors of monkish tales and legendary fiction, — fit emblem how reluctantly they admitted the fairer light of truth amidst these dark recesses, and how much they have debased its genuine lustre! The low cells, the long and narrow aisles, the gloomy arches, the damp and secret caverns which wind beneath the hollow ground, far from impressing on the mind the idea of the God of truth and love, seem only fit for those dark places of the earth in which are the habitations of cruelty. These massy stones and scattered reliques of the vast edifice, like the large bones and gigantic armor of a once formidable ruffian, produce emotions of mingled dread and exultation. Farewell, ye once venerated seats! enough of you remains, and may it always remain, to remind us from what we have escaped, and make posterity forever thankful for this fairer age of liberty and light.

Such were for a while my meditations; but it is cruel to insult a fallen enemy, and I gradually fell into a different train of thought. I began to consider whether something might not be advanced in favor of these institutions during the barbarous ages in which they flourished; and, though they have been productive of much mischief and superstition, whether they might not have spread the glimmering of a feeble ray of knowledge through that thick night which once involved the Western hemisphere.

And where, indeed, could the precious remains of classical learning, and the divine monuments of ancient taste, have been safely lodged amidst the ravages of that age of ferocity and rapine which succeeded the desolation of the Roman Empire, except in sanctuaries like these, consecrated by the superstition of the times beyond their intrinsic merit? The frequency of wars, and the

licentious cruelty with which they were conducted, left
neither the hamlet of the peasant nor the castle of the
baron free from depredation; but the church and monastery generally remained inviolate. There Homer and
Aristotle were obliged to shroud their heads from the
rage of Gothic ignorance; and there the sacred records
of Divine truth were preserved, like treasure hid in the
earth in troublesome times, safe, but unenjoyed. Some
of the barbarous nations were converted before their
conquests, and most of them soon after their settlement
in the countries they overran. Those buildings which
their new faith taught them to venerate, afforded a shelter for those valuable manuscripts which must otherwise
have been destroyed in the common wreck. At the
revival of learning, they were produced from their
dormitories. A copy of the Pandects of Justinian, that
valuable remain of Roman law which first gave to
Europe the idea of a more perfect jurisprudence, and
gave men a relish for a new and important study, was
discovered in a monastery of Amalphi. Most of the
classics were recovered by the same means; and to this
is owing, — to the books and learning preserved in these
repositories, — that we were not obliged to begin anew,
and trace every art by slow and uncertain steps from
its first origin. Science, already full-grown and vigorous, awaked as from a trance, shook her pinions, and
soon soared to the heights of knowledge.

Nor was she entirely idle during her recess; at least we cannot but confess that what little learning remained in the world was amongst the priests and religious orders. Books, before the invention of paper and the art of printing, were so dear, that few private persons possessed any. The only libraries were in convents; and the monks were often employed in transcribing manuscripts, which was a very tedious, and at that time a very necessary task. It was frequently enjoined as a penance for some slight offence, or given as an exercise to the younger part of the community. The monks were obliged by their rules to spend some stated hours every day in reading and study; nor was any one to be chosen abbot without a competent share of learning. They were the only historians; and though their accounts be interwoven with many a legendary tale, and darkened by much superstition, still they are better than no histories at all; and we cannot but think ourselves obliged to them for transmitting to us, in any dress, the annals of their country.

They were likewise almost the sole instructors of youth. Towards the end of the tenth century there were no schools in Europe but the monasteries, and those which belonged to Episcopal residences; nor any masters but the Benedictines. It is true, their course of education extended no further than what they called the seven liberal arts, and these were taught in a very

dry and uninteresting manner.   But this was the genius
of the age, and it should not be imputed to them as a
reproach that they did not teach well, when no one
taught better.   We are guilty of great unfairness when
we compare the schoolmen with the philosophers of a
more enlightened age.   We should contrast them with
those of their own times; with a high-constable of
France who could not read; with kings who made the
sign of the cross in confirmation of their charters, because
they could not write their names; with a whole people
without the least glimmering of taste or literature.
Whatever was their real knowledge, there was a much
greater difference between men of learning and the bulk
of the nation at that time than there is at present; and
certainly some of the disciples of those schools who,
though now fallen into disrepute, were revered in their
day by the names of the subtle or the angelic doctors,
showed an acuteness and strength of genius which, if
properly directed, would have gone far in philosophy;
and they only failed because their inquiries were not
the objects of the human powers.   Had they exercised
half that acuteness on facts and experiments, they had
been truly great men.   However, there were not wanting some, even in the darkest ages, whose names will
be always remembered with pleasure by the lovers of
science.   Alcuin, the preceptor of Charlemagne, the
first who introduced a taste for polite literature into

France, and the chief-instrument that prince made use of in his noble endeavors for the encouragement of learning, — to whom the universities of Soissons, Tours, and Paris owe their origin; the historians, Matthew Paris and William of Malmsbury; the elegant and unfortunate Abelard; and, to crown the rest, the English Franciscan, Roger Bacon.

It may be here observed, that forbidding the vulgar tongue in the offices of devotion, and in reading the Scriptures, though undoubtedly a great corruption in the Christian church, was of infinite service to the interests of learning. When the ecclesiastics had locked up their religion in a foreign tongue, they would take care not to lose the key. This gave an importance to the learned languages; and every scholar could not only read, but wrote and disputed in Latin, which without such a motive would probably have been no more studied than the Chinese. And at the time when the modern languages of Europe were yet unformed and barbarous, Latin was of great use as a kind of universal tongue by which learned men might converse and correspond with each other.

Indeed, the monks were almost the only set of men who had leisure or opportunity to pay the least attention to literary subjects. A learned education (and a very little went to that title) was reckoned peculiar to the religious. It was almost esteemed a blemish on the savage and martial character of the gentry to have any tincture of letters. A man, therefore, of a studious and retired turn, averse to quarrels, and not desirous of the fierce and sanguinary glory of those times, beheld in the cloister a peaceful and honorable sanctuary; where, without the reproach of cowardice, or danger of invasion, he might devote himself to learning, associate with men of his own turn, and have free access to libraries and manuscripts. In this enlightened and polished age, where learning is diffused through every rank, and many a merchant's clerk possesses more real knowledge than half the literati of that era, we can scarcely conceive how gross an ignorance overspread those times, and how totally all useful learning might have been lost amongst us, had it not been for an order of men vested with peculiar privileges, and protected by even a superstitious degree of reverence.

Thus the Muses, with their attendant arts, in strange disguise indeed, and uncouth trappings, took refuge in the peaceful gloom of the convent. Statuary carved a madonna or a crucifix; Painting illuminated a missal; Eloquence made the panegyric of a saint; and History composed a legend. Yet still they breathed, and were ready, at any happier period, to emerge from obscurity with all their native charms and undiminished lustre.

But there were other views in which those who devoted themselves to a monastic life might be supposed useful to society. They were often employed either in cultivating their gardens, or in curious mechanical works; as indeed the nuns are still famous for many elegant and ingenious manufactures. By the constant communication they had with those of their own order, and with their common head at Rome, they maintained some intercourse between nations at a time when travelling was dangerous, and commerce had not, as now, made the most distant parts of the globe familiar to each other; and they keep up a more intimate bond of union amongst learned men of all countries, who would otherwise have been secluded from all knowledge of each other. A monk might travel with more convenience than any one else; his person was safe, and he was sure of meeting with proper accommodations. The intercourse with Rome must have been peculiarly favorable to these Northern nations, as Italy for a long time led the way in every improvement of politeness or literature; and if we imported their superstitions, we likewise imported their manufactures, their knowledge, and their taste. Thus Alfred sent for Italian monks when he wanted to civilize his people, and introduce among them some tincture of letters. It may likewise be presumed that they tempered the rigor of monarchy. Indeed they, as well as the sovereigns, endeavored to enslave the people; but subjection was not likely to be so abject and unlimited where the object of it was divided, and each showed by turns that the other might be opposed. It must have been of service to the cause of liberty to have a set of men whose laws, privileges, and immunities the most daring kings were afraid to trample on; and this, before a more enlightened spirit of freedom had arisen, might have its effect in preventing the states of Christendom from falling into such entire slavery as the Asiatics.

Such an order would in some degree check the excessive regard paid to birth. A man of mean origin and obscure parentage saw himself excluded from almost every path of secular preferment, and almost treated as a being of an inferior species by the high and haughty spirit of the gentry; but he was at liberty to aspire to the highest dignities of the Church; and there have been many who, like Sextus V., have by their industry and personal merit alone raised themselves to a level with kings.

It should likewise be remembered that many of the orders were charitable institutions; as the *knights of faith and charity* in the thirteenth century, who were associated for the purpose of suppressing those bands of robbers which infested the public roads in France; the *brethren of the Order of the Redemption*, for redeeming slaves from the Mahometans; the *Order of St. Anthony*, first established for the relief of the poor under certain disorders; and the *brethren and sisters of the pious and Christian schools*, for educating poor children. These supplied the place of hospitals and such other foundations, which are now established on the broader basis of public benevolence. To bind up the wounds of the stranger was peculiarly the office of the inhabitants of the convent; and they often shared the charities they received. The exercise of hospitality is still their characteristic, and must have been of particular use formerly, when there were not the conveniences and accommodations for travelling which we now enjoy. The learned stranger was always sure of an agreeable residence amongst them; and as they all understood Latin, they served him for interpreters, and introduced him to a sight of whatever was curious or valuable in the countries which he visited. They checked the spirit of savage fierceness, to which our warlike ancestors were so prone, with the mildness and sanctity of religious influences; they preserved some respect to law and order, and often decided controversies by means less bloody than the sword, though confessedly more superstitious.

A proof that these institutions had a favorable aspect towards civilization may be drawn from a late history of Ireland. "Soon after the introduction of Christianity into that kingdom," says Dr. Leland, "the monks fixed their habitations in deserts, which they cultivated with their own hands, and rendered the most delightful spots

10 *   o

in the kingdom. These deserts became well-policed
cities; and it is remarkable enough, that to the monks
we owe so useful an institution in Ireland as the bringing great numbers together into one civil community.
In these cities the monks set up schools, and taught
not only the youth of Ireland, but the neighboring
nations, furnishing them also with books. They became umpires between contending chiefs, and when
they could not confine them within the bounds of
reason and religion, at least terrified them by denoun-
cing Divine vengeance against their excesses."

Let it be considered, too, that when the minds of men
began to open, some of the most eminent reformers
sprung from the bosom of the Church, and even of the
convent. It was not the laity who began to think.
The ecclesiastics were the first to perceive the errors
they had introduced. The Church was reformed from
within, not from without; and, like the silk-worm, when
ripened in their cells to maturer vigor and perfection,
they pierced the cloud themselves had spun, and within
which they had so long been enveloped.

And let not the good Protestant be too much startled
if I here venture to insinuate that the monasteries
were schools of some high and respectable virtues.
Poverty, chastity, and a renunciation of the world,
were certainly intended in the first plan of these institutions; and though, from the unavoidable frailty of

human nature, they were not always observed, certain it is that many individuals amongst them have been striking examples of the self-denying virtues ; and as the influence they acquired was only built upon the voluntary homage of the mind, it may be presumed such an ascendency was not originally gained without some species of merit. The fondness for monkery is easily deduced from some of the best principles in the human heart. It was indeed necessity that in the third century first drove the Christians to shelter themselves from the Decian persecution in the solitary deserts of Thebais ; but the humor soon spread, and numbers under the name of hermits, or eremites, secluded themselves from the commerce of mankind, choosing the wildest solitudes, living in caves and hollows of the rocks, and subsisting on such roots and herbs as the ground afforded them. About the fourth century they were gathered into communities, and increased with surprising rapidity. It was then that, by a great and sudden revolution, the fury of persecution had ceased, and the governing powers were become friendly to Christianity. But the agitation of men's minds did not immediately subside with the storm. The Christians had so long experienced the necessity of resigning all the enjoyments of life, and were so detached from every tie which might interfere with the profession of their faith, that upon a more favorable turn of affairs they hardly dared open their minds to pleasurable emotions. They thought the life of a good man must be a continual warfare between mind and body ; and having been long used to see ease and safety on the one side and virtue on the other, no wonder if the association was so strong in their minds as to suggest the necessity of voluntary mortification, and lead them to inflict those sufferings upon themselves which they no longer apprehended from others. They had continually experienced the amazing effects of Christianity in supporting its followers under hardship, tortures, and death ; and they thought little of its influence in regulating the common behavior of life, if it produced none of those great exertions they had been used to contemplate. They were struck with the change from heathen licentiousness to the purity of the gospel ; and thought they could never be far enough removed from that bondage of the senses which it had just cost them so violent a struggle to escape. The minds of men were working with newly received opinions, not yet mellowed into a rational faith ; and the young converts, astonished at the grandeur and sublimity of the doctrines which then first entered their hearts with irresistible force, thought them worthy to engross their whole attention. The mystic dreams of the Platonist mingled with the enthusiasm of the martyr ; and it soon became the prevailing opinion that silence, solitude, and contemplation were necessary for the reception of Divine truth. Mistaken ideas prevailed of a purity and perfection far superior to the rules of common life, which was only to be attained by those who denied themselves all the indulgences of sense ; and thus the ascetic severities of the cloister succeeded in some degree to the philosophic poverty of the Cynic school and the lofty virtues of the Stoic.

Indeed, it is now the prevailing taste in morals to decry every observance which has the least appearance of rigor, and to insist only on the softer virtues. But let it be remembered that self-command and self-denial are as necessary to the practice of benevolence, charity, and compassion, as to any other duty ; that it is impossible to live to others without denying ourselves ; and that the man who has not learned to curb his appetites and passions is ill qualified for those sacrifices which the friendly affections are continually requiring of him. The man who has that one quality of self-command will find little difficulty in the practice of any other duty ; as, on the contrary, he who has it not, though possessed of the gentlest feelings and most refined sensibilities, will soon find his benevolence sink into a mere companionable easiness of temper, neither useful to others nor happy for himself. A noble enthusiasm is sometimes of use to show how far human nature can go. Though it may not be proper or desirable that numbers should seclude themselves from the common duties and ordinary avocations of life for the austerer lessons of the cloister; yet it is not unuseful that some should push their virtues to even a romantic height; and it is encouraging to reflect, in the hour of temptation, that the love of ease, the aversion to pain, every appetite and passion, and even the strongest propensities in our nature, have been controlled; that the empire of the mind over the body has been asserted in its fullest extent; and that there have been men in all ages capable of voluntarily renouncing all the world offers, voluntarily suffering all it dreads, and living independent, and unconnected with it. Nor was it a small advantage, or ill calculated to support the dignity of science, that a man of learning might be respectable in a coarse gown, a leathern girdle, and barefooted. Cardinal Ximenes preserved the severe simplicity of a convent amidst the pomp and luxury of palaces; and to those who thus thought it becoming in the highest stations to affect the appearance of poverty, the reality surely could not be very dreadful.

There is yet another light in which these institutions may be considered. It is surely not improper to provide a retreat for those who, stained by some deep and enormous crime, wish to expiate by severe and uncommon penitence those offences which render them unworthy of freer commerce with the world. Repentance is never so secure from a relapse as when it breaks off at once from every former connection, and, entering upon a new course of life, bids adieu to every object that might revive the idea of temptations which have once prevailed. In these solemn retreats, the stillness and acknowledged sanctity of the place, with the striking novelty of everything around them, might have great influence in calming the passions ; might break the force of habit, and suddenly induce a new turn of thinking. There are likewise afflictions so overwhelming to humanity that they leave no relish in the mind for anything else than to enjoy its own melancholy in silence and solitude ; and to a heart torn with remorse, or oppressed with sorrow, the gloomy severities of La Trappe are really a relief. Retirement is also the favorite wish of age. Many a statesman and many a warrior, sick of the bustle of that world to which they had devoted the prime of their days, have longed for some quiet cell, where, like Cardinal Wolsey or Charles V., they might shroud their gray hairs, and lose sight of the follies with which they had been too much tainted.

Though there is, perhaps, less to plead for immuring beauty in a cloister, and confining that part of the species who are formed to shine in families and sweeten society to the barren duties and austere discipline of a monastic life, yet circumstances might occur in which they would, even to a woman, be a welcome refuge. A

young female, whom accident or war had deprived of
her natural protectors, must, in an age of barbarism, be
peculiarly exposed and helpless. A convent offered her
an asylum where she might be safe, at least, if not
happy; and add to the consciousness of unviolated virtue the flattering dreams of angelic purity and perfection. There were orders, as well among the women as
the men, instituted for charitable purposes, such as that
of the *virgins of love*, or *daughters of mercy*, founded in
1660 for the relief of the sick poor, with others for instructing their children. These must have been peculiarly suited to the softness and compassion of the sex;
and to this it is no doubt owing, that still, in Catholic
countries, ladies of the highest rank often visit the hospitals and houses of the poor, waiting on them with the
most tender assiduity, and performing such offices as
our Protestant ladies would be shocked at the thoughts
of. We should also consider that most of the females
who now take the veil are such as have no agreeable
prospects in life. Why should not these be allowed to
quit a world which will never miss them? It is easier
to retire from the public than to support its disregard.
The convent is to them a shelter from poverty and neglect. Their little community grows dear to them. The
equality which subsists among these sisters of obscurity, the similarity of their fate, the peace, the leisure
they enjoy, give rise to the most endearing friendships.

Their innocence is shielded by the simplicity of their life from even the idea of ill; and they are flattered by the notion of a voluntary renunciation of pleasures, which, probably, had they continued in the world, they would have had little share in.

After all that can be said, we have reason enough to rejoice that the superstitions of former times are now fallen into disrepute. What might be a palliative at one time, soon became a crying evil in itself. When the fuller day of science began to dawn, the monkish orders were willing to exclude its brightness, that the dim lamp might still glimmer in their cell. Their growing vices have rendered them justly odious to society, and they seem in a fair way of being forever abolished. But may we not still hope that the world was better than it would have been without them, and that He who knows to bring good out of evil has made them, in their day, subservient to some useful purposes? The corruptions of Christianity, which have been accumulating for so many ages, seem to be now gradually clearing away, and some future period may perhaps exhibit our religion in all its native simplicity.

> So the pure, limpid stream, when foul with stains
> Of rushing torrents and descending rains,
> Works itself clear, and as it runs refines,
> Till by degrees the floating mirror shines;
> Reflects each flower that on its borders grows,
> And a new heaven in its fair bosom shows.

AGAINST INCONSISTENCY IN OUR EXPECTATIONS.

" What is more reasonable, than that they who take pains for anything should get most in that particular for which they take pains ? They have taken pains for power, you for right principles; they for riches, you for a proper use of the appearance of things : see whether they have the advantage of you in that for which you have taken pains, and which they neglect. If they are in power, and you not, why will not you speak the truth to yourself, that you do nothing for the sake of power, but that they do everything ? No, but since I take care to have right principles, it is more reasonable that I should have power. Yes, in respect to what you take care about, your principles. But give up to others the things in which they have taken more care than you. Else it is just as if, because you have right principles, you should think it fit that, when you shoot an arrow, you should hit the mark better than an archer, or that you should forge better than a smith." — CARTER's *Epictetus*.

AS most of the unhappiness in the world arises rather from disappointed desires than from positive evil, it is of the utmost consequence to attain just notions of the laws and order of the universe, that we may not vex ourselves with fruitless wishes, or give way to groundless and unreasonable discontent. The laws of natural philosophy, indeed, are tolerably understood and attended to ; and though we may suffer inconveniences, we are seldom disappointed in consequence of them. No man expects to preserve orange-

trees in the open air through an English winter; or,
when he has planted an acorn, to see it become a large
oak in a few months. The mind of man naturally
yields to necessity; and our wishes soon subside when
we see the impossibility of their being gratified. Now,
upon an accurate inspection, we shall find, in the moral
government of the world, and the order of the intellectual system, laws as determinate, fixed, and invariable
as any in Newton's " Principia." The progress of vege-
tation is not more certain than the growth of habit;
nor is the power of attraction more clearly proved than
the force of affection or the influence of example. The
man, therefore, who has well studied the operations of
nature in mind as well as matter will acquire a certain
moderation and equity in his claims upon Providence.
He never will be disappointed either in himself or
others. He will act with precision, and expect that
effect and that alone from his efforts, which they are
naturally adapted to produce. For want of this, men
of mind and integrity often censure the dispositions of
Providence for suffering characters they despise to run
away with advantages which, they yet know, are purchased by such means as a high and noble spirit could
never submit to. If you refuse to pay the price, why
expect the purchase ? We should consider this world as
a great mart of commerce, where fortune exposes to our
view various commodities,—riches, ease, tranquillity,

fame, integrity, knowledge. Everything is marked at
a settled price. Our time, our labor, our ingenuity, is
so much ready money which we are to lay out to the
best advantage. Examine, compare, choose, reject; but
stand to your own judgment; and do not, like children, when you have purchased one thing, repine that
you do not possess another which you did not purchase.
Such is the force of well-regulated industry, that a
steady and vigorous exertion of our faculties, directed
to one end, will generally insure success. Would you,
for instance, be rich ? Do you think that single point
worth the sacrificing everything else to ? You may
then be rich. Thousands have become so from the
lowest beginnings by toil, and patient diligence, and
attention to the minutest articles of expense and profit.
But you must give up the pleasures of leisure, of a
vacant mind, of a free, unsuspicious temper. If you
preserve your integrity, it must be a coarse-spun and
vulgar honesty. Those high and lofty notions of morals
which you brought with you from the schools must be
considerably lowered, and mixed with the baser alloy
of a jealous and worldly-minded prudence. You must
learn to do hard, if not unjust things; and for the nice
embarrassments of a delicate and ingenuous spirit, it is
necessary for you to get rid of them as fast as possible.
You must shut your heart against the Muses, and be
content to feed your understanding with plain house-

hold truths. In short, you must not attempt to enlarge
your ideas, or polish your taste, or refine your sentiments; but must keep on in one beaten track, without
turning aside either to the right hand or to the left.
"But I cannot submit to drudgery like this, — I feel a
spirit above it." 'T is well: be above it, then, only do
not repine that you are not rich.

Is knowledge the pearl of price ? That too may be
purchased — by steady application, and long, solitary
hours of study and reflection. Bestow these, and you
shall be wise. "But (says the man of letters) what a
hardship it is that many an illiterate fellow who cannot
construe the motto of the arms on his coach shall raise
a fortune and make a figure, while I have little more
than the common conveniences of life !" *Et tibi magna
satis !* Was it in order to raise a fortune that you
consumed the sprightly hours of youth in study and
retirement ? Was it to be rich that you grew pale over
the midnight lamp, and distilled the sweetness from
the Greek and Roman spring ? You have then mistaken your path, and ill employed your industry.
"What reward have I, then, for all my labors ? " What
reward ! A large, comprehensive soul, well purged from
vulgar fears and perturbations and prejudices ; able
to comprehend and interpret the works of man — of
God. A rich, flourishing, cultivated mind, pregnant
with inexhaustible stores of entertainment and reflec-

tion. A perpetual spring of fresh ideas, and the conscious dignity of superior intelligence. Good heaven! and what reward can you ask besides?

" But is it not some reproach upon the economy of Providence that such a one, who is a mean, dirty fellow, should have amassed wealth enough to buy half a nation?" Not in the least. He made himself a mean, dirty fellow for that very end. He has paid his health, his conscience, his liberty, for it; and will you envy him his bargain? Will you hang your head and blush in his presence because he outshines you in equipage and show? Lift up your brow with a noble confidence, and say to yourself, I have not these things, it is true; but it is because I have not sought, because I have not desired them; it is because I possess something better. I have chosen my lot. I am content and satisfied.

You are a modest man. You love quiet and independence, and have a delicacy and reserve in your temper which renders it impossible for you to elbow your way in the world, and be the herald of your own merits. Be content, then, with a modest retirement, with the esteem of your intimate friends, with the praises of a blameless heart, and a delicate, ingenuous spirit; but resign the splendid distinctions of the world to those who can better scramble for them.

The man whose tender sensibility of conscience and strict regard to the rules of morality make him scru-

pulous and fearful of offending is often heard to complain of the disadvantages he lies under in every path
of honor and profit. "Could I but get over some nice
points, and conform to the practice and opinion of
those about me, I might stand as fair a chance as others
for dignities and preferment." And why can you not?
What hinders you from discarding this troublesome
scrupulosity of yours which stands so grievously in
your way? If it be a small thing to enjoy a healthful
mind, sound at the very core, that does not shrink from
the keenest inspection; inward freedom from remorse
and perturbation; unsullied whiteness and simplicity
of manners; a genuine integrity,

> "Pure in the last recesses of the mind," —

if you think these advantages an inadequate recompense for what you resign, dismiss your scruples this
instant, and be a slave-merchant, a parasite, or — what
you please.

> "If these be motives weak, break off betimes";

and as you have not spirit to assert the dignity of
virtue, be wise enough not to forego the emoluments
of vice.

I much admire the spirit of the ancient philosophers,
in that they never attempted, as our moralists often do,
to lower the tone of philosophy, and make it consistent
with all the indulgences of indolence and sensuality.

They never thought of having the bulk of mankind for their disciples, but kept themselves as distinct as possible from a worldly life. They plainly told men what sacrifices were required, and what advantages they were which might be expected.

> " Si virtus hoc una potest dare, fortis omissis
>   Hoc age deliciis . . . . "

If you would be a philosopher, these are the terms. You must do thus and thus: there is no other way. If not, go and be one of the vulgar.

There is no one quality gives so much dignity to a character as consistency of conduct. Even if a man's pursuits be wrong and unjustifiable, yet if they are prosecuted with steadiness and vigor, we cannot withhold our admiration. The most characteristic mark of a great mind is to choose some one important object, and pursue it through life. It was this made Cæsar a great man. His object was ambition; he pursued it steadily, and was always ready to sacrifice to it every interfering passion or inclination.

There is a pretty passage in one of Lucian's dialogues, where Jupiter complains to Cupid that, though he has had so many intrigues, he was never sincerely beloved. In order to be loved, says Cupid, you must lay aside your ægis and your thunder-bolts, and you must curl and perfume your hair, and place a garland on your head, and walk with a soft step, and assume a winning, obsequious deportment. But, replied Jupiter, I am not willing to resign so much of my dignity. Then, returns Cupid, leave off desiring to be loved. He wanted to be Jupiter and Adonis at the same time.

It must be confessed that men of genius are of all others most inclined to make these unreasonable claims. As their relish for enjoyment is strong, their views large and comprehensive, and they feel themselves lifted above the common bulk of mankind, they are apt to slight that natural reward of praise and admiration which is ever largely paid to distinguished abilities, and to expect to be called forth to public notice and favor, without considering that their talents are commonly very unfit for active life; that their eccentricity and turn for speculation disqualifies them for the business of the world, which is best carried on by men of moderate genius; and that society is not obliged to reward any one who is not useful to it. The poets have been a very unreasonable race, and have often complained loudly of the neglect of genius and the ingratitude of the age. The tender and pensive Cowley and the elegant Shenstone had their minds tinctured by this discontent; and even the sublime melancholy of Young was too much owing to the stings of disappointed ambition.

The moderation we have been endeavoring to inculcate will likewise prevent much mortification and

disgust in our commerce with mankind. As we ought
not to wish in ourselves, so neither should we expect
in our friends, contrary qualifications. Young and sanguine, when we enter the world, and feel our affections
drawn forth by any particular excellence in a character,
we immediately give it credit for all others; and are
beyond measure disgusted when we come to discover,
as we soon must discover, the defects in the other side
of the balance. But nature is much more frugal than
to heap together all manner of shining qualities in one
glaring mass. Like a judicious painter, she endeavors
to preserve a certain unity of style and coloring in
her pieces. Models of absolute perfection are only to
be met with in romance; where exquisite beauty, and
brilliant wit, and profound judgment, and immaculate
virtue are all blended together to adorn some favorite
character. As an anatomist knows that the racer
cannot have the strength and muscles of the draught-
horse, and that winged men, griffins, and mermaids
must be mere creatures of the imagination; so the philosopher is sensible that there are combinations of moral
qualities which never can take place but in idea. There
is a different air and complexion in characters as well
as in faces, though perhaps each equally beautiful; and
the excellences of one cannot be transferred to the
other. Thus if one man possesses a stoical apathy of
soul, acts independent of the opinion of the world, and

fulfils every duty with mathematical exactness, you must not expect that man to be greatly influenced by the weakness of pity or the partialities of friendship: you must not be offended that he does not fly to meet you after a short absence, or require from him the convivial spirit and honest effusions of a warm, open, susceptible heart. If another is remarkable for a lively, active zeal, inflexible integrity, a strong indignation against vice, and freedom in reproving it, he will probably have some little bluntness in his address not altogether suitable to polished life; he will want the winning arts of conversation; he will disgust by a kind of haughtiness and negligence in his manner, and often hurt the delicacy of his acquaintance with harsh and disagreeable truths.

We usually say, that man is a genius, *but* he has some whims and oddities; such a one has a very general knowledge, *but* he is superficial, etc. Now, in all such cases we should speak more rationally did we substitute *therefore* for *but*. He is a genius, *therefore* he is whimsical; and the like.

It is the fault of the present age, owing to the freer commerce that different ranks and professions now enjoy with each other, that characters are not marked with sufficient strength; the several classes run too much into one another. We have fewer pedants, it is true, but we have fewer striking originals. Every one is expected to have such a tincture of general knowledge as is incompatible with going deep into any science; and such a conformity to fashionable manners as checks the free workings of the ruling passion, and gives an insipid sameness to the face of society, under the idea of polish and regularity.

There is a cast of manners peculiar and becoming to each age, sex, and profession; one, therefore, should not throw out illiberal and commonplace censures against another. Each is perfect in its kind. A woman as a woman; a tradesman as a tradesman. We are often hurt by the brutality and sluggish conceptions of the vulgar; not considering that some there must be to be hewers of wood and drawers of water, and that cultivated genius, or even any great refinement and delicacy in their moral feelings, would be a real misfortune to them.

Let us then study the philosophy of the human mind. The man who is master of this science will know what to expect from every one. From this man, wise advice; from that, cordial sympathy; from another, casual entertainment. The passions and inclinations of others are his tools, which he can use with as much precision as he would the mechanical powers; and he can as readily make allowance for the workings of vanity, or the bias of self-interest in his friends, as for the power of friction or the irregularities of the needle.

ON EDUCATION.

THE other day I paid a visit to a gentleman with whom, though greatly my superior in fortune, I have long been in habits of easy intimacy. He rose in the world by honorable industry; and married, rather late in life, a lady to whom he had been long attached, and in whom centred the wealth of several expiring families. Their earnest wish for children was not immediately gratified. At length they were made happy by a son, who, from the moment he was born, engrossed all their care and attention. My friend received me in his library, where I found him busied in turning over books of education, of which he had collected all that were worthy of notice, from Xenophon to Locke, and from Locke to Catherine Macaulay. As he knows I have been engaged in the business of instruction, he did me the honor to consult me on the subject of his researches, hoping, he said, that, out of all the systems before him, we should be able to form a plan equally complete and comprehensive; it being the determination of both himself and his lady to choose the best that could be had, and to spare neither pains nor expense in making their child all

that was great and good. I gave him my thoughts
with the utmost freedom, and, after I returned home,
threw upon paper the observations which had occurred
to me.

The first thing to be considered, with respect to
education, is the object of it. This appears to me to
have been generally misunderstood. Education, in its
largest sense, is a thing of great scope and extent. It
includes the whole process by which a human being
is formed to be what he is, in habits, principles, and
cultivation of every kind. But of this, a very small
part is in the power even of the parent himself; a small-
er still can be directed by purchased tuition of any
kind. You engage for your child masters and tutors
at large salaries; and you do well, for they are competent to instruct him; they will give him the means,
at least, of acquiring science and accomplishments;
but in the business of education, properly so called,
they can do little for you. Do you ask, then, what
will educate your son? Your example will educate
him; your conversation with your friends, the business he sees you transact, the likings and dislikings
you express, these will educate him; — the society
you live in will educate him; your domestics will educate him; above all, your rank and situation in life,
your house, your table, your pleasure-grounds, your
hounds and your stables, will educate him. It is not

in your power to withdraw him from the continual influence of these things, except you were to withdraw yourself from them also. You speak of *beginning* the education of your son. The moment he was able to form an idea, his education was already begun; the education of circumstances, — insensible education, — which, like insensible perspiration, is of more constant and powerful effect, and of infinitely more consequence to the habit, than that which is direct and apparent. This education goes on at every instant of time; it goes on like time; you can neither stop it nor turn its course. What these have a tendency to make your child, that he will be. Maxims and documents are good precisely till they are tried, and no longer; they will teach him to talk, and nothing more. The *circumstances* in which your son is placed will be even more prevalent than your example; and you have no right to expect him to become what you yourself are, but by the same means. You, that have toiled during youth, to set your son upon higher ground, and to enable him to begin where you left off, do not expect that son to be what you were, — diligent, modest, active, simple in his tastes, fertile in resources. You have put him under quite a different master. Poverty educated you; wealth will educate him. You cannot suppose the result will be the same. You must not even expect that he will be what you now are; for, though relaxed perhaps from

the severity of your frugal habits, you still derive
advantage from having formed them; and in your
heart you like plain dinners, and early hours, and old
friends, whenever your fortune will permit you to enjoy
them.   But it will not be so with your son; his tastes
will be formed by your present situation, and in no
degree by your former one.   But I take great care, you
will say, to counteract these tendencies, and to bring
him up in hardy and simple manners; I know their
value, and am resolved that he shall acquire no other.
Yes, you make him hardy; that is to say, you take a
country-house in a good air, and make him run, well
clothed and carefully attended, for, it may be, an hour,
in a clear, frosty winter's day upon your gravelled ter-
race; or perhaps you take the puny, shivering infant
from his warm bed, and dip him in an icy-cold bath, —
and you think you have done great matters.   And so
you have; you have done all you can.   But you were
suffered to run abroad half the day on a bleak heath,
in weather fit and unfit, wading barefoot through dirty
ponds, sometimes losing your way benighted, scram-
bling over hedges, climbing trees, in perils every hour,
both of life and limb.   Your life was of very little consequence to any one; even your parents, encumbered
with a numerous family, had little time to indulge the
softnesses of affection or the solicitude of anxiety; and
to every one else it was of no consequence at all.   It is

not possible for you, it would not even be right for you, in your present situation, to pay no more attention to your child than was paid to you. In these mimic experiments of education there is always something which distinguishes them from reality; some weak part left unfortified, for the arrows of misfortune to find their way into. Achilles was a young nobleman, *dios Achilleus*, and therefore, though he had Charon for his tutor, there was one foot left undipped. You may throw by Rousseau; your parents practised without having read it; you may read, but imperious circumstances forbid you the practice of it.

You are sensible of the advantages of simplicity of diet; and you make a point of restricting that of your child to the plainest food, for you are resolved that he shall not be nice. But this plain food is of the choicest quality, prepared by your own cook; his fruit is ripened from your walls; his cloth, his glasses, all the accompaniments of the table, are such as are only met with in families of opulence; the very servants who attend him are neat, well dressed, and have a certain air of fashion. You may call this simplicity; but I say he will be nice, — for it is a kind of simplicity which only wealth can attain to, and which will subject him to be disgusted at all common tables. Besides, he will from time to time partake of those delicacies which your table abounds with; you yourself will give

11 *

him of them occasionally; you would be unkind if you did not. Your servants, if good-natured, will do the same. Do you think you can keep the full stream of luxury running by his lips, and he not taste of it? Vain imagination!

I would not be understood to inveigh against wealth, or against the enjoyments of it; they are real enjoyments, and allied to many elegancies in manners and in taste;—I only wish to prevent unprofitable pains and inconsistent expectations.

You are sensible of the benefit of early rising; and you may, if you please, make it a point that your daughter shall retire with her governess, and your son with his tutor, at the hour when you are preparing to see company. But their sleep, in the first place, will not be so sweet and undisturbed amidst the rattle of carriages, and the glare of tapers glancing through the rooms, as that of the village child in his quiet cottage, protected by silence and darkness; and, moreover, you may depend upon it, that, as the coercive power of education is laid aside, they will in a few months slide into the habitudes of the rest of the family, whose hours are determined by their company and situation in life. You have, however, done good, as far as it goes; it is something gained, to defer pernicious habits, if we cannot prevent them.

There is nothing which has so little share in education as direct precept. To be convinced of this, we need only reflect that there is no one point we labor more to establish with children than that of their speaking truth; and there is not any in which we succeed worse. And why? Because children readily see we have an interest in it. Their speaking truth is used by us as an engine of government. "Tell me, my dear child, when you have broken anything, and I will not be angry with you." "Thank you for nothing," says the child. "If I prevent you from finding it out, I am sure you will not be angry"; and nine times out of ten he can prevent it. He knows that, in the common intercourses of life, you tell a thousand falsehoods. But these are necessary lies on important occasions.

Your child is the best judge how much occasion he has to tell a lie; he may have as great occasion for it as you have to conceal a bad piece of news from a sick friend, or to hide your vexation from an unwelcome visitor. That authority which extends its claims over every action and even every thought, which insists upon an answer to every interrogation, however indiscreet or oppressive to the feelings, will, in young or old, produce falsehood; or, if in some few instances the deeply imbibed fear of future and unknown punishment should restrain from direct falsehood, it will produce a habit of dissimulation which is still worse. The child, the slave, or the subject, who, on proper occasions, may not say "I do not choose to tell," will certainly, by the circumstances in which you place him, be driven to have recourse to deceit, even should he not be countenanced by your example.

I do not mean to assert that sentiments inculcated in education have no influence, — they have much, though not the most; but it is the sentiments we let drop occasionally, the conversation they overhear when playing unnoticed in a corner of the room, which has an effect upon children, and not what is addressed directly to them in the tone of exhortation. If you would know precisely the effect these set discourses have upon your child, be pleased to reflect upon that which a discourse from the pulpit, which you have reason to think merely professional, has upon you. Children have almost an intuitive discernment between the maxims you bring forward for their use and those by which you direct your own conduct. Be as cunning as you will, they are always more cunning than you. Every child knows whom his father and mother love, and see with pleasure, and whom they dislike; for whom they think themselves obliged to set out their best plate and china; whom they think it an honor to visit, and upon whom they confer honor by admitting them to their company. "Respect nothing so much as virtue," says Eugenio to his son; "virtue and talents are the only grounds of distinction." The child pres-

ently has occasion to inquire why his father pulls off
his hat to some people and not to others; he is told
that outward respect must be proportioned to different
stations in life. This is a little difficult of comprehen-
sion; however, by dint of explanation, he gets over it
tolerably well. But he sees his father's house in the
bustle and hurry of preparation; common business laid
aside, everybody in movement, an unusual anxiety to
please and to shine. Nobody is at leisure to receive
his caresses or attend to his questions; his lessons are
interrupted, his hours deranged. At length a guest
arrives; it is my Lord ——, whom he has heard you
speak of twenty times as one of the most worthless
characters upon earth. Your child, Eugenio, has received a lesson of education. Resume, if you will, your
systems of morality on the morrow, you will in vain
attempt to eradicate it. "You expect company, mamma;
must I be dressed to-day?" "No, it is only good Mrs.
Such-a-one." Your child has received a lesson of education; one which he well understands and will long
remember. You have sent your child to a public
school; but to secure his morals against the vice which
you too justly apprehend abounds there, you have giv-
en him a private tutor, — a man of strict morals and
religion. He may help him to prepare his tasks; but
do you imagine it will be in his power to form his
mind? His school-fellows, the allowance you give him,

the manners of the age and of the place, will do that;
and not the lectures which he is obliged to hear. If
these are different from what you yourself experienced,
you must not be surprised to see him gradually recede
from the principles, civil and religious, which you hold,
and break off from your connections, and adopt manners
different from your own. This is remarkably exempli-
fied amongst those of the Dissenters who have risen to
wealth and consequence. I believe it would be difficult to find an instance of families who for three generations have kept their carriage and continued Dissenters.

Education, it is often observed, is an expensive thing.
It is so; but the paying for lessons is the smallest part
of the cost. If you would go to the price of having
your son a worthy man, you must be so yourself; your
friends, your servants, your company, must be all of
that stamp. Suppose this to be the case, much is done:
but there will remain circumstances which perhaps you
cannot alter, that will still have their effect. Do you
wish him to love simplicity? Would you be content
to lay down your coach, to drop your title? Where is
the parent who would do this to educate his son? You
carry him to the workshops of artisans, and show him
different machines and fabrics, to awaken his ingenuity.
The necessity of getting his bread would awaken it
much more effectually. The single circumstance of

having a fortune to get, or a fortune to spend, will probably operate more strongly upon his mind, not only than your precepts, but even than your example. You wish your.child to be modest and unassuming; you are so, perhaps, yourself, — and you pay liberally a preceptor for giving him lessons of humility. You do not perceive that the very circumstance of having a man of letters and accomplishments retained about his person, for his sole advantage, tends more forcibly to inspire him with an idea of self-consequence than all the lessons he can give him to repress it. "Why do not you look sad, you rascal?" says the undertaker to his man in the play of "The Funeral"; "I give you I know not how much money for looking sad, and the more I give you, the gladder I think you are." So will it be with the wealthy heir. The lectures that are given him on condescension and affability only prove to him upon how much higher ground he stands than those about him; and the very pains that are taken with his moral character will make him proud, by showing him how much he is the object of attention. You cannot help these things. Your servants, out of respect to you, will bear with his petulance; your company, out of respect to you, will forbear to check his impatience; and you yourself, if he is clever, will repeat his observations.

In the exploded doctrine of sympathies you are

directed, if you have cut your finger, to let that alone, and put your plaster upon the knife. This is very bad doctrine, I must confess, in philosophy, but very good in morals. Is a man luxurious, self-indulgent? do not apply your *physic of the soul* to him, but cure his fortune. Is he haughty? cure his rank, his title. Is he vulgar? cure his company. Is he diffident or mean-spirited? cure his poverty, give him consequence, — but these prescriptions go far beyond the family recipes of education.

What, then, is the result? In the first place, that we should contract our ideas of education, and expect no more from it than it is able to perform. It can give instruction. There will always be an essential difference between a human being cultivated and uncultivated. Education can provide proper instructors in the various arts and sciences, and portion out to the best advantage those precious hours of youth which never will return. It can likewise give, in a great degree, personal habits; and even if these should afterwards give way under the influence of contrary circumstances, your child will feel the good effects of them, for the later and the less will he go into what is wrong. Let us also be assured that the business of education, properly so called, is not transferable. You may engage masters to instruct your child in this or the other accomplishment, but you must educate him yourself.

You not only ought to do it, but you must do it, whether you intend it or no. As education is a thing necessary for all, — for the poor and for the rich, for the illiterate as well as for the learned, — Providence has not made it dependent upon systems uncertain, operose, and difficult of investigation. It is not necessary, with Rousseau or Madame Genlis, to devote to the education of one child the talents and the time of a number of grown men ; to surround him with an artificial world ; and to counteract, by maxims, the natural tendencies of the situation he is placed in, in society. Every one has time to educate his child : the poor man educates him while working in his cottage ; the man of business while employed in his counting-house.

Do we see a father who is diligent in his profession, domestic in his habits, whose house is the resort of well-informed, intelligent people, — a mother whose time is usefully filled, whose attention to her duties secures esteem, and whose amiable manners attract affection ? Do not be solicitous, respectable couple, about the moral education of your offspring; do not be uneasy because you cannot surround them with the apparatus of books and systems, or fancy you must retire from the world to devote yourselves to their improvement. In your world they are brought up much better than they could be under any plan of factitious education which you could provide for them ;

they will imbibe affection from your caresses, taste
from your conversation, urbanity from the commerce
of your society, and mutual love from your example.
Do not regret that you are not rich enough to provide
tutors and governors, to watch his steps with sedulous
and servile anxiety, and furnish him with maxims it is
morally impossible he should act upon when grown up.
Do not you see how seldom this over-culture produces
its effect, and how many shining and excellent characters start up every day from the bosom of obscurity,
with scarcely any care at all ?

Are children, then, to be neglected ? Surely not; but,
having given them the instruction and accomplishments which their situation in life requires, let us
reject superfluous solicitude, and trust that their characters will form themselves from the spontaneous influence of good examples, and circumstances which
impel them to useful action.

But the education of your house, important as
it is, is only a part of a more comprehensive system.
Providence takes your child where you leave him.
Providence continues his education upon a larger scale,
and by a process which includes means far more effica-
cious. Has your son entered the world at eighteen,
opinionated, haughty, rash, inclined to dissipation ? Do
not despair; he may yet be cured of these faults, if it
pleases Heaven. There are remedies which you could

not persuade yourself to use, if they were in your
power, and which are specific in cases of this kind.
How often do we see the presumptuous, giddy youth
changed into the wise counsellor, the considerate, steady
friend! How often the thoughtless, gay girl, into the
sober wife, the affectionate mother! Faded beauty,
humbled self-consequence, disappointed ambition, loss of
fortune,— this is the rough physic provided by Providence to meliorate the temper, to correct the offensive
petulancies of youth, and bring out all the energies of
the finished character. Afflictions soften the proud;
difficulties push forward the ingenious; successful industry gives consequence and credit, and develops a
thousand latent good qualities. There is no malady of
the mind so inveterate, which this education of events
is not calculated to cure, if life were long enough; and
shall we not hope that He in whose hand are all the
remedial..processes of nature will renew the discipline
in another state, and finish the imperfect man?

States are educated as individuals, — by circumstances : the prophet may cry aloud and spare not;
the philosopher may descant on morals ; eloquence may
exhaust itself in invective against the vices of the age;
these vices will certainly follow certain states of poverty
or riches, ignorance or high civilization. But what
these gentle alteratives fail of doing may be accomplished by an unsuccessful war, a loss of trade, or any

of those great calamities by which it pleases Providence
to speak to a nation in such language as *will* be
heard.   If, as a nation, we would be cured of pride, it
must be by mortification; if of luxury, by a national
bankruptcy perhaps; if of injustice, or the spirit of
domination, by a loss of national consequence.   In
comparison of these strong remedies, a fast or a sermon
are prescriptions of very little efficacy.

ON PREJUDICE.

IT is to speculative people, fond of novel doctrines, and who, by accustoming themselves to make the most fundamental truths the subject of discussion, have divested their minds of that reverence which is generally felt for opinions and practices of long standing, that the world is ever to look for its improvement or reformation. But it is also these speculatists who introduce into it absurdities and errors more gross than any which have been established by that common consent of numerous individuals, which opinions long acted upon must have required for their basis. For systems of the latter class must at least possess one property, — that of being practicable; and there is likewise a presumption that they are, or at least originally were, useful; whereas the opinions of the speculatist may turn out to be utterly incongruous and eccentric. The speculatist may invent machines which it is impossible to put in action, or which, when put in action, may possess the tremendous power of tearing up society by the roots. Like the chemist, he is not sure in the moment of projection whether he shall blow up his own dwelling and that of his neighbor, or whether he shall be rewarded with a discovery which will secure the health and prolong the existence of future generations. It becomes us, therefore, to examine with peculiar care those maxims which, under the appearance of following a closer train of reasoning, militate against the usual practices or genuine feelings of mankind. No subject has been more canvassed than education. With regard to that important object, there is a maxim avowed by many sensible people, which seems to me to deserve particular investigation. "Give your child," it is said, "no *prejudices :* let reason be the only foundation of his opinions; where he cannot reason, let him suspend his belief. Let your great care be, that as he grows up he has nothing to unlearn; and never make use of authority in matters of opinion, for authority is no test of truth." The maxim sounds well, and flatters perhaps the secret pride of man, in supposing him more the creature of reason than he really is; but I suspect on examination we shall find it exceedingly fallacious. We must first consider what a *prejudice* is. A prejudice is a sentiment in favor or disfavor of any person, practice, or opinion previous to and independent of examining their merits by reason and investigation. Prejudice is prejudging; that is, judging previously to evidence. It is therefore sufficiently apparent that no *philosophical belief* can be founded on mere prejudice; because it is

the business of philosophy to go deep into the nature and
properties of things ; nor can it be allowable for those to
indulge prejudice who aspire to lead the public opinion;
those to whom the high office is appointed of sifting
truth from error, of canvassing the claims of different
systems, of exploding old and introducing new tenets.
These must investigate with a kind of audacious bold-
ness every subject that comes before them ; these, neither
impressed with awe for all that mankind have been
taught to reverence, nor swayed by affection for whatever the sympathies of our nature incline us to love, must
hold the balance with a severe and steady hand while
they are weighing the doubtful scale of probabilities,
and with a stoical apathy of mind yield their assent to
nothing but a preponderancy of evidence. But is this
an office for a child ? Is it an office for more than one
or two men in a century ? And is it desirable that a
child should grow up without opinions to regulate his
conduct, till he is able to form them fairly by the
exercise of his own abilities ? Such an exercise requires at least the sober period of matured reason :
reason not only sharpened by argumentative discussion,
but informed by experience. The most sprightly child
can only possess the former; for, let it be remembered
that, though the reasoning powers put forth pretty early
in life, the faculty of using them to effect does not come
till much later. The first efforts of a child in reasoning

resemble those quick and desultory motions by which
he gains the play of his limbs; they show agility and
grace, they are pleasing to look at, and necessary for
the gradual acquirement of his bodily powers; but
his joints must be knit into more firmness, and his
movements regulated with more precision, before he is
capable of useful labor and manly exertion. A reasoning child is not yet a reasonable being. There is great
propriety in the legal phraseology which expresses
maturity, not by having arrived at the possession of
reason, but of that power, the late result of information, thought, and experience, — discretion, which alone
teaches, with regard to reason, its powers, its limits,
and its use. This the child of the most sprightly parts
cannot have; and therefore his attempts at reasoning,
whatever acuteness they may show, and how much
soever they may please a parent with the early promise
of future excellence, are of no account whatever in the
sober search after truth. Besides, taking it for granted
(which, however, is utterly impossible) that a youth
could be brought up to the age of fifteen or sixteen
without prejudice in favor of any opinions whatever,
and that he is then set to examine for himself some
important proposition, — how is he to set about it?
Who is to recommend books to him? Who is to give
him the previous information necessary to comprehend
the question? Who is to tell him whether or no it is

important ? Whoever does these will infallibly lay a
bias upon his mind according to the ideas he himself
has received upon the subject. Let us suppose the
point in debate was the preference between the Roman
Catholic and Protestant modes of religion. Can a youth
in a Protestant country, born of Protestant parents,
with access, probably, to hardly a single controversial
book on the Roman Catholic side of the question, —
can such a one study the subject without prejudice ?
His knowledge of history, if he has such knowledge,
must, according to the books he has read, have already
given him a prejudice on the one side or the other ; so
must the occasional conversation he has been witness
to, the appellations he has heard used, the tone of
voice with which he has heard the words monk or priest
pronounced, and a thousand other evanescent circumstances. It is likewise to be observed, that every
question of any weight and importance has numerous
dependencies and points of connection with other
subjects, which make it impossible to enter upon the
consideration of it without a great variety of previous
knowledge. There is no object of investigation perfectly insulated ; we must not conceive therefore of a
man's sitting down to it with a mind perfectly new and
untutored: he must have passed more or less through a
course of studies ; and, according to the color of those
studies, his mind will have received a tincture, — that

is, a prejudice. — But it is, in truth, the most absurd of
all suppositions, that a human being can be educated,
or even nourished and brought up, without imbibing
numberless prejudices from everything which passes
around him. A child cannot learn the signification of
words, without receiving ideas along with them; he
cannot be impressed with affection to his parents and
those about him, without conceiving a predilection for
their tastes, opinions, and practices. He forms numberless associations of pain or pleasure, and every
association begets a prejudice; he sees objects from a
particular spot, and his views of things are contracted
or extended according to his position in society : as no
two individuals can have the same horizon, so neither
can any two have the same associations ; and different
associations will produce different opinions, as neces-
sarily as, by the laws of perspective, different distances
will produce different appearances of visible objects.
Let us confess a truth, humiliating perhaps to human
pride : a very small part only of the opinions of the
coolest philosopher are the result of fair reasoning;
the rest are formed by his education, his temperament,
by the age in which he lives, by trains of thought
directed to a particular track through some accidental
association, — in short, by *prejudice*. But why, after
all, should we wish to bring up children without prejudices ? A child has occasion to act long before he

can reason. Shall we leave him destitute of all the
principles that should regulate his conduct, till he can
discover them by the strength of his own genius ? If
it were possible that one whole generation could be
brought up without prejudices, the world must return
to the infancy of knowledge, and all the beautiful fabric
which has been built up by successive generations
must be begun again from the very foundation. Your
child has a claim to the advantage of your experience,
which it would be cruel and unjust to deprive him of.
Will any father say to his son, " My dear child, you
are entering upon a world full of intricate and perplexed paths, in which many miss their way, to their
final misery and ruin. Amidst many false systems,
and much vain science, there is also some true knowledge ; there is a right path : I believe I know it, for I
have the advantage of years and experience, but I will
instil no prejudices into your mind ; I shall therefore
leave you to find it out as -you can ; whether your
abilities are great or small, you must take the chance
of them. There are various systems in morals ; I have
examined and found some of a good, others of a bad
tendency. There is such a thing as religion ; many
people think it the most important concern of life :
perhaps I am one of them : perhaps I have chosen
from amidst the various systems of belief — many of
which are extremely absurd, and some even pernicious

—that which I cherish as the guide of my life, my comfort in all my sorrows, and the foundation of my dearest hopes: but far be it from me to influence you in any manner to receive it; when you are grown up, you must read all the books upon these subjects which you can lay your hands on, for neither in the choice of these would I presume to prejudice your mind; converse with all who pretend to any opinions upon the subject; and whatever happens to be the result, you must abide by it. In the mean time, concerning these important objects you must keep your mind in a perfect equilibrium. It is true you want these principles more now than you can do at any other period of your life; but I had rather you never had them at all, than that you should not come fairly by them." Should we commend the wisdom or the kindness of such a parent? The parent will perhaps plead, in his behalf, that it is by no means his intention to leave the mind of his child in the uncultivated state I have supposed. As soon as his understanding begins to open, he means to discuss with him those propositions on which he wishes him to form an opinion. He will make him read the best books on the subject, and by free conversation, and explaining the arguments on both sides, he does not doubt but the youth will soon be enabled to judge satisfactorily for himself. I have no objection to make against this mode of proceeding:

as a mode of *instruction*, it is certainly a very good
one; but he must know little of human nature, who
thinks that after this process the youth will be really
in a capacity of judging for himself, or that he is less
under the dominion of prejudice than if he had received
the same truths from the mere authority of his parents;
for most assuredly the arguments on either side will
not have been set before him with equal strength or
with equal warmth. The persuasive tone, the glowing
language, the triumphant retort, will all be reserved
for the side on which the parent has formed his own
conclusions. It cannot be otherwise; he cannot be
convinced himself of what he thinks a truth, without
wishing to convey that conviction, nor without thinking all that can be urged on the other side weak and
futile. He cannot in a matter of importance neutralize
his feelings: perfect impartiality can be the result only
of indifference. He does not perhaps seem to dictate,
but he wishes gently to guide his pupil; and that wish
is seldom disappointed. The child adopts the opinion
of his parent, and seems to himself to have adopted it
from the decisions of his own judgment; but all these
reasonings must be gone over again, and these opinions
undergo a fiery ordeal, if ever he comes really to think
and determine for himself.

The fact is, that no man, whatever his system may
be, refrains from instilling prejudices into his child in

any matter he has much at heart. Take a disciple of
Rousseau, who contends that it would be very pernicious to give his son any ideas of a Deity till he is of an
age to read Clarke or Leibnitz, and ask him if he waits
so long to impress on his mind the sentiments of
patriotism, — the civic affection. O no! you will find
his little heart is early taught to beat at the very name
of liberty, and that, long before he is capable of forming a single political idea, he has entered with warmth
into all the party sentiments and connections of his
parents. He learns to love and hate, to venerate or
despise, by rote; and he soon acquires decided opinions,
of the real ground of which he can know absolutely
nothing. Are not ideas of female honor and decorum
impressed first as prejudices; and would any parent wish
they should be so much as canvassed till the most
settled habits of propriety have rendered it safe to do
it? In teaching first by prejudice that which is afterwards to be proved, we do but follow Nature. Instincts
are the prejudices she gives us: we follow them im-
plicitly, and they lead us right; but it is not till long
afterwards that reason comes and justifies them. Why
should we scruple to lead a child to right opinions in
the same way by which Nature leads him to right
practices!

Still it will be urged that man is a rational being,
and therefore reason is the only true ground of belief,

and authority is not reason. This point requires a
little discussion. That he who receives a truth upon
authority has not a reasonable belief is in one sense true,
since he has not drawn it from the result of his own
inquiries; but in another it is certainly false, since the
authority itself may be to him the best of all reasons
for believing it. There are few men who, from the
exercise of the best powers of their minds, could derive
so good a reason for believing a mathematical truth as
the authority of Sir Isaac Newton. There are two
principles deeply implanted in the mind of man, without which he could never attain knowledge,—curiosity
and credulity; the former to lead him to make discoveries himself, the latter to dispose him to receive
knowledge from others. The credulity of a child to
those who cherish him is in early life unbounded.
This is one of the most useful instincts he has, and
is, in fact, a precious advantage put into the hands
of the parent for storing his mind with ideas of all
kinds. Without this principle of assent he could never
gain even the rudiments of knowledge. He receives
it, it is true, in the shape of prejudice; but the
prejudice itself is founded upon sound reasoning, and
conclusive though imperfect experiment. He finds
himself weak, helpless, and ignorant; he sees in his
parent a being of knowledge and powers more than
his utmost capacity can fathom,—almost a god to him.

He has often done him good, therefore he believes he
loves him; he finds him capable of giving him information upon all the subjects he has applied to him
about; his knowledge seems unbounded, and his information has led him right whenever he has had
occasion to try it by actual experiment: the child does
not draw out his little reasonings into a logical form,
but this is to him a ground of belief, that his parent
knows everything, and is infallible. Though the proposition is not exactly true, it is sufficiently so for him
to act upon: and when he believes in his parent with
implicit faith, he believes upon grounds as truly rational
as when, in after life, he follows the deductions of his
own reason.

But you will say, I wish my son may have nothing to
unlearn, and therefore I would have him wait to form
an opinion till he is able to do it on solid grounds. And
why do you suppose he will have less to unlearn if he
follows his own reason than if he followed yours? If
he thinks, if he inquires, he will no doubt have a great
deal to unlearn, whichever course you take with him;
but it is better to have some things to unlearn than to
have nothing learned. Do you hold your own opinions
so loosely, so hesitatingly, as not to think them safer
to abide by than the first results of his stammering
reason? Are there no truths to learn so indubitable
as to be without fear of their not approving themselves

to his mature and well-directed judgment ? Are there
none you esteem so useful as to feel anxious that he be
put in possession of them ? We are solicitous not only
to put our children in a capacity of acquiring their
daily bread, but to bequeath to them riches which they
may receive as an inheritance. Have you no mental
wealth you wish to transmit, no stock of ideas he may
begin with, instead of drawing them all from the labor of
his own brain ? If, moreover, your son should not adopt
your prejudices, he will certainly adopt those of other
people ; or, if on subjects of high interest he *could* be
kept totally indIfferent, the consequence would be, that
he would conceive either that such matters were not
worth the trouble of inquiry, or that nothing satisfac-
tory was to be learned about them : for there are nega-
tive prejudices as well as positive.

Let parents, therefore, not scruple to use the power
God and Nature have put into their hands for the
advantage of their offspring. Let them not fear to
impress them with prejudices for whatever is fair and
honorable in action, — whatever is useful and important
in systematic truth. Let such prejudices be wrought
into the very texture of the soul. Such truths let
them appear to know by intuition. Let the child
never remember the period when he did not know
them. Instead of sending him to that cold and hesitating belief which is founded on the painful and

uncertain consequences of late investigation, let his conviction of all the truths you deem important be mixed up with every warm affection of his nature, and identified with his most cherished recollections; the time will come soon enough when his confidence.in you will have received a check. The growth of his own reason and the development of his powers will lead him with a sudden impetus to examine everything, to canvass everything, to suspect everything. If he finds, as he certainly will find, the results of his reasoning different in some respects from those you have given him, far from being now disposed to receive your assertions as proofs, he will rather feel disinclined to any opinion you profess, and struggle to free himself from the net you have woven about him.

The calm repose of his mind is broken, the placid lake is become turbid, and reflects distorted and broken images of things; but be not you alarmed at the new workings of his thoughts, — it is the angel of reason which descends and troubles the waters. To endeavor to influence by authority would be as useless now as it was salutary before. Lie by in silence, and wait the result. Do not expect the mind of your son is to resemble yours, as your figure is reflected by the image in the glass; he was formed, like you, to use his own judgment, and he claims the high privilege of his nature. His reason is mature, his mind must now form itself. Happy must you esteem yourself, if amidst all lesser differences of opinion, and the wreck of many of your favorite ideas, he still preserves those radical and primary truths which are essential to his happiness, and which different trains of thought and opposite modes of investigation will very often equally lead to.

Let it be well remembered that we have only been recommending those prejudices which go before reason, not those which are contrary to it. To endeavor to make children, or others over whom we have influence, receive systems which we do not believe, merely because it is convenient to ourselves that they should believe them, though a very fashionable practice, makes no part of the discipline we plead for. These are not prejudices, but impositions. We may also grant that nothing should be received as a prejudice which can be easily made the subject of experiment. A child may be allowed to find out for himself that boiling water will scald his fingers and mustard bite his tongue; but he must be *prejudiced* against ratsbane, because the experiment would be too costly. In like manner it may do him good to have experienced that little instances of inattention or perverseness draw upon him the displeasure of his parent; but that profligacy is attended with loss of character is a truth one would rather wish him to take upon trust.

There is no occasion to inculcate by prejudices those truths which it is of no importance for us to know till our powers are able to investigate them. Thus the metaphysical questions, of space and time, necessity and free-will, and a thousand others, may safely be left for that age which delights in such discussions. They have no connection with conduct; and none have any business with them at all but those who are able by such studies to exercise and sharpen their mental powers: but it is not so with those truths on which our well-being depends; these must be taught to all, not only before they can reason upon them, but independently of the consideration whether they will ever be able to reason upon them as long as they live. What has hitherto been said relates only to instilling prejudices into *others;* how far a man is to allow them in himself, or, as a celebrated writer expresses it, to *cherish* them, is a different question, on which perhaps I may some time offer my thoughts. In the mean time I cannot help concluding, that to reject the influence of prejudice in education is itself one of the most unreasonable of prejudices.

ON FEMALE STUDIES.

LETTER I.

MY DEAR YOUNG FRIEND, — If I had not been afraid you would feel some little reluctance in addressing me first, I should have asked you to begin the correspondence between us; for I am at present ignorant of your particular pursuits. I cannot guess whether you are climbing the hill of science, or wandering among the flowers of fancy; whether you are stretching your powers to embrace the planetary system, or examining with a curious eye the delicate veining of a green leaf and the minute ramifications of a sea-weed; or whether you are toiling through the intricate and thorny mazes of grammar. Whichever of these is at present your employment, your general aim, no doubt, is the improvement of your mind; and we will therefore spend some time in considering what kind and degree of literary attainments sit gracefully upon the female character.

Every woman should consider herself as sustaining the general character of a rational being, as well as the more confined one belonging to the female sex; and therefore the motives for acquiring general knowledge

and cultivating the taste are nearly the same to both
sexes. The line of separation between the studies of
a young man and a young woman appears to me to be
chiefly fixed by this, — that a woman is excused from
all professional knowledge. Professional knowledge
means all that is necessary to fit a man for a peculiar
profession or business. Thus men study in order to
qualify themselves for the law, for physic, for various
departments in political life, for instructing others from
the pulpit or the professor's chair. These all require
a great deal of severe study and technical knowledge ;
much of which is nowise valuable in itself, but as a
means to that particular profession. Now, as a woman
can never be called to any of these professions, it is
evident you have nothing to do with such studies.
A woman is not expected to understand the myste-
ries of politics, because she is not called to govern ;
she is not required to know anatomy, because she is
not to perform surgical operations ; she need not embarrass herself with theological disputes, because she
will neither be called upon to make nor to explain
creeds.

Men have various departments in active life ; women
have but one, and all women have the same, differently
modified indeed by their rank in life and other incidental circumstances. It is to be a wife, a mother, a
mistress of a family. The knowledge belonging to

these duties is your professional knowledge, the want
of which nothing will excuse. Literary knowledge,
therefore, in men, is often an indispensable duty; in
women, it can be only a desirable accomplishment. In
women it is more immediately applied to the purposes
of adorning and improving the mind, of refining the sentiments, and supplying proper stores for conversation.
For general knowledge women have, in some respects,
more advantages than men. Their avocations often
allow them more leisure; their sedentary way of life
disposes them to the domestic, quiet amusement of
reading; the share they take in the education of their
children throws them in the way of books. The uniform tenor and confined circle of their lives makes
them eager to diversify the scene by descriptions which
open to them a new world; and they are eager to gain
an idea of scenes on the busy stage of life from which
they are shut out by their sex. It is likewise particularly desirable for women to be able to give spirit and
variety to conversation by topics drawn from the stores
of literature, as the broader mirth and more boisterous
gayety of the other sex are to them prohibited. As
their parties must be innocent, care should be taken
that they do not stagnate into insipidity. I will venture to add that the purity and simplicity of heart
which a woman ought never, in her freest commerce
with the world, to wear off, her very seclusion from

the jarring interests and coarser amusements of society,
fit her in a peculiar manner for the worlds of fancy
and sentiment, and dispose her to the quickest relish
of what is pathetic, sublime, or tender. To you, therefore, the beauties of poetry, of moral painting, and all,
in general, that is comprised under the term of polite
literature, lie particularly open, and you cannot neglect them without neglecting a very copious source of
enjoyment.

Languages are on some accounts particularly adapted
to female study, as they may be learned at home without
experiments or apparatus, and without interfering with
the habits of domestic life ; as they form the style, and
as they are the immediate inlet to works of taste. But
the learned languages, the Greek especially, require a
great deal more time than a young woman can conveniently spare. To the Latin there is not an equal
objection ; and if a young person has leisure, has an
opportunity of learning it at home by being connected
with literary people, and is placed in a circle of society
sufficiently liberal to allow her such an accomplishment,
I do not see, if she has a strong inclination, why she
should not make herself mistress of so rich a store of
original entertainment : it will not in the present state
of things excite either a smile or a stare in fashionable
company. To those who do not intend to learn the
language, I would strongly recommend the learning so

much of the grammar of it as will explain the name and nature of cases, genders, inflection of verbs, etc.; of which, having only the imperfect rudiments in our own language, a mere English scholar can with difficulty form a clear idea. This is the more necessary, as all our grammars, being written by men whose early studies had given them a partiality for the learned languages, are formed more upon those than upon the real genius of our own tongue.

I was going now to mention French, but perceive I have written a letter long enough to frighten a young correspondent, and for the present I bid you adieu.

***

LETTER II.

FRENCH you are not only permitted to learn, but you are laid under the same necessity of acquiring it as your brother is of acquiring Latin. Custom has made the one as much expected from an accomplished woman, as the other from a man who has had a liberal education. The learning French, or indeed any language completely, includes reading, writing, and speaking it. But here I must take the liberty to offer my ideas, which differ something from those generally entertained, and you will give them what weight you think they deserve. It seems to me that the efforts of young

ladies in learning French are generally directed to what
is unattainable; and if attained, not very useful, — the
speaking it.   It is utterly impossible, without such advantages as few enjoy, to speak a foreign language with
fluency and a proper accent; and if even by being in
a French family some degree of both is attained, it is
soon lost by mixing with the world at large.   As to
the French which girls are obliged to speak at boarding-
schools, it does very well to speak in England, but at
Paris it would probably be less understood than English
itself.

I do not mean by this to say that the speaking of
French is not a very elegant accomplishment; and to
those who mean to spend some time in France, or who,
being in very high life, often see foreigners of distinction, it may be necessary; but in common life it is very
little so: and for English people to meet together to
talk a foreign language is truly absurd.   There is a sar-
casm against this practice as old as Chaucer's time: —

> ". . . . Frenche she spake ful fayre and fetisely,
> After the schole of Stratford atte Bowe,
> For Frenche of Paris was to her unknowe."

But with regard to reading French, the many charming publications in that language, particularly in polite
literature, of which you can have no adequate idea
by translation, render it a very desirable acquisition.

Writing it is not more useful in itself than speaking, except a person has foreign letters to write; but it is necessary for understanding the language grammatically and fixing the rules in the mind. A young person who reads French with ease and is so well grounded as to write it grammatically, and has what I should call a good English pronunciation of it, will, by a short residence in France, gain fluency and the accent; whereas one not grounded would soon forget all she had learned, though she had acquired some fluency in speaking. For speaking, therefore, love and cultivate your own : know all its elegancies, its force, its happy turns of expression, and possess yourself of all its riches. In foreign languages you have only to learn ; but with regard to your own you have probably to unlearn, and to avoid vulgarisms and provincial barbarisms.

If, after you have learned French, you should wish to add Italian, the acquisition will not be difficult. It is valuable on account of its poetry — in which it far excels the French — and its music. The other modern languages you will hardly attempt, except led to them by some peculiar bent.

History affords a wide field of entertaining and useful reading. The chief thing to be attended to in studying it is to gain a clear, well-arranged idea of facts in chronological order, and illustrated by a knowl-

edge of the places where such facts happened. Never
read without tables and maps : make abstracts of what
you read. Before you embarrass yourself in the detail
of this, endeavor to fix well in your mind the arrange-
ment of some leading facts which may serve as landmarks to which to refer the rest. Connect the history
of different countries together. In the study of history
the different genius of a woman, I imagine, will show
itself. The detail of battles, the art of sieges, will not
interest her so much as manners and sentiment; this
is the food she assimilates to herself.

The great laws of the universe, the nature and properties of those objects which surround us, it is unpardonable not to know : it is more unpardonable to know,
and not to feel the mind struck with lively gratitude.
Under this head are comprehended natural history,
astronomy, botany, experimental philosophy, chemistry,
physics. In these you will rather take what belongs
to sentiment and to utility than abstract calculations
or difficult problems. You must often be content to
know a thing is so, without understanding the proof.
It belongs to a Newton to prove his sublime problems,
but we may all be made acquainted with the result.
You cannot investigate ; you may remember. This
will teach you not to despise common things; will
give you an interest in everything you see. If you are
feeding your poultry, or tending your bees, or extract-

ing the juice of herbs, with an intelligent mind, you
are gaining real knowledge; it will open to you an
inexhaustible fund of wonder and delight, and effectually prevent you from depending for your entertainment on the poor novelties of fashion and expense.

But of all reading, what most ought to engage your
attention are works of sentiment and morals. Morals
is that study in which alone both sexes have an equal
interest; and in sentiment yours has even the advantage. The works of this kind often appear under the
seducing form of novel and romance : here, great care
and the advice of your older friends is requisite in the
selection. Whatever is true, however uncouth in the
manner or dry in the subject, has a value from being
true ; but fiction in order to recommend itself must give
us *la belle Nature.* You will find fewer plays fit for your
perusal than novels, and fewer comedies than tragedies.

What particular share any one of the studies I have
mentioned may engage of your attention will be determined by your peculiar turn and bent of mind. But
I shall conclude with observing that a woman ought
to have that general tincture of them all which marks
the cultivated mind. She ought to have enough of
them to engage gracefully in general conversation. In
no subject is she required to be deep, — of none ought
she to be ignorant. If she knows not enough to speak
well, she should know enough to keep her from speak-

ing at all ; enough to feel her ground and prevent her from exposing her ignorance ; enough to hear with intelligence, to ask questions with propriety, and to receive information where she is not qualified to give it. A woman who to a cultivated mind joins that quickness of intelligence and delicacy of taste which such a woman often possesses in a superior degree, with that nice sense of propriety which results from the whole, will have a kind of *tact* by which she will be able on all occasions to discern between pretenders to science and men of real merit. On subjects upon which she cannot talk herself, she will know whether a man talks with knowledge of his subject. She will not judge of systems, but by their systems she will be able to judge of men. She will distinguish the modest, the dogmatical, the affected, the over-refined, and give her esteem and confidence accordingly. She will know with whom to confide the education of her children, and how to judge of their progress and the methods used to improve them. From books, from conversation, from learned instructors, she will gather the flower of every science ; and her mind, in assimilating every-thing to itself, will adorn it with new graces. She will give the tone to the conversation even when she chooses to bear but an inconsiderable part in it. The modesty which prevents her from an unnecessary display of what she knows, will cause it to be supposed that her knowledge is deeper than in reality it is : as when the landscape is seen through the veil of a mist, the bounds of the horizon are hid. As she will never obtrude her knowledge, none will ever be sensible of any deficiency in it, and her silence will seem to proceed from discretion rather than a want of information. She will seem to know everything by leading every one to speak of what he knows; and when she is with those to whom she can give no real information, she will yet delight them by the original turns of thought and sprightly elegance which will attend her manner of speaking on any subject. Such is the character to whom professed scholars will delight to give information, from whom others will equally delight to receive it : — the character I wish you to become, and to form which your application must be directed.

ON THE CLASSICS.

THE authors known by the name of the Greek and
Roman Classics have laid the foundation of all
that is excellent in modern literature; and are so frequently referred to both in books and conversation,
that a person of a cultivated mind cannot easily be
content without obtaining some knowledge of them,
even though he should not be able to read them in
their original tongues. A clear and short account of
these authors in a chronological series, together with
a sketch of the character of their several productions,
for the use of those who have either none or a very
superficial knowledge of the languages they are written
in, is, as far as I know, a desideratum which it is much
to be wished that some elegant scholar should supply:
in the mean time a few general remarks upon them
may be not unacceptable.

In the larger sense of the word, an author is called
a Classic when his work has stood the test of time
long enough to become a permanent part of the literature of his country. Of the number of writings
which in their day have attained a portion of fame,

very few in any age have survived to claim this honorable distinction. Every circumstance which gave temporary celebrity must be forgotten; party must have subsided; the voice of friends and of enemies must be silent; and the writer himself must have long mouldered in the dust, before the gates of immortality are opened to him. It is in vain that he attempts to flatter or to soothe his contemporaries, they are not called to the decision; his merits are to be determined by a race he has never seen; the judges are not yet born who are to pronounce on the claims of Darwin and of Cowper. The severe impartiality of Posterity stands aloof from every consideration but that of excellence, and from her verdict there is no appeal.

It is true, indeed, that amidst the revolutions of ages; particularly before the invention of printing, accidental circumstances must often have had great influence in the preservation of particular writings; and we know and lament that many are lost which the learned world would give treasures of gold to recover. But it cannot easily happen that a work should be preserved without superior merit; and indeed we know from the testimony of antiquity, that the works which have come down to us, and which we read and admire, are in general the very works which by the Greeks and Romans themselves were esteemed most excellent.

It is impossible to contemplate without a sentiment

of reverence and enthusiasm these venerable writings which have survived the wreck of empires; and, what is more, of languages which have received the awful stamp of immortality, and are crowned with the applause of so many successive ages. It is wonderful that words should live so much longer than marble temples; — words, which at first are only uttered breath; and, when afterwards enshrined and fixed in a visible form by the admirable invention of writing, committed to such frail and perishable materials: yet the light paper bark floats down the stream of time, and lives through the storms which have sunk so many stronger-built vessels. Homer is read, though *the grass now grows where Troy town stood:* and nations once despised as barbarous appreciate the merit of Cicero's orations on the banks of the Thames, when the long honors of the Consulate are vanished, and the language of Rome is no longer spoken on the shores of the Tiber.

> Still green with bays each ancient altar stands,
> Above the reach of sacrilegious hands;
> Secure from flames, from envy's fiercer rage,
> Destructive war and all-involving age.
> See from each clime the learn'd their incense bring,
> Hear in all tongues consenting Pæans ring !

It is owing to the preservation of a few books of the kind we are speaking of, that at the revival of letters the world had not to go back to the very beginnings of science. When the storm of barbaric rage had passed over and spent itself, they were drawn from the mould of ruins and dust of convents, and were of essential service in forming our taste and giving a direction to the recovered energies of the human mind. Oral instruction can benefit but one age and one set of hearers; but these silent teachers address all ages and all nations. They may sleep for a while and be neglected; but whenever the desire of information springs up in the human breast, there they are with their mild wisdom ready to instruct and please us. The Philosopher opens again his school; his maxims have lost nothing of their truth: the harmony of the Poet's numbers, though locked up for a time, becomes again vocal, and we find that what was nature and passion two thousand years ago is nature and passion still.

Books are a kind of perpetual censors on men and manners; they judge without partiality, and reprove without fear or affection. There are times when the flame of virtue and liberty seems almost to be extinguished amongst the existing generation; but their animated pages are always at hand to rekindle it. The despot trembles on his throne, and the bold bad man turns pale in his closet at the sentence pronounced against him ages before he was born.

In addition to their intrinsic value there is much

incidental entertainment in consulting authors who
flourished at so remote a period. Every little circumstance becomes curious as we discover allusions to
customs now obsolete, or draw indications of the
temper of the times from the various slight hints and
casual pieces of information which may be gathered
up by the ingenious critic. Sometimes we have the
pleasure of being admitted into the cabinet of a great
man, and leaning as it were over his shoulder while
he is pouring himself out in the freedom of a confidential
intercourse which was never meant to meet the eye
even of his contemporaries. At another time we are
delighted to witness the conscious triumph of a genius
who, with a generous confidence in his powers, prophe-
sies his own immortality, and to feel, as we read, that his
proud boast has not been too presumptuous. Another
advantage of reading the ancients is, that we trace the
stream of ideas to their spring. It is always best to
go to the fountain-head. We can never have a just
idea of the comparative merit of the moderns, without
knowing how much they have derived from imitation.
It is amusing to follow an idea from century to century, and observe the gradual accession of thought and
sentiment; to see the jewels of the ancients new set,
and the wit of Horace sparkling with additional lustre
in the lines of Pope.

The real sources of history can only be known by

some acquaintance with the original authors. This indeed will often be found to betray the deficiency of our documents, and the difficulty of reconciling jarring accounts. It will sometimes unclothe and exhibit in its original bareness what the art of the moderns has dressed up and rounded into form. It will show the unsightly chasms and breaks which the modern compiler passes over with a light foot, and perhaps make us sceptical with regard to many particulars of which we formerly thought we had authentic information. But it is always good to know the real measure of our knowledge. That knowledge would be greater, if the treasures of antiquity had come to us undiminished; but this is not the case. Besides the loss of many mentioned with honor by their contemporaries, few authors are come down to us entire; and of some exquisite productions only fragments are extant. The full stream. of narration is sometimes suddenly checked at the most interesting period, and the sense of a brilliant passage is clouded by the obscurity of a single word. The literary productions are come to us in a similar state with the fine statues of antiquity: of which some have lost an arm, others a leg, some a little finger only; scarce any have escaped some degree of mutilation; and sometimes a trunk is dug up so shorn of its limbs that the antiquaries are puzzled to make out to what god or hero it originally belonged.   To the frequent loss of part of an author must be added the difficulty of deciphering what remains.

Ancient manuscripts are by no means easy to read. You are not to imagine, when you see a fair edition of Virgil or Horace, divided into verses and accurately pointed, that you see it in anything like its original state. The oldest manuscripts are written wholly in capitals, and without any separation of letters into words. Passing through many hands, they have suffered from the mistakes or carelessness of transcribers ; by which so great an obscurity is thrown on many passages that very often he who makes the happiest guess is the best commentator.   But this very obscurity has usefully exercised the powers of the human mind.   It became a great object, at the revival of letters, to compare different readings ; to elucidate a text by parallel passages ; to supply by probable conjecture what was necessary to make an author speak sense ; and by every possible assistance of learning and sound criticism, together with typographical advantages, to restore the beauty and splendor of the classic page.   Verbal criticism was at that time of great and- real use ; and those who are apt to undervalue it are little aware how much labor was requisite to reduce the confused or mutilated work of a thousand years back to form and order.

This task was well fitted for an age recently emerged

out of barbarism. The enthusiastic admiration with which men were struck on viewing the masterpieces of human genius, and even the superstitious veneration with which they regarded everything belonging to them, tended to form their taste by a quicker process than if they had been left to make the most of their own abilities. By degrees the moderns felt their own powers; they learned to imitate, and perhaps to excel, what before they idolized. But a considerable period had passed before any of the modern languages were thought worthy of being the vehicle of the discoveries of science or even of the effusions of fancy. Christianity did not, as might have been expected, bring into discredit the pagan philosophy. Aristotle reigned in the schools, where he was regarded with a veneration fully equal to what was expressed for the sainted fathers of the Church; and as to the mythology of the ancients, it is so beautiful that all our earlier poetry has been modelled upon it. Even yet the predilection for the Latin language is apparent in our inscriptions, in the public exercises of our schools and universities, and the general bent of the studies of youth. In short, all our knowledge and all our taste has been built upon the foundation of the ancients; and without knowing what they have done, we cannot estimate rightly the merit of our own authors.

It may naturally be asked why the Greek and

Roman writers alone are called by the name of the
Classics. It is true the Hebrew might be esteemed so,
if we did not receive them upon a higher ground of
merit. As to the Persian and Arabic, with other
languages of countries once highly cultivated, their
authors are not taken into the account, partly because
they are understood by so few, and partly because their
idioms and modes of expression, if not of feeling, are so
remote from ours that we can scarcely enter into their
merits. Their writings are comprehended under the
name of Oriental literature. It has been more cultivated of late, particularly by Sir William Jones; and
our East India possessions will continue to draw our
attention that way; but curiosity is gratified, rather
than taste. We are pleased, indeed, with occasional
beauties, sometimes a pure maxim of morality and
sometimes a glowing figure of speech; but they do
not enter into the substance of the mind, which ever
must be fed and nourished by the classic literature of
Greece and Rome.

I shall subjoin a few specimens of the mythological
stories of the ancients.

ATALANTA.

ATALANTA was a beautiful young woman, exceedingly
swift of foot. She had many lovers; but she resolved

not to marry till she could meet with one who should
conquer her in running. A great many young men
proposed themselves, and lost their lives; for the
conditions were, that, if they were overcome in the
race, they should be put to death. At length she was
challenged by Hippomenes, a brave and handsome
youth. " Do you know," said Atalanta, " that nobody
has yet been found who excels me in swiftness,
and that you must be put to death if you do not
win the race ? I should be sorry to have any more
young men put to death." "I am not afraid," said
Hippomenes; "I think I shall win the race and win
you too."

So the ground was marked out and the day appointed, and a great number of spectators gathered
together; and Atalanta stood with her garments tucked
up, and Hippomenes by her, waiting impatiently for
the signal. At length it was given; and immediately
they both started at the same instant, and ran with
their utmost speed across the plain. But Atalanta flew
like the wind, and soon outstripped the young man.
Then Hippomenes drew from his vest a golden apple,
which had been given him by Venus from the gardens
of the Hesperides, and threw it from him with all his
force. The virgin saw it glittering as it rolled across
the plain, and ran out of the course to pick it up.
While she was doing so Hippomenes passed her, and

13 *

the spectators shouted for joy. However, Atalanta redoubled her speed, soon overtook Hippomenes, and again got before him. Upon this Hippomenes produced another golden apple, and threw it as before. It rolled a great way out of the course, and the virgin was very far behind by picking it up. She had great difficulty this time to recover her lost ground, and the spectators shouted, "Hippomenes will win! Hippomenes will win!" But Atalanta was so light, so nimble, and exerted herself so much, that at length she passed him as before, and flew as if she had wings towards the goal. And now she had but a little way to run; and the people said, "Poor Hippomenes! he will lose, after all, and be put to death like the rest; see, see how she gains ground of him! how near the goal she is! Atalanta will win the race." Then Hippomenes took another golden apple, — it was the last he had, — and prayed to Venus to give him success, and threw it behind him. Atalanta saw it, and considered a moment whether she should venture to delay herself again by picking it up. She knew she ran the risk of losing the race, but she could not withstand the beautiful glittering of the apple as it rolled along; and she said to herself, "I shall easily overtake Hippomenes, as I did before." But she was mistaken; for they had now so little a way to run, that, though she skimmed along the plain like a bird, and exerted all her strength, she was too late. Hippomenes reached the goal before her; she was obliged to own herself conquered, and to marry him according to the agreement.

ARION.

ARION was a poet of Lesbos, who sung his own verses to his harp. He had been a good while at the court of Periander, tyrant of Corinth, and had acquired great riches, with which he was desirous to return to his native country. He therefore made an agreement with a captain of a ship to carry him to Mitylene in Lesbos, and they set sail. But the captain and crew, tempted by the wealth which he had on board, determined to seize his gold and throw him into the sea. When poor Arion heard their cruel intention he submitted to his fate, for he knew he could not resist, and only begged they would allow him to give them one tune upon his harp before he died. This they complied with; and Arion, standing on the deck, drew from his harp such melodious strains, accompanied with such moving verses, that anybody but these cruel sailors would have been touched with them. When he had finished they threw him into the sea, where they supposed he was swallowed up: but that was not the case, for a dolphin, which had been drawn towards the ship by

the sweetness of Arion's voice, swam to him, took him
gently upon his back, conveyed him safely over the
waves, and landed him at Tenæra, whence he returned
to Periander. Periander was very much surprised to
see him come again in such a forlorn and destitute
condition, and asked him the reason. Arion told his
story. Periander bade him conceal himself till the
sailors should return from their voyage, and he would
do him justice. When the ship returned from its
voyage, Periander ordered the sailors to be brought
before him, and asked them what they had done with
Arion. They said he had died during the voyage, and
that they had buried him. Then Periander ordered
Arion to appear before them in the clothes he wore
when they cast him into the sea. At this plain proof
of their guilt they were quite confounded, and Periander put them all to death. It is said further, that the
dolphin was taken up into the heavens and turned into
a constellation. It is a small constellation, of moderate
brightness, and has four stars in the form of a rhombus;
you will find it south of the Swan, and a little west
of the bright star Alcair.

VENUS AND ADONIS.

THE goddess Venus loved Adonis, a mortal. Beautiful Venus loved the beautiful Adonis. She often said

to him, " O Adonis! be content to lie crowned with
flowers by the fresh fountains, and to feed upon honey
and nectar, and to be lulled to sleep by the warbling
of birds ; and do not expose your life by hunting the
tawny lion, or the tusky boar, or any savage beast.
Take care of that life which is so dear to Venus!"
But Adonis would not listen to her. He loved to rise
early in the morning, while the dew was upon the grass,
and to beat the thickets with his well-trained hounds,
whose ears swept the ground. With his darts he
pierced the nimble fawns and the kids with budding
horns, and brought home the spoil upon his shoulders.
But one day he wounded a fierce bristly boar; the
arrow stuck in his side, and made the animal mad
with pain : he rushed upon Adonis, and gored his thigh
with his sharp tusks. Beautiful Adonis fell to the
ground like a lily that is rooted up by a sudden storm :
his blood flowed in crimson streams down his fair side ;
and his eyelids closed, and the shades of death hovered
over his pale brow.

In the mean time the evening came on, and Venus
had prepared a garland of fresh leaves and flowers to
bind around the glowing temples of Adonis when he
should come hot and tired from the chase, and a couch
of rose-leaves to rest his weary limbs; and she said,
" Why does not Adonis come ? Return Adonis! let
me hear the sound of your feet! let me hear the voice

of your dogs! let them lick my hands, and make me understand that their master is approaching!" But Adonis did not return; and the dark night came, and the rosy morning appeared again, and still he did not appear. Then Venus sought him in the plains, and through the thickets, and amidst the rough brakes; and her veil was torn with the thorns, and her feet bruised and bleeding with the sharp pebbles, for she ran hither and thither like a distracted person. And at length upon the mountain she found him whom she loved so dearly; but she found him cold and dead, with his faithful dogs beside him.

Then Venus rent her beautiful tresses, and beat her breast, and pierced the air with her loud lamentations; and the little Cupids that accompany her broke their ivory bows for grief, and scattered upon the ground the arrows of their golden quivers: and they said, "We mourn Adonis; Venus mourns for beautiful Adonis; the Loves mourn along with her. Beautiful Adonis lies dead upon the ground, his side gored with the tooth of a boar, — his white thigh with a white tooth. Venus kisses the cold lips of Adonis; but Adonis does not know that he is kissed, and she cannot revive him with her warm breath."

Then Venus said, "You shall not quite die, my Adonis! I will change you into a flower." And she shed nectar on the ground, which mixed with the blood, and presently a crimson flower sprang up in the room of Adonis; and also the river was tinged with his blood and became red.

And every year, on the day that Adonis died, the nymphs mourned and lamented for him, and ran up and down shrieking, and crying " Beautiful Adonis is dead ! "

SELÁMA;

AN IMITATION OF OSSIAN.

WHAT soft voice of sorrow is in the breeze? what lovely sunbeam of beauty trembling on the rock? Its bright hair is bathed in showers; and it looks, faint and dim, through its mist on the rushy plain. Why art thou alone, maid of the mournful look? The cold, dropping rain is on the rocks of Torléna, the blast of the desert lifts thy yellow locks. Let thy steps be in the hall of shells, by the blue winding stream of Clutha: let the harp tremble beneath thy fingers; and the sons of heroes listen to the music of songs.

Shall my steps be in the hall of shells, and the aged low in the dust? The father of Seláma is low behind this rock, on his bed of withered leaves; the thistle's down is strewed over him by the wind, and mixes with his gray hair. Thou art fallen, chief of Etha! without thy fame; and there is none to revenge thy death. But thy daughter will sit, pale, beside thee, till she sinks, a faded flower, upon thy lifeless form. Leave the maid of Clutha, son of the stranger! in the red eye of her tears.

How fell the car-borne Connal, blue-eyed mourner of the rock? Mine arm is not weakened in battle; nor my sword without its fame.

Connal was a fire in his youth, that lightened through fields of renown: but the flame weakly glimmered through gray ashes of age. His course was like a star moving through the heavens: it walketh in brightness, but leaveth no track behind; its silver path cannot be found in the sky. The strength of Etha is rolled away like a tale of other years; and his eyes have failed. Feeble and dark, he sits in his hall, and hears the distant tread of a stranger's steps; the haughty steps of Tonthormo, from the roar of Duvranno's echoing stream. He stood in the hall like a pillar of darkness, on whose top is the red beam of fire: wide rolled his eyes beneath the gloomy arch of his bent brow; as flames in two caves of a rock, overhung with the black pine of the desert. They had rolled on Seláma, and he asked the daughter of Connal. Tonthormo! breaker of shields! thou art a meteor of death in war, whose fiery hair streams on the clouds, and the nations are withered beneath its path. Dwell, Tonthormo! amidst thy hundred hills, and listen to thy torrent's roar; but the soft sigh of the virgins is with the chief of Crono; Hidallan is the dream of Seláma, the dweller of her secret thoughts. A rushing storm in war, a breeze that sighs over the fallen foe, pleasant

T

are thy words of peace, and thy songs at the mossy
brook. Thy smiles are like the moonbeams trembling
on the waves. Thy voice is the gale of summer that
whispers among the reeds of the lake, and awakens the
harp of Moilena with all its lightly trembling strings.
O that thy calm light was around me! my soul should
not fear the gloomy chief of Duvranno. He came with
his stately steps. — My shield is before thee, maid of
my love! a wall of shelter from the lightning of
swords. They fought. Tonthormo bends, in all his
pride, before the arm of youth. But a voice was in
the breast of Hidallan, shall I slay the lover of Seláma?
Seláma dwells in thy dark bosom, shall my steel enter
there? Live, thou storm of war! He gave again his
sword. But, careless as he strode away, rage arose in
the troubled thoughts of the vanquished. He marked
his time, and sidelong pierced the heart of the generous son of Semo. His fair hair is spread on the dust,
his eyes are bent on the trembling beam of Clutha.
Farewell, light of my soul! They are closed in darkness. Feeble wast thou then, my father! and in vain
didst thou call for help. Thy gray locks are scattered,
as a wreath of snow on the top of ·a withered trunk;
which the boy brushes away with his staff; and careless singeth as he walks. Who shall defend thee, my
daughter! said the broken voice of Etha's chief. Fair
flower of the desert! the tempest shall rush over thee;

and thou shalt be low beneath the foot of the savage
son of prey. But I will wither, my father! on thy
tomb. Weak and alone I dwell amidst my tears, there
is no young warrior to lift the spear, no brother of
love! O that mine arm were strong! I would rush
amidst the battle. Seláma has no friend!

But Seláma has a friend, said the kindling soul of
Reuthamir. I will fight thy battles, lovely daughter
of kings; and the sun of Duvranno shall set in blood.
But when I return in peace, and the spirits of thy foes
are on my sword, meet me with thy smiles of love,
maid of Clutha! with thy slow-rolling eyes. Let the
soft sound of thy steps be heard in my halls, that the
mother of Reuthamir may rejoice. Whence, she will
say, is this beam of the distant land? Thou shalt
dwell in her bosom.

My thoughts are with him who is low in the dust,
son of Cormac! But lift the spear, thou friend of the
unhappy! the light of my soul may return.

He strode in his rattling arms. Tall, in a gloomy
forest, stood the surly strength of Duvranno. Gleaming behind the dark trees was his broad shield; like
the moon when it rises in blood, and the dusky clouds
sail low and heavy athwart its path. Thoughts, like
the troubled ocean, rushed over his soul, and he struck,
with his spear, the sounding pine. Starting, he mixed
in battle with the chief of woody Morna. Long was

the strife of arms; and the giant sons of the forest
trembled at their strokes. At length Tonthormo fell —
the sword of Reuthamir waved, a blue flame, around
him. He bites the ground in rage. His blood is
poured, a dark red stream, into Oithona's trembling
waves. Joy brightened in the soul of Reuthamir;
when a young warrior came, with his forward spear.
He moved in the light of beauty; but his words were
haughty and fierce. Is Tonthormo fallen in blood, the
friend of my early years? Die, thou dark-souled chief!
for never shall Selàma be thine, the maid of his love.
Lovely shone her eyes, through tears, in the hall of her
grief, when I stood by the chief of Duvranno, in the
rising strife of Clutha.

Retire, thou swelling voice of pride! thy spear is
light as the taper reed. Pierce the roes of the desert,
and call the hunter to the feast of songs, but speak not
of the daughter of Connal, son of the feeble arm!
Selàma is the love of heroes.

Try thy strength with the feeble arm, said the rising
pride of youth. Thou shalt vanish like a cloud of mist
before the sun, when he looks abroad in the power of
his brightness, and the storms are rolled away from before his face.

But thou thyself didst fall before Reuthamir, in all
thy boasting words. As a tall ash of the mountain,
when the tempest takes its green head and lays it level
on the plain.

Come from thy secret cave, Seláma! thy foes are silent and dark. Thou dove that hidest in the clefts of the rocks! the storm is over and past. Come from thy rock, Seláma! and give thy white hand to the chief who never fled from the face of glory, in all its terrible brightness.

She gave her hand, but it was trembling and cold, for the spear was deep in her side. Red, beneath her mail, the current of crimson wandered down her white breast, as the track of blood on Cromla's mountains of snow, when the wounded deer slowly crosses the heath, and the hunter's cries are in the breeze. Blest be the spear of Reuthamir! said the faint voice of the lovely, I feel it cold in my heart. Lay me by the son of Semo. Why should I know another love? Raise the tomb of the aged, his thin form shall rejoice, as he sails on a low-hung cloud, and guides the wintry storm. Open your airy halls, spirits of my love.

And have I quenched the light which was pleasant to my soul? said the chief of Morna. My steps moved in darkness, why were the words of strife in thy tale? Sorrow, like a cloud, comes over my soul, and shades the joy of mighty deeds. Soft be your rest in the narrow house, children of grief! The breeze in the long whistling grass shall not awaken you. The tempest shall rush over you, and the bulrush bow its head upon your tomb, but silence shall dwell in your habitation;

long repose, and the peace of years to come. The voice of the bard shall raise your remembrance in the distant land, and mingle your tale of woe with the murmur of other streams. Often shall the harp send forth a mournful sound, and the tear dwell in the soft eyes of the daughters of Morna.

Such were the words of Reuthamir, while he raised the tombs of the fallen. Sad were his steps towards the towers of his fathers, as, musing, he crossed the dark heath of Lena, and struck, at times, the thistle's beard.

LETTER ON WATERING-PLACES.

SIR, — I am a country gentleman, and enjoy an estate in Northamptonshire, which formerly enabled
its possessors to assume some degree of consequence in
the country; but which for several generations has
been growing less, only because it has not grown bigger. I mean, that though I have not yet been obliged
to mortgage my land or fell my timber, its relative
value is every day diminishing by the prodigious influx
of wealth, real and artificial, which for some time past
has been pouring into this kingdom. Hitherto, however, I have found my income equal to my wants. It
has enabled me to inhabit a good house in town for
four months of the year, and to reside amongst my tenants and neighbors for the remaining eight with credit
and hospitality. I am indeed myself so fond of the
country, and so averse in my nature to everything of
hurry and bustle, that if I consulted only my own taste
I should never feel a wish to leave the shelter of my
own oaks in the dreariest season of the year; but I
looked upon our annual visit to London as a proper
compliance with the gayer disposition of my wife and
the natural curiosity of the younger part of the family;

besides, to say the truth, it had its advantages in avoiding a round of dinners and card-parties, which we must otherwise have engaged in for the winter season, or have been branded with the appellation of unsociable. Our journey gave me an opportunity of furnishing my study with some new books and prints, and my wife of gratifying her neighbors with some ornamental trifles before their value was sunk by becoming common, or of producing at her table or in her furniture some new-invented refinement of fashionable elegance. Our hall was the first that was lighted by an Argand lamp; and I still remember how we were gratified by the astonishment of our guests when my wife with an audible voice called to the footman for the tongs to help to the asparagus with. We found it pleasant, too, to be enabled to talk of capital artists and favorite actors; and I made the better figure in my political debates from having heard the most popular speakers in the House.

Once, too, to recruit my wife's spirits after a tedious confinement from a lying-in, we passed a season at Bath. In this manner, therefore, things went on very well in the main, till of late my family have discovered that we lead a very dull kind of life; and that it is impossible to exist with comfort, or indeed to enjoy a tolerable share of health, without spending a good part of every summer at a watering-place. I held out as long as I could. One may be allowed to resist the plans of dissipation, but the plea of health cannot decently be withstood.

It was soon discovered that my eldest daughter wanted bracing; and my wife had a bilious complaint, against which our family physician declared that sea-bathing would be particularly serviceable. Therefore, though it was my own private opinion that my daughter's nerves might have been as well braced by morning rides upon the Northamptonshire hills as by evening dances in the public rooms, and that my wife's bile would have been greatly lessened by compliance with her husband, I acquiesced; and preparations were made for our journey. These indeed were but slight, for the chief gratification proposed in this scheme was an entire freedom from care and form. We should find everything requisite in our lodgings; it was of no consequence whether the rooms we should occupy for a few months in the summer were elegant or not; the simplicity of a country life would be the more enjoyed by the little shifts we should be put to; and all necessaries would be provided in our lodgings. It was not, therefore, till after we had taken them that we discovered how far ready-furnished lodgings were from affording every article in the catalogue of necessaries. We did not indeed give them a very scrupulous examination; for the place was so full, that when we arrived, — late at night, and tired with our journey, —

all the beds in the inn were taken up, and an easy-
chair and a carpet were all the accommodations we
could obtain for our repose. The next morning, therefore, we eagerly engaged the first lodgings we found
vacant, and have ever since been disputing about the
terms, which from the hurry were not sufficiently
ascertained ; and it is not even yet settled whether the
little blue garret, which serves us as a powdering room,
is ours of right or by favor. The want of all sorts of
conveniences is a constant excuse for the want of all
order and neatness, which is so visible in our apart-
ment ; and we are continually lamenting that we are
obliged to buy things of which we have such plenty at
home.

It is my misfortune that I can do nothing without
all my little conveniences about me, and in order to
write a common letter I must have my study-table to
lean my elbows on in sedentary luxury ; you will judge,
therefore, how little I am able to employ my leisure,
when I tell you that the only room they have been
able to allot for my use is so filled with my daughters'
hat-boxes, bandboxes, wig-boxes, etc., that I can scarcely move about in it, and am at this moment writing
upon a spare trunk for want of a table. I am therefore driven to saunter about with the rest of the party ;
but instead of the fine clumps of trees and waving
fields of corn I have been accustomed to have before

my eyes, I see nothing but a naked beach almost without a tree, exposed by turns to the cutting eastern
blast and the glare of a July sun, and covered with a
sand equally painful to the eyes and to the feet. The
ocean is indeed an object of unspeakable grandeur; but
when it has been contemplated in a storm and in a
calm, when we have seen the sun rise out of its bosom
and the moon silver its extended surface, its variety is
exhausted, and the eye begins to require the softer and
more interesting scenes of cultivated nature. My family have indeed been persuaded several times to enjoy
the sea still more by engaging in a little sailing-party;
but as, unfortunately, Northamptonshire has not afforded
them any opportunity of becoming seasoned sailors,
these parties of pleasure are always attended with the
most dreadful sickness. This, likewise, I am told, is
very good for the constitution; it may be so for aught
I know; but I confess I am apt to imagine that taking
an emetic at home would be equally salutary, and I am
sure it would be more decent. Nor can I help imagin-
ing that my youngest daughter's lover has been less
assiduous since he has contemplated her in the indeli-
cate situation of a ship-cabin. I have endeavored to
amuse myself with the company, but without much
success. It consists of a very few great people, who
make a set by themselves, and think they are entitled
by the freedom of a watering-place to indulge them-

selves in all manner of *polissonneries ;* and the rest is a
motley group of sharpers, merchants' clerks, kept mis-
tresses, idle men, and nervous women.   I have been
accustomed to be nice in my choice of acquaintance,
especially for my family ; but the greater part of our
connections here are such as we should be ashamed to
acknowledge anywhere else ; and the few we have seen
above ourselves will equally disclaim us when we meet
in town next winter.   As to the settled inhabitants of
the place, all who do not get by us view us with dislike, because we raise the price of provisions ; and
those who do — which in one way or other comprehends all the lower class — have lost every trace of
rural simplicity, and are versed in all arts of low
cunning and chicane.   The spirit of greediness and ra-
pacity is nowhere so conspicuous as in lodging-houses.
At our seat in the country our domestic concerns went
on as by clock-work ; a quarter of an hour in a week
settled the bills, and few tradesmen wished, and none
dared, to practise any imposition where all were
known, and the consequence of their different behavior
must have been their being marked for life for encouragement or for distrust.   But here the continual fluc-
tuation of company takes away all regard to character ;
the most respectable and ancient families have no
influence any further than as they scatter their ready
cash, and neither gratitude nor respect are felt where

there is no bond of mutual attachment besides the
necessities of the present day. I should be happy if
we had only to contend with this spirit during our
present excursion ; but the effect it has upon servants
is most pernicious. Our family used to be remarkable
for having its domestics grow gray in its service, but
this expedition has already corrupted them ; two we
have this evening parted with, and the rest have
learned so much of the tricks of their station that we
shall be obliged to discharge them as soon as we return
home. In the country I had been accustomed to do
good to the poor ; there are charities here too : we
have joined in a subscription for a crazy poetess, a raf-
fle for the support of a sharper who passes under the
title of a German count, and a benefit-play for a *gentleman* on board the hulks. Unfortunately, to balance
these various expenses, this place, which happens to be
a great resort of smugglers, affords daily opportunities
of making *bargains.* We drink spoiled teas under the
idea of their being cheap ; and the little room we have
is made less by the reception of cargoes of India taffe-
ties, shawl-muslins, and real chintzes. All my authority here would be exerted in vain ; for (I do not know
whether you know it or no) the buying of a bargain is
a temptation which is not in the nature of any woman
to resist. I am in hopes, however, the business may
receive some little check from an incident which hap-

pened a little time since : an acquaintance of ours,
returning from Margate, had his carriage seized by the
custom-house officers, on account of a piece of silk
which one of his female cousins, without his knowledge, had stowed in it ; and it was only released by its
being proved that what she had bought with so much
satisfaction as contraband was in reality the home-bred
manufacture of Spitalfields.

My family used to be remarkable for regularity in
their attendance on public worship; but that, too, here
is numbered amongst the amusements of the place.
Lady Huntingdon has a chapel, which sometimes at-
tracts us; and when nothing promises us any particular
entertainment, a tea-drinking at the Rooms, or a concert of what is called sacred music, is sufficient to draw
us from a church where no one will remark either our
absence or our presence. Thus we daily become more
lax in our conduct, for want of the salutary restraint
imposed upon us by the consciousness of being looked
up to as an example by others.

In this manner, sir, has the season passed away. I
spend a great deal of money, and make no figure; I am
in the country, and see nothing of country simplicity
or country occupations ; I am in an obscure village,
and yet cannot stir out without more observers than
if I were walking in St. James's Park ; I am cooped up
in less room than my own dog-kennel, while my spa-

cious halls are injured by standing empty; and I am
paying for tasteless, unripe fruit, while my own choice
wall-fruit is rotting by bushels under the trees.   In
recompense for all this we have the satisfaction of
knowing that we occupy the very rooms which my
Lord —— had just quitted; of picking up anecdotes,
true or false, of people in high life ; and of seizing the
ridicule of every character as they pass by us in the
moving show-glass of the place, — a pastime which
often affords us a good deal of mirth, but which, I
confess, I can never join in without reflecting that
what is our amusement is theirs likewise.   As to the
great ostensible object of our excursion, health, I
am afraid we cannot boast of much improvement.   We
have had a wet and cold summer; and these houses,
which are either old tenements vamped up, or new
ones slightly run up for the accommodation of bathers
during the season, have more contrivances for letting
in the cooling breezes than for keeping them out, a
circumstance which I should presume sagacious physicians do not always attend to when they order patients
from their own warm, compact, substantial houses to
take the air in country lodgings; of which the best
apartments, during the winter, have only been inhab-
ited by the rats, and where the poverty of the landlord
prevents him from laying out more in repairs than will
serve to give them a showy and attractive appearance.

Be that as it may ; the rooms we at present inhabit are so pervious to the breeze, that in spite of all the ingenious expedients of listing the doors, pasting paper on the inside of cupboards, laying sand-bags, puttying crevices, and condemning closet doors, it has given me a severe touch of my old rheumatism, and all my family are in one way or other affected with it: my eldest daughter, too, has got cold with her bathing, though the sea-water never gives anybody cold !

In answer to these complaints, I am told by the good company here that I have stayed too long in the same air, and that now I ought to take a trip to the Continent, and spend the winter at Nice, which would complete the business. I am entirely of their opinion, that it *would* complete the business, and have therefore taken the liberty of laying my case before you ; and am, sir,

Yours, etc.,

HENRY HOMELOVE.

DIALOGUE

BETWEEN MADAME COSMOGUNIA AND A PHILOSOPHICAL EN-
QUIRER OF THE EIGHTEENTH CENTURY, JANUARY 1, 1793.

E. I rejoice, my good madam, to see you. You bear
your years extremely well. You really look as fresh
and blooming this morning as if you were but just out
of your leading-strings; and yet you have — I forget
how many centuries upon your shoulders.

C. Do not you know, son, that people of my standing are by no means fond of being too nicely questioned
about their years? Besides, my age is a point by no
means agreed upon.

E. I thought it was set down in the church register?

C. That is true; but everybody does not go by your
register. The people who live eastward of us, and have
sold tea time out of mind, by the Great Wall, say I am
older by a vast deal; and that long before the time
when your people pretend I was born, I had near as
much wisdom and learning as I have now.

E. I do not know how that matter might be; one
thing I am certain of, that you did not know your

14 *   U

letters then ; and everybody knows that these tea-dealers, who are very vain, and want to go higher than anybody else for the antiquity of their family, are noted for lying.

C. On the other hand, old *Isaac*, the great chronicler, who was so famous for casting a figure, used to say that the register itself had been altered, and that he could prove I was much younger than you have usually reckoned me to be. It may be so ; — for my part, I cannot be supposed to remember so far back. I could not write in my early youth, and it was a long time before I had a pocket-almanac to set down all occurrences in, and the ages of my children, as I do now.

E. Well ; your exact age is not so material ; — but there is one point which I confess I wish much to ascertain. I have often heard it asserted that as you increase in years you grow wiser and better, and that you are at this moment more candid, more liberal, a better manager of your affairs, and, in short, more amiable in every respect, than ever you were in the whole course of your life ; and others — you will excuse me, madam — pretend that you are almost in your dotage ; that you grow more intolerable every year you live ; and that whereas in your childhood you were a sprightly, innocent young creature, that rose with the lark, lay down with the lamb, and thought or said no harm of any one, you are become

suspicious, selfish, interested, fond of nothing but indulging your appetites, and continually setting your
own children together by the ears for straws. Now I
should like to know where the truth lies?

C. As to that, I am, perhaps, too nearly concerned
to answer you properly. I will therefore only observe
that I do not remember the time when I have not
heard exactly the same contradictory assertions.

E. I believe the best way to determine the question
will be by facts. Pray be so good as to tell me how
you have employed yourself in the different periods
of your life; from the earliest time you can remember,
for instance.

C. I have a very confused remembrance of living in
a pleasant garden full of fruit, and of being turned out
because I had not minded the injunctions that were
laid upon me. After that I became so very naughty
that I got a severe ducking, and was in great danger
of being drowned.

E. A hopeful beginning, I must allow! Pray what
was the first piece of work you recollect being engaged
in?

C. I remember setting myself to build a prodigious
high house of cards, which I childishly thought I could
raise up to the very skies. I piled them up very high,
and at last left off in the middle, and had my tongue
slit for being so self-conceited. Afterwards I baked

dirt in the sun, and resolved to make something very
magnificent, I hardly knew what; so I built a great
many mounds in the form of sugar-loaves, very broad
at bottom and pointed at top: they took me a great
many years to make, and were fit for no earthly purpose
when they were done. They are still to be seen, if you
choose to take the trouble of going so far. Travellers
call them my *folly*.

E. Pray what studies took your attention when you
first began to learn ?

C. At first I amused myself, as all children do, with
pictures, and drew, or rather attempted to draw, figures
of lions and serpents, and men with the heads of ani-
mals, and women with fishes' tails; to all which I
affixed a meaning, often whimsical enough. Many of
these my first scratches are still to be seen upon old
walls and stones, and have greatly exercised the ingenuity of the curious to find out what I could possibly
mean by them. Afterwards, when I had learned to read,
I was wonderfully entertained with stories of giants,
griffins, and mermaids; and men and women turned
into trees, and horses that spoke, and of an old man
that used to eat up his children, till his wife deceived
him by giving him a stone to eat instead of one of
them ; and of a conjurer that tied up the wind in bags,
and —

E. Hold, hold, my good madam ! you have given me

a very sufficient proof of that propensity to the marvellous which I have always remarked in you. I suppose, however, you soon grew too old for such nursery stories as these.

C. On the contrary, I amused myself with putting them into verse, and had them sung to me on holidays; and, at this very day, I make a point of teaching them to all my children in whose education I take any pains.

E. I think I should rather whip them for employing their time so idly; I hope at least these pretty stories kept you out of mischief?

C. I cannot say they did; I never was without a scratched face, or a bloody nose, at any period I can remember.

E. Very promising dispositions, truly!

C. My amusements were not all so mischievous. I was very fond of star-gazing, and telling fortunes, and trying a thousand tricks for good luck, many of which have made such an impression on my mind, that I remember them even to this day.

E. I hope, however, your reading was not all of the kind you have mentioned?

C. No. It was at some very famous races, which were held every four years for my diversion, and which I always made a point to be at, that a man once came upon the race-ground, and read a history-book aloud to the whole company : there were, to be sure, a number of stories in it not greatly better than those I have been telling you; however, from that time I began to take to more serious learning, and likewise to reckon and date all my accounts by these races, which, as I told you, I was very fond of.

E. I think you afterwards went to school, and learnt philosophy and mathematics ?

C. I did so.   I had a great many famous masters.

E. Were you a teachable scholar ?

C. One of my masters used always to weep when he saw me; another used always to burst into a fit of laughter.   I leave you to guess what they thought of me.

E. Pray what did you do when you were in middle age ? — that is usually esteemed the most valuable part of life.

C. I somehow got shut up in a dark cell, where I took a long nap.

E. And after you waked —

C. I fell a disputing with all my might.

E. What were the subjects that interested you so much ?

C. Several.

E. Pray let us have a specimen ?

C. Whether the light of Tabor was created or uncreated ; whether *one* be a number ; whether men should cross themselves with two fingers or with three; whether the creation was finished in six days because it is the most perfect number, or whether six is the most perfect number because the creation was finished in six days; whether two and one make three, or only one.

E. And pray what may be your opinion of the last proposition, particularly?

C. I have by no means made up my mind about it; in another century, perhaps, I may be able to decide upon the point.

E. These debates of yours had one advantage, however; you could not possibly put yourself in a passion on such kind of subjects.

C. There you are very much mistaken. I was constantly in a passion upon one or the other of them; and if my opponent did not agree with me, my constant practice was to knock him down, even if it were in the church. I have the happiness of being able to interest myself in the most indifferent questions, as soon as I am contradicted upon it. I can make a very good dispute out of the question whether the preference be due to blue or green in the color of a jockey's cap; and would desire no better cause of a quarrel than whether a person's name should be spelt with C or with K.

E. These constant disputes must have had a very

bad effect on your younger children. How do you hope ever to have a quiet house?

C. And yet, I do assure you, there is no one point that I have labored more than that important one of family harmony.

E. Indeed.

C. Yes; for the sake of that order and unanimity which has always been dear to me, I have constantly insisted that all my children should sneeze and blow their nose at the same time and in the same manner.

E. May I presume to ask the reason of this injunction?

C. Is it possible you do not see the extreme danger, as well as indecorum, of suffering every one to blow his nose his own way? Could you trust any one with the keys of your offices, who sneezed to the right when other people sneezed to the left, or to the left when they sneezed to the right?

E. I confess I am rather dull in discerning the inconvenience that would ensue: — but pray have you been able to accomplish this desirable uniformity?

C. I acknowledge I have not; and indeed I have met with so much obstinate resistance to this my wise regulation, that, to tell you the truth, I am almost on the point of giving it up. You would hardly believe the perverseness my children have shown on the occasion; blowing their noses, locked up in their rooms, or in dark corners about the house, in every possible way; so that, in short, on pretence of colds, tender noses, or want of pocket-handkerchiefs, or one plea or another, I have been obliged to tolerate the uncomplying, very much against my will. However, I contrived to show my disapprobation, at least, of such scandalous irregularities, by never saying *God bless you*, if a person sneezes in the family contrary to established rule.

E. I am glad, at least, you are in this respect got a little nearer to common-sense. As you seem to have been of so imperious a disposition, I hope you were not trusted with any mischievous weapons?

C. At first I used to fight with clubs and stones; afterwards with other weapons; but at length I contrived to get at gunpowder, and then I did glorious mischief.

E. Pray had you never anybody who taught you better?

C. Yes; several wise men, from time to time, attempted to mend my manners, and reform me, as they called it.

E. And how did you behave to them?

C. Some I hunted about; some I poisoned; some I contrived to have thrown into prison; some I made bonfires of; others I only laughed at. It was but the other day that one of them wanted to give me some hints for the better regulation of my family; upon which I pulled his house down: I was often, however, the better for the lesson, though the teacher had seldom the pleasure of seeing it.

E. I have heard it said you are very partial to your children; that you pamper some and starve others. Pray who are your favorites?

C. Generally, those who do the most mischief.

E. Had you not once a great favorite called Louis, whom you used to style the immortal man?

C. I had so. I was continually repeating his name: I set up a great number of statues to him, and ordered that every one should pull off his hat to them as he went by.

E. And what is become of them now?

C. The other day, in a fit of spleen, I kicked them all down again.

E. I think I have read that you were once much under the influence of an old man with a high-crowned hat, and a bunch of keys by his side?

C. It is true. He used to frighten me by setting his arms akimbo and swearing most terribly; besides which he was always threatening to put me in a dark hole, if I did not do as he would have me. He has conjured many *pence* out of my pocket, I assure you; and he used to make me believe the strangest stories! But I have now pretty nearly done with him; he dares not speak so big as he used to do: hardly a shoeblack will pull off his hat to him now; it is even as much as he can do to keep his own tight upon his head; nay, I have been assured that the next high wind will certainly blow it off.

E. You must doubtless have made great advances in the art of reasoning, from the various lights and experiments of modern times: pray what was the last philosophical study that engaged your attention?

C. One of the last was a system of quackery called Animal Magnetism.

E. And what in theology?

C. A system of quackery called Swedenborgianism.

E. And pray what are you doing at this moment?

C. I am going to turn over quite a new leaf. I am singing Ça Ira.

E. I do not know whether you are going to turn over a new leaf or no; but I am sure, from this account, it is high time you should. All I can say is, that if I cannot mend you, I will endeavor to take care you do not spoil me; and one thing more, that I wish you would lay your commands on Miss Burney to write a new novel, and make you laugh.

DIALOGUE IN THE SHADES.

Clio. There is no help for it, — they must go. The river Lethe is here at hand; I shall tear them off and throw them into the stream.

Mercury. Illustrious daughter of Mnemosyne, Clio! the most respected of the Muses, — you seem disturbed. What is it that brings us the honor of a visit from you in these infernal regions?

Clio. You are a god of expedients, Mercury; I want to consult you. I am oppressed with the continually increasing demands upon me. I have had more business for these last twenty years than I have often had for two centuries; and if I had, as old Homer says, " a throat of brass and adamantine lungs," I could never get through it. And what did he want this throat of brass for? for a paltry list of ships, canoes rather, which would be laughed at in the Admiralty Office of London. But I must inform you, Mercury, that my roll is so full, and I have so many applications which cannot in decency be refused, that I see no other way than striking off some hundreds of names in order to make room; and I am come to inform the shades of my determination.

Mercury. I believe, Clio, you will do right; and as one end of your roll is a little mouldy, no doubt you will begin with that; but the ghosts will raise a great clamor.

Clio. I expect no less; but necessity has no law. All the parchment in Pergamus is used up, — my roll is long enough to reach from earth to heaven; it is grown quite cumbrous; it takes a life, as mortals reckon lives, to unroll it.

Mercury. Yet consider, Clio, how many of these have passed a restless life, and encountered all manner of dangers, and bled and died, only to be placed upon your list, — and now to be struck off!

Clio. And committed all manner of crimes, you might have added; but go they must. Besides, they have been sufficiently recompensed. Have they not been praised and sung and admired for some thousands of years? Let them give place to others. What! have they no conscience? no modesty? Would Xerxes, think you, have reason to complain, when his parading expeditions have already procured him above two thousand years of fame, though a Solyman or a Zingis Khan should fill up his place?

Mercury. Surely you are not going to blot out Xerxes from your list of names?

Clio. I do not say that I am; but that I keep him is more for the sake of his antagonists than his own.

And yet their places might be well supplied by the Swiss heroes of Morgarten, or the brave though unsuccessful patriot Aloys Reding. — But pray what noise is that at the gate?

Mercury. A number of the shades, who have received an intimation of your purpose, and are come to remonstrate against it.

Clio. In the name of all the gods whom have we here? Hercules, Theseus, Jason, Œdipus, Bacchus, Cadmus with a bag of dragons' teeth, and a whole tribe of strange, shadowy figures! I shall expect to see the Centaurs and Lapithæ, or Perseus on his flying courser. Away with them; they belong to my sisters, not to me; Melpomene will receive them gladly.

Mercury. You forget, Clio, that Bacchus conquered India.

Clio. And had horns like Moses, as Vossius is pleased to say. No, Mercury, I will have nothing to do with these; if ever I received them, it was when I was young and credulous. As I have said, let my sisters take them; or let them be celebrated in tales for children.

Mercury. That will not do, Clio. Children in this age read none but wise books; stories of giants and dragons are all written for grown-up children now.

Clio. Be that as it may, I shall clear my hands of them and of a great many more, I do assure you.

Mercury. I hope "the tale of Troy divine — "

Clio. Divine let it be, but my share in it is very small; I recollect furnishing the catalogue. Mercury, I will tell you the truth. When I was young, my mother (as arrant a gossip as ever breathed) related to me a great number of stories; and as in those days people could not read or write, I had no better authority for what I recorded; but after letters were found out, and now since the noble invention of printing, — why, do you think, Mercury, any one would dare to tell lies in print?

Mercury. Sometimes, perhaps. I have seen a splendid victory in the gazette of one country dwindle into an honorable retreat in that of another.

Clio. In newspapers, very possibly; but with regard to myself, when I have time to consider and lay things together, I assure you you may depend upon me. Whom have we in that group which I see indistinctly in a sort of twilight?

Mercury. Very renowned personages: Ninus, Sesostris, Semiramis, Cheops who built the largest pyramid.

Clio. If Cheops built the largest pyramid, people are welcome to inquire about him at the spot, — room must be made. As to Semiramis, tell her her place shall be filled up by an empress and a conqueror from the shores of the wintry Baltic.

Mercury. The renowned Cyrus is approaching with a

look of confidence, for he is introduced by a favorite of yours, the elegant Xenophon.

Clio. Is that Cyrus ? Pray desire him to take off that dress which Xenophon has given him. Truly I took him for a Greek philosopher ; I fancy Queen To-myris would scarcely recognize him.

Mercury. Aspasia hopes, for the honor of her sex, that she shall continue to occupy a place among those you celebrate.

Clio. Tell the mistress of Pericles we can spare her without inconvenience. Many ladies are to be found in modern times who possess her eloquence and her talents, with the modesty of a vestal; and should a more perfect likeness be required, modern times may furnish that also.

Mercury. Here are two figures who approach you with a very dignified air.

Solon and *Lycurgus.* We present ourselves, divine Clio, with confidence. We have no fear that you should strike from your roll the lawgivers of Athens and Sparta.

Clio. Most assuredly not. Yet I must inform you that a name higher than either of yours, and a constitution more perfect, is to be found in a vast continent, of the very existence of which you had not the least suspicion.

Mercury. I see approaching a person of a noble and

spirited air, if he did not hold his head a little on one side as if his neck were awry.

Alexander. Clio, I need not introduce myself; I am, as you well know, the son of Jupiter Ammon, and my arms have reached even to the remote shore of the Indus.

Clio. Pray burn your genealogy; and for the rest, suffer me to inform you that the river Indus and the whole peninsula which you scarcely discovered, with sixty millions of inhabitants, is at this moment subject to the dominion of a few merchants in a remote island of the Northern Ocean, the very name of which never reached your ears.

Mercury. Here is Empedocles, who threw himself into Etna merely to be placed upon your roll; and Calanus, who mounted his funeral pile before Alexander from the same motive.

Clio. They have been remembered long enough, in all reason; their places may be supplied by the two next madmen who shall throw themselves under the wheels of the chariot of Juggernaut, — fanatics are the growth of every age.

Mercury. Here is a ghost preparing to address you with a very self-sufficient air ; his robe is embroidered with flower-de-luces.

. *Louis XIV.* I am persuaded, Clio, you will recognize *the immortal man.* I have always been a friend and patron of the Muses ; my actions are well known ;

all Europe has resounded with my name, — the terror
of other countries, the glory of my own; I am well
assured you are not going to strike me off.

Clio. To strike you off? certainly not; but to place
you many degrees lower in the list; to reduce you
from a sun, your favorite emblem, to a star in the
galaxy. My sisters have certainly been partial to you:
you bought their favor with — how many livres a year?
not much more than a London bookseller will give for
a quarto poem. But me you cannot bribe.

Louis. But, Clio, you have yourself recorded my
exploits; — the passage of the Rhine, Namur, Flanders,
Franche Comté.

Clio. O Louis, if you could but guess the extent of
the present French Empire; — but no, it could never
enter into your imagination.

Louis. I rejoice at what you say; I rejoice that my
posterity have followed my steps, and improved upon
my glory.

Clio. Your posterity have had nothing to do with it.

Louis. Remember, too, the urbanity of my character,
how hospitably I received the unfortunate James of
England, — England, the natural enemy of France.

Clio. Your hospitality has been well returned. Your
descendants, driven from their thrones, are at this
moment supported by the bounty of the nation and
king of England.

Louis. O Clio, what is it that you tell me! let me hide my diminished head in the deepest umbrage of the grove; let me seek out my dear Maintenon, and tell my beads with her till I forget that I have been either praised or feared.

Clio. Comfort yourself, however; your name, like the red letter which marks the holiday, though insignificant in itself, shall still enjoy the honor of designating the age of taste and literature.

Mercury. Here is a whole crowd coming, Clio, I can scarcely keep them off with my wand: they have all got notice of your intentions, and the infernal regions are quite in an uproar, — what is to be done?

Clio. I cannot tell; the numbers distract me: to examine their pretensions one by one is impossible; I must strike off half of them at a venture: the rest must make room, — they must crowd, they must fall into the background; and where I used to write a name all in capitals, with letters of gold illuminated, I must put it in *small pica.* I do assure you, Mercury, I cannot stand the fatigue I undergo much longer. I am not provided, as you very well know, with either chariot or wings, and I am expected to be in all parts of the globe at once. In the good old times my business lay almost entirely between the Hellespont and the Pillars of Hercules, with sometimes an excursion to the mouths (then seven) of the Nile or the banks of the Euphrates. But now I am required to be in a hundred places at once; I am called from Jena to Austerlitz, from Cape Trafalgar to Aboukir, and from the Thames to the Ganges and Burampooter; besides a whole continent, a world by itself, fresh and vigorous, which I foresee will find me abundance of employment.

Mercury. Truly I believe so; I am afraid the old leaven is working in the new world.

Clio. I am puzzled at this moment how to give the account, which always is expected of me, of the august sovereigns of Europe.

Mercury. How so?

Clio. I do not know where to find them; they are most of them upon their *travels.*

Mercury. You must have been very much employed in the French Revolution.

Clio. Continually; the actors in the scene succeeded one another with such rapidity that the hero of to-day was forgotten on the morrow. Necker, Mirabeau, Dumourier, La Fayette, appeared successively like pictures in a magic lantern, — shown for a moment and then withdrawn: and now the space is filled by one tremendous gigantic figure, that throws his broad shadow over half the globe.

Mercury. The ambition of Napoleon has indeed procured you much employment.

Clio. Employment! There is not a goddess so harassed as I am; my sisters lead quite idle lives in comparison. Melpomene has in a manner slept through the last half-century, except when now and then she dictated to a certain favorite nymph. Urania, indeed, has employed herself with Herschel in counting the stars; but her task is less than mine. Here am I expected to calculate how many hundred thousands of rational beings cut one another's throats at Austerlitz, and to take the tale of two hundred and thirteen thousand human bodies and ninety-five thousand horses, that lie stiff, frozen, and unburied on the banks of the Berecina; — and do you think, Mercury, this can be a pleasant employment?

Mercury. I have had a great increase of employment myself lately, on account of the multitude of shades I have been obliged to convey; and poor old Charon is almost laid up with the rheumatism: we used to have a holiday comparatively during the winter months; but of late, winter and summer I have observed are much alike to heroes.

Clio. I wish to Jupiter I could resign my office! Son of Maia, I declare to you I am sick of the horrors I record; I am sick of mankind. For above these three thousand years have I been warning them and reading lessons to them, and they will not mend: Robespierre was as cruel as Sylla, and Napoleon has no more moderation than Pyrrhus. The human frame, of curious texture, delicately formed, feeling, and irritable by the least annoyance, with face erect and animated with Promethean fire, they wound, they lacerate, they mutilate with most perverted ingenuity. I will go and record the actions of the tigers of Africa; in them such fierceness is natural. Nay, the human race will be exterminated if this work of destruction goes on much longer.

Mercury. With regard to that matter, Clio, I can set your heart at rest. A great philosopher has lately discovered that the world is in imminent danger of being overpeopled, and that if twenty or forty thousand men could not be persuaded every now and then to stand and be shot at, we should be forced to eat one another. This discovery has had a wonderful effect in quieting tender consciences. The calculation is very simple, any school-boy will explain it to you.

Clio. O what a number of fertile plains and green savannas, and tracts covered with trees of beautiful foliage, have never yet been pressed by human footsteps! My friend Swift's project of eating children was not so cruel as these bloody and lavish sacrifices to Mars, the most savage of all the gods.

Mercury. You forget yourself, Clio; Mars is not worshipped now in Christian Europe.

Clio. By Jupiter, but he is! Have I not seen the bloody and torn banners, with martial music and military procession, brought into the temple, — and whose temple thinkest thou ? and to whom have thanks been given on both sides, amidst smoking towns and wasted fields, after the destruction of man and devastation of the fair face of nature ! And Mercury, god of wealth and frauds, you have your temple too, though your name is not inscribed there.

Mercury. I am afraid men will always love wealth.

Clio. O if I had to record only such pure names as Washington or a Howard !

Mercury. It would be very gratifying certainly ; but then, Clio, you would have very little to do, and might almost as well burn your roll.

KNOWLEDGE AND HER DAUGHTER:

A FABLE.

KNOWLEDGE, the daughter of Jupiter, descended from the skies to visit man. She found him naked and helpless, living on the spontaneous fruits of the earth, and little superior to the ox that grazed beside him. She clothed and fed him; she built him palaces; she showed him the hidden riches of the earth, and pointed with her finger the course of the stars as they rose and set in the horizon. Man became rich with her gifts and accomplished from her conversation. In process of time Knowledge became acquainted with the schools of the philosophers; and being much taken with their theories and their conversation, she married one of them. They had many beautiful and healthy children; but among the rest was a daughter of a different complexion from all the rest, whose name was Doubt. She grew up under many disadvantages; she had a great hesitation in her speech; a cast in her eye, which, however, was keen and piercing; and was subject to nervous tremblings. Her mother saw her with dislike: but her father, who was of the sect of the Pyrrhonists, cherished and taught her logic, in which she made a great progress. The Muse of History was much troubled with her intrusions: she would tear out whole leaves, and blot over many pages of her favorite works. With the divines her depredations were still worse: she was forbidden to enter a church; notwithstanding which she would slip in under the surplice, and spend her time in making mouths at the priest. If she got at a library, she destroyed or blotted over the most valuable manuscripts. A most undutiful child; she was never better pleased than when she could unexpectedly trip up her mother's heels, or expose a rent or an unseemly patch in her flowing and ample garment. With mathematicians she never meddled; but in all other systems of knowledge she intruded herself, and her breath diffused a mist over the page which often left it scarcely legible. Her mother at length said to her, "Thou art my child, and I know it is decreed that while I tread this earth thou must accompany my footsteps; but thou art mortal, I am immortal; and there will come a time when I shall be freed from thy intrusion, and shall pursue my glorious track from star to star, and from system to system, without impediment and without check."

15*

TRUE MAGICIANS.

TO MISS C.

MY DEAR SARAH, — I have often reflected, since I left you, on the wonderful powers of magic exhibited by you and your sister. The dim obscurity of that grotto hollowed out by your hands under the laurel hedge, where you used to mix the ingredients of your incantations, struck us with awe and terror; and the broom which you so often brandished in your hands made you look very like witches indeed. I must confess, however, that some doubts have now and then arisen in my mind, whether or no you were truly initiated in the secrets of your art; and these suspicions gathered strength after you had suffered us and yourself to be so drenched as we all were on that rainy Tuesday; which to say the least was a very odd circumstance, considering you had the command of the weather. — As I was pondering these matters alone in the chaise between Epsom and London, I fell asleep and had the following dream.

I thought I had been travelling through an unknown country, and came at last to a thick wood cut out into several groves and avenues, the gloom of which inspired thoughtfulness, and a certain mysterious dread of unknown powers came upon me. I entered, however, one of the avenues, and found it terminated in a magnificent portal, through which I could discern confusedly, among thick foliage, cloistered arches and Grecian porticos, and people walking and conversing amongst the trees. Over the portal was the following inscription: "*Here dwell the true magicians. Nature is our servant. Man is our pupil. We change, we conquer, we create.*"

As I was hesitating whether or no I should presume to enter, a pilgrim who was sitting under the shade offered to be my guide, assuring me that these magicians would do me no harm, and that, so far from having any objection to be observed in their operations, they were pleased with any opportunity of exhibiting them to the curious. In, therefore, I went, and addressed the first of the magicians I met with, who asked me whether I liked panoramas. On replying that I thought them very entertaining, she took me to a little eminence and bade me look round. I did so, and beheld the representation of the beautiful vale of Dorking, with Norbury Park and Box Hill to the north, Reigate to the east, and Leith tower with the Surry hills to the south. After I had admired for some time the beauty and accuracy of the painting, a vast curtain

seemed to be drawn gradually up, and my view extended on all sides.   On one hand I traced the windings of the Thames up to Oxford, and stretched my eye
westward over Salisbury Plain, and across the Bristol
Channel into the romantic country of South Wales;
northward the view extended to Lincoln cathedral, and
York minster towering over the rest of the churches.
Across the Sussex downs I had a clear view of the
British Channel, and the opposite coast of France with
its ports blockaded by our fleets.   As the horizon of
the panorama still extended, I spied the towers of
Notre Dame and the Tuileries, and my eye wandered
at large over "the vine-covered hills and gay regions
of France," quite down to the source of the Loire.   At
the same time the great Atlantic Ocean opened to my
view; and on the other hand I saw the Lake of Geneva,
and the dark ridge of Mount Jura, and discovered the
summits of the Alps covered with snow; and beyond,
the orange-groves of Italy, the majestic dome of St.
Peter's, and the smoking crater of Vesuvius.   As the
curtain still rose, I stretched my view over the Medi-
terranean, the scene of ancient glory, the Archipelago
studded with islands, the shores of the Bosphorus, and
the gilded minarets and cypress-groves of Constanti-
nople.   Throwing back a look to the less attractive
north, I saw pictured the rugged, broken coast of Nor-
way, the cheerless moors of Lapland, and the intermi-

nable desolation of the plains of Siberia. Turning my
eye again southward, the landscape extended to the
plains of Barbary, covered with date-trees; and I dis-
cerned the points of pyramids appearing above the
horizon, and saw the Delta and the seven-mouthed
Nile. In short, the curtain still rose, and the view
extended further and further till the panorama took in
the whole globe. I cannot express to you the pleasure
I felt as I saw mountains, seas, and islands spread out
before me. Sometimes my eye wandered over the vast
plains of Tartary, sometimes it expatiated in the savannas of America. I saw men with dark skins, white
cotton turbans wreathed about their heads, and long
flowing robes of silk; others almost naked under a ver-
tical sun. I saw whales sporting in the northern seas,
and elephants trampling amidst fields of maize and
forests of palm-trees. I seemed to have put a girdle
about the earth, and was gratified with an infinite variety of objects which I thought I never could be weary
of contemplating. At length, turning towards the magician who had entertained me with such an agreeable
exhibition, and asking her name, she informed me it
was *Geography*.

My attention was next arrested by a sorceress, who,
I was told, possessed the power of calling up from the
dead whomsoever she pleased, man or woman, in their
proper habits and figures, and obliging them to con-

verse and answer questions. She held a roll of parchment in her hand, and had an air of great dignity. I confess that I felt a little afraid; but having been somewhat encouraged by the former exhibition, I ventured to ask her to give me a specimen of her power, in case there was nothing unlawful in it. "Whom," said she, "do you wish to behold?" After considering some time, I desired to see Cicero the Roman orator. She made some talismanic figures on the sand, and presently he arose to my view, his neck and head bare, the rest of his body in a flowing toga, which he gathered round him with one hand, and stretching out the other very gracefully he recited to me one of his orations against Catiline. He also read to me, which was more than I could in reason have expected, several of his familiar letters to his most intimate friends. I next desired that Julius Cæsar might be called up: on which he appeared, his hair nicely arranged, and the fore-part of his head, which was bald, covered with wreaths of laurel; and he very obligingly gave me a particular account of his expedition into Gaul. I wished to see the youth of Macedon, but was a little disappointed in his figure, for he was low in stature and held his head awry; but I saw him manage Bucephalus with admirable courage and address, and was afterwards introduced with him into the tent of Darius, where I was greatly pleased with the generosity and politeness of his behavior. I afterwards expressed some curiosity to see a battle, if I might do it with safety, and was gratified with the sea-fight of Actium. I saw, after the first onset, the galleys of Cleopatra turning their prows and flying from the battle, and Antony, to his eternal shame, quitting the engagement and making sail after her. I then wished to call up all the kings of England, and they appeared in order one after the other, with their crowns and the insignia of their dignity, and walked over the stage for my amusement, much like the descendants of Banquo in Macbeth. Their queens accompanied them, trailing their robes upon the ground, and the bishops with their mitres, and judges, and generals, and eminent persons of every class. I asked many questions as they passed, and received a great deal of information relative to the laws, manners, and transactions of past times. I did not, however, always meet with direct answers to my questions. For instance, when I called up Homer, and after some other conversation asked him where he was born, he only said, "Guess!" And when I asked Louis the Fourteenth who was the man in the iron mask, he frowned and would not tell me. I took a great deal of pleasure in calling up the shades of distinguished people in different ages and countries, making them stand close by one another, and comparing their manners and costume. Thus I measured Catha-

rine of Russia against Semiramis, and Aristotle against
Lord Bacon. I could have spent whole years in conversation with so many celebrated persons, and promised myself that I would often frequent this obliging
magician. Her name, I found, was in heaven *Clio*, on
earth *History*.

I saw another who was making a charm for two
friends, one of whom was going to the East Indies;
they were bitterly lamenting that when they were
parted at so great a distance from each other they
could no longer communicate their thoughts, but must
be cut off from each other's society. Presenting them
with a talisman inscribed with four-and-twenty black
marks, " Take this," she said ; " I have breathed a voice
upon it: by means of this talisman you shall still converse, and hear one another as distinctly when half the
globe is between you as if you were talking together in
the same room." The two friends thanked her for such
an invaluable present, and retired. Her name was
Abracadabra.

I was next invited to see a whispering gallery of a
most curious and uncommon structure. To make the
experiment of its powers, a young poet of a very modest appearance, who was stealing along in a retired
walk, was desired to repeat a verse in it. He applied
his lips to the wall, and whispered in a low voice,
" *Rura mihi et rigui placcant in vallibus amnes.*" The

sound ran along the walls for some time in a kind of
low whisper; but every minute it grew louder and
louder, till at length it was echoed and re-echoed from
every part of the gallery, and seemed to be pronounced
by a multitude of voices at once, in different languages,
till the whole dome was filled with the sound. There
was a strong smell of incense. The gallery was con-
structed by *Fame.*

The good pilgrim next conducted me to a cave where
several sorceresses, very black and grim, were amusing
themselves with making lightning, thunder, and earth-
quakes. I saw two vials of cold liquor mixed together,
and flames burst forth from them. I saw some insig-
nificant-looking black grains, which would throw palaces and castles into the air. I saw — and it made my
hair stand on end — a headless man who lifted up his
arm and grasped a sword. I saw men flying through
the air without wings, over the tops of towns and castles, and come down unhurt. The cavern was very
black, and the smoke and fires and mephitic blasts and
sulphureous vapors that issued from it gave the whole
a very tremendous appearance. I did not stay long,
but as I retired I saw *Chemistry* written on the walls
in letters of flame, with several other names which I
do not now remember.

My companion whispered me that some of these
were suspected of communication with the evil genii,

W

and that the demon of War had been seen to resort to the cave. "But now," said the pilgrim, "I will lead you to enchanters who deserve all your veneration, and are even more beneficent than those you have already seen." He then led me to a cavern that opened upon the sea-shore; it blew a terrible storm, the waves ran mountain high, the wind roared, and vessels were driven against each other with a terrible shock. A female figure advanced and threw a little oil upon the waves; they immediately subsided, the winds were still, the storm was laid, and the vessels pursued their course in safety. "By what magic is this performed?" exclaimed I. "The magician is *Meekness*," replied my conductor; "she can smooth the roughest sea and allay the wildest storm."

My view was next directed to a poor wretch who lay groaning in a most piteous manner, and crushed to the earth with a mountain on his breast; he uttered piercing shrieks, and seemed totally unable to rise or help himself. One of these good magicians, whose name I found was *Patience*, advanced, and struck the mountain with a wand; on which, to my great surprise, it diminished to a size not more than the load of an ordinary porter, which the man threw over his shoulders with something very like a smile, and marched off with a firm step and very composed air.

I must not pass over a charmer of a very pleasing

appearance and lively aspect. She possessed the power (a very useful one in a country so subject to fogs and rains as this is) of gilding a landscape with sunshine whenever she breathed upon it. Her name was *Cheerfulness*. Indeed, you may remember that your papa brought her down with him on that very rainy day when we could not go out at all, and he played on his flute to you, and you all danced.

I was next struck, on ascending an eminence, with a most dreary landscape. All the flat country was one stagnant marsh. Amidst the rushy grass lay the fiend Ague, listless and shivering. On the bare and bleak hills sat Famine, with a few shells of acorns before her, of which she had eaten the fruit. The woods were tangled and pathless; the howl of wolves was heard. A few smoky huts, or caves, not much better than the dens of wild beasts, were all the habitations of men that presented themselves. "Miserable country!" I exclaimed; "step-child of Nature!" "This," said my conductor, " is Britain as our ancestors possessed it." " And by what magic," I replied, " has it been converted into the pleasant land we now inhabit ? " " You shall see," said he. " It has been the work of one of our most powerful magicians. Her name is *Industry*." At the word she advanced and waved her wand over the scene. Gradually the waters ran off into separate channels, and left rich meadows covered

with innumerable flocks and herds.   The woods disap-
peared, except what waved gracefully on the tops of
the hills, or filled up the unsightly hollows. ` When-
ever she moved her wand, roads, bridges, and canals
laid open and improved the face of the country.   A
numerous population, spread abroad in the fields, were
gathering in the harvest.   Smoke from warm cottages
ascended through the trees, pleasant towns and villages
marked the several points of distance.   Last, the
Thames was filled with forests of masts, and proud
London appeared with all its display of wealth and
grandeur.

I do not know whether it was the pleasure I received
from this exhilarating scene, or the carriage having just
got upon the pavement, which awakened me; but I
determined to write out my dream, and advise you to
cultivate your acquaintance with all the *true Arts of
Magic.*

THE PINE AND THE OLIVE.

A FABLE.

A STOIC, swelling with the proud consciousness of his own worth, took a solitary walk; and straying amongst the groves of Academus, he sat down between an Olive and a Pine tree. His attention was soon excited by a murmur which he heard among the leaves. The whispers increased; and listening attentively, he plainly heard the Pine say to the Olive as follows: " Poor tree! I pity thee. Thou now spreadest thy green leaves and exultest in all the pride of youth and spring; but how soon will thy beauty be tarnished! The fruit which thou exhaustest thyself to bear shall hardly be shaken from thy boughs before thou shalt grow dry and withered; thy green veins, now so full of juice, shall be frozen; naked and bare thou wilt stand exposed to all the storms of winter, whilst my firmer leaf shall resist the change of the seasons. *Unchangeable* is my motto; and through the various vicissitudes of the year I shall continue equally green and vigorous as I am at present."

The Olive, with a graceful wave of her boughs,

replied: "It is true thou wilt always continue as thou art at present. Thy leaves will keep that sullen and gloomy green in which they are now arrayed, and the stiff regularity of thy branches will not yield to those storms which will bow down many of the feebler tenants of the grove. Yet I wish not to be like thee. I rejoice when Nature rejoices; and when I am desolate, Nature mourns with me. I fully enjoy pleasure in its season, and I am contented to be subject to the influences of those seasons and that economy of Nature by which I flourish. When the spring approaches I feel the kindly warmth; my branches swell with young buds, and my leaves unfold; crowds of singing birds which never visit thy noxious shade sport on my boughs; my fruit is offered to the gods, and rejoices men; and when the decay of nature approaches, I shed my leaves over the funeral of the falling year, and am well contented not to stand a single exemption to the mournful desolation I see everywhere around me."

The Pine was unable to frame a reply; and the philosopher turned away his steps rebuked and humbled.

ON RIDDLES.

MY DEAR YOUNG FRIENDS, — I presume
you are now all come home for the holidays,
and that the brothers and sisters and cousins, papas
and mammas, uncles and aunts, are all met cheerfully
round a Christmas fire, enjoying the company of their
friends and relations, and eating plum-pudding and
mince-pie. These are very good things; but one
cannot always be eating plum-pudding and mince-pie:
the days are short, and the weather bad, so that you
cannot be much abroad; and I think you must want
something to amuse you. Besides, if you have been
employed as you ought to be at school, and if you are
quick and clever, as I hope you are, you will want some
employment for that part of you which thinks, as well
as that part of you which eats; and you will like
better to solve a riddle than to crack a nut or a walnut.
Finding out riddles is the same kind of exercise to the
mind which running and leaping and wrestling in sport
are to the body. They are of no use in themselves, —
they are not work, but play; but they prepare the
body, and make it alert and active for anything it may
be called to perform in labor or war. So does the finding

out of riddles, if they are good especially, give quickness of thought, and a facility of turning about a problem every way, and viewing it in every possible light. When Archimedes, coming out of the bath, cried in transport "*Eureka !*" (I have found it!) he had been exercising his mind precisely in the same manner as you will do when you are searching about for the solution of a riddle.

And pray, when you are got together, do not let any little Miss or Master say, with an affected air, " O, do not ask me ; I am so stupid I never can guess." They do not mean you should think them stupid and dull ; they mean to imply that these things are too trifling to engage their attention. If they are employed better, it is very well ; but if not, say, "I am very sorry indeed you are so dull, but we that are clever and quick will exercise our wits upon these; and as our arms grow stronger by exercise, so will our wits."

Riddles are of high antiquity, and were the employment of grave men formerly. The first riddle that we have on record was proposed by Samson at a wedding feast to the young men of the Philistines, who were invited upon the occasion. The feast lasted seven days ; and if they found it out within the seven days, Samson was to give them thirty suits of clothes and thirty sheets ; and if they could not guess it, they were to forfeit the same to him. The riddle was : " Out of the eater came forth meat, and out of the strong came forth sweetness." He had killed a lion, and left its carcass; on returning soon after, he found a swarm of bees had made use of the skeleton as a hive, and it was full of honeycomb. Struck with the oddness of the circumstance, he made a riddle of it. They puzzled about it the whole seven days, and would not have found it out at last if his wife had not told them.

The Sphinx was a great riddle-maker. According to the fable, she was half a woman and half a lion. She lived near Thebes, and to everybody that came she proposed a riddle; and if they did not find it out, she devoured them. At length Œdipus came, and she asked him, "What is that animal which walks on four legs in the morning, two at noon, and three at night?" Œdipus answered, "Man:—in childhood, which is the morning of life, he crawls on his hands and feet; in middle age, which is noon, he walks erect on two; in old age he leans on a crutch, which serves for a supplementary third foot."

The famous wise men of Greece did not disdain to send puzzles to each other. They are also fond of riddles in the East. There is a pretty one in some of their tales. "What is that tree which has twelve branches, and each branch thirty leaves, which are all black on one side and white on the other?" The tree is the year; the branches, the months; the leaves, black on one side and white on the other, signify day and night. Our Anglo-Saxon ancestors also had riddles, some of which are still preserved in a very ancient manuscript.

A riddle is a description of a thing without the name; but as it is meant to puzzle, it appears to belong to something else than what it really does, and often seems contradictory; but when you have guessed it, it appears quite clear. It is a bad riddle if you are at all in doubt, when you have found it out, whether you are right or no. A riddle is not verbal, as charades, conundrums, and rebuses are: it may be translated into any language, which the others cannot. Addison would put them all in the class of false wit: but Swift, who was as great a genius, amused himself with making all sorts of puzzles; and therefore I think you need not be ashamed of reading them. It would be pretty entertainment for you to make a collection of the better ones, — for many are so dull that they are not worth spending time about. I will conclude by sending you a few which will be new to you.

I.

I often murmur, yet I never weep;
I always lie in bed, yet never sleep;
My mouth is wide, and larger than my head,

And much disgorges though it ne'er is fed;
I have no legs or feet, yet swiftly run,
And the more falls I get, move faster on.

II.

Ye youths and ye virgins, come list to my tale,
With youth and with beauty my voice will prevail.
My smile is enchanting, and golden my hair,
And on earth I am fairest of all that is fair;
But my name it perhaps may assist you to tell,
That I 'm banished alike both from heaven and hell.
There's a charm in my voice, 't is than music more sweet,
And my tale oft repeated, untired I repeat.
I flatter, I soothe, I speak kindly to all,
And wherever you go, I am still within call.
Though I thousands have blest, 't is a strange thing to say,
That not one of the thousands e'er wishes my stay,
But when most I enchant him, impatient the more,
The minutes seem hours till my visit is o'er.
In the chase of my love I am ever employed,
Still, still he's pursued, and yet never enjoyed;
O'er hills and o'er valleys unwearied I fly,
But should I o'ertake him, that instant I die;
Yet I spring up again, and again I pursue,
The object still distant, the passion still new.
Now guess, — and to raise your astonishment most,
While you seek me you have me, when found I am lost.

III.

I never talk but in my sleep;
I never cry, but sometimes weep;
My doors are open day and night; .
Old age I help to better sight;
I, like camelion, feed on air,
And dust to me is dainty fare.

IV.

We are spirits all in white,
On a field as black as night;
There we dance and sport and play,
Changing every changing day:
Yet with us is wisdom found,
As we move in mystic round.
Mortals, wouldst thou know the grains
That Ceres heaps on Libya's plains,
Or leaves that yellow Autumn strews,
Or the stars that Herschel views,
Or find how many drops would drain
The wide-scooped bosom of the main,
Or measure central depths below, —
Ask of us, and thou shalt know.
With fairy feet we compass round
The pyramid's capacious bound,
Or step by step ambitious climb
The cloud-capt mountain's height sublime.

Riches though we do not use,
'T is ours to gain, and ours to lose.
From Araby the Blest we came,
In every land our tongue 's the same ;
And if our number you require,
Go count the bright Aonian quire.
Wouldst thou cast a spell to find
The track of light, the speed of wind,
Or when the snail with creeping pace
Shall the swelling globe embrace ;
Mortal, ours the powerful spell ; —
Ask of us, for we can tell.

V.

An unfortunate maid,
I by love was betrayed,
And wasted and pined by my grief ;
To deep solitudes then,
Of rock, mountain, and glen,
From the world I retired for relief.

Yet there by the sound
Of my voice I am found,
Though no footstep betrays where I tread ;
The poet and lover,
My haunts to discover,
Still leave at the dawn their soft bed.

If the poet sublime
Address me in rime,
In rime I support conversation;
To the lover's fond moan
I return groan for groan,
And by sympathy give consolation.

Though I 'm apt, 't is averred,
To love the last word,
Nor can I pretend 't is a fiction;
I shall ne'er be so rude
On your talk to intrude
With anything like contradiction.

The fair damsels of old
By their mothers were told,
That maids should be seen and not heard;
The reverse is my case,
For you 'll ne'er see my face,
To my voice all my charms are transferred.

VI.

From rosy bowers we issue forth,
From east to west, from south to north,
Unseen, unfelt, by night, by day,
Abroad we take our airy way:
We foster love and kindle strife,

The bitter and the sweet of life ;
Piercing and sharp, we wound like steel ;
Now, smooth as oil, those wounds we heal :
Not strings of pearl are valued more,
Or gems enchased in golden ore ;
Yet thousands of us every day,
Worthless and vile, are thrown away.
Ye wise, secure with bars of brass
The double doors through which we pass ;
For, once escaped, back to our cell
No human art can us compel.

ENIGMA.

TO THE LADIES.

HARD is my stem and dry, no root is found
    To draw nutritious juices from the ground;
Yet of your ivory fingers' magic touch
The quickening power and strange effect is such,
My shrivelled trunk a sudden shade extends,
And from rude storms your tender frame defends;
A hundred times a day my head is seen
Crowned with a floating canopy of green;
A hundred times, as struck with sudden blight,
The spreading verdure withers to the sight.
Not Jonah's gourd by power unseen was made
So soon to flourish, and so soon to fade.
Unlike the Spring's gay race, I flourish most
When groves and gardens all their blooms have lost;
Lift my green head against the rattling hail,
And brave the driving snows and freezing gale;
And faithful lovers oft, when storms impend,
Beneath my friendly shade together bend,
There join their heads within the green recess,
And in the close-wove covert nearer press.
But lately am I known to Britain's isle,
Enough — You 've guessed — I see it by your smile.

THE KING IN HIS CASTLE.

M<small>Y</small> DEAR LUCY, — Have you made out who the Four Sisters are ? If you have, I will tell you another story. It is about a monarch who lives in a sumptuous castle, raised high above the ground and built with exquisite art. He takes a great deal of state upon him, and, like Eastern monarchs, transacts everything by means of his ministers; for he never appears himself, and indeed lives in so retired a manner that, though it has often excited the curiosity of his subjects, his residence is hidden from them with as much jealous care as that of Pygmalion was from the Tyrians; and it has never been discovered with any certainty which of the chambers of the castle he actually inhabits, though by means of his numerous spies he is acquainted with what passes in every one of them.

But I must proceed to give you some account of his chief ministers; and I will begin with two who are mutes. Their office is to bring him quick and faithful intelligence of all that is going forward; this they perform in a very ingenious manner. You have heard of the Mexicans, who, not having the art of writing, sup-

plied the deficiency by painting everything they have
a mind to communicate; so that when the Spaniards
came amongst them they sent regular accounts to the
king of their landing and all their proceedings, in very
intelligible language, without writing a single word.
Now this is just the method of these two mutes; they
are continually employed in making pictures of everything that passes, which they do with wonderful quickness and accuracy, all in miniature, but in exact pro-
portion, and colored after life. These pictures they
bring every moment to a great gate of the palace,
where the king receives them.

The next I shall mention are two drummers. These
have each a great drum, on which they beat soft or
loud, quick or slow, according to the occasion. They
often entertain the king with music; besides which
they are arrived at such wonderful perfection upon
their instrument, and make the strokes with such precision, that by the different beats accompanied by
proper pauses and intervals they can express anything
they wish to tell; and the king relies upon them as
much as upon his mutes. There is a sort of covered
way, made in the form of a labyrinth, from the station
of the drummers to the inner rooms of the palace.

There is a pair of officers — for you must know the
offices go mightily by pairs — whose department it is
to keep all nuisances from the palace. They are

lodged for that purpose under a shed or penthouse built with that view before the front of the palace. They likewise gather and present to the monarch sweet odors, essences, and perfumes, with which he regales himself. They likewise inspect the dishes that are served up at his table; and if any of them are not fit to be eaten, they give notice for their removal; and sometimes, if anything offensive is about to enter the palace, they order the agents to shut two little doors which are in their keeping, and by that means prevent its entrance.

The agents are two very active officers of long reach and quick execution. The executive part of government is chiefly intrusted to them; they obey the king's commands with a readiness and vigor truly admirable; they defend the castle from all assaults, and are vigilant in keeping at a distance every annoyance. Their office is branched out into ten subordinate ones, but in cases which require great exertion they act together.

I must not omit the beef-eaters. These stand in rows at the great front gate of the palace, much as they do at St. James's, only that they are dressed in white. Their office is to prepare the viands for the king, who is so very lazy and so much accustomed to have everything done for him, that, like the king of Bantam and some other Eastern monarchs, he requires his meat to be chewed before it is presented to him.

Close by the beef-eaters lives the king's orator, a fat, portly gentleman, of something of a Dutch make, but remarkably voluble and nimble in his motions notwithstanding. He delivers the king's orders and explains his will. This gentleman is a good deal of an epicure, which I suppose is the reason he has his station so near to the beef-eaters. He is a perfect connoisseur in good eating, and assumes a right of tasting all the dishes; and the king pays the greatest regard to his opinion. Justice obliges me to confess that this orator is one of the most flippant and ungovernable of the king's subjects.

Among the inferior officers are the porters, two stout, lusty fellows who carry the king about from place to place (for I am sure you are by this time too well acquainted with his disposition to suppose he performs that office for himself); but as most great men's officers have their deputies, so these lazy porters are very apt to get their business done by deputy, and to have people to carry *them* about.

I should never have done if I were to mention all the particulars of the domestic establishment and internal economy of the castle, which is all arranged with wonderful art and order; how the outgoings are proportioned to the income, and what a fellow-feeling there is between all the members of the family from the greatest to the meanest. The king, from his high birth, on which he values himself much, — being of a race and lineage quite different from any of his subjects, — and from his superior capacity, claims the most absolute obedience; though, as is frequently the case with kings, he is in fact most commonly governed by his ministers, who lead him where they please without his being sensible of it. As you, my dear Lucy, have had more conversation with this king than most of your age have been honored with, I dare say you will be at no loss in pointing him out. I therefore add no more, but that I am

Yours, etc.

THE MISSES.*

ADDRESSED TO A CARELESS GIRL.

WE were talking last night, my dear Anne, of a family of misses whose acquaintance is generally avoided by people of sense. They are most of them old maids; which is not very surprising, considering that the qualities they possess are not the most desirable for a helpmate. They are a pretty numerous clan, and I shall endeavor to give you such a description of them as may enable you to decline their visits; especially as, though many of them are extremely unlike in feature and temper, and indeed very distantly related, yet they have a wonderful knack at introducing each other, so that if you open your doors to one of them, you are very likely in process of time to be troubled with the whole tribe.

The first I shall mention — and indeed she deserves to be mentioned first, for she always was fond of being a ringleader of her company — is *Miss Chief*. This young lady was brought up, until she was fourteen, in a large rambling mansion in the country, where she was allowed to romp all day with the servants and idle

* Juvenile Forget-me-not of 1830.

boys of the neighborhood. There she employed herself
in the summer in milking into her bonnet, tying the
grass together across the path to throw people down,
and in the winter making slides before the door for the
same purpose; and the accidents these gave rise to
always procured her the enjoyment of a hearty laugh.
She was a great lover of fun, and at Christmas time
distinguished herself by various tricks, such as putting
furze balls into the beds, drawing off the clothes in the
middle of the night, and pulling people's seats from
under them. At length as a lady who was coming to
visit the family, mounted on rather a skittish horse,
rode up to the door, Miss Chief ran up and unfurled
an umbrella full in the horse's face, which occasioned
him to throw his rider, who broke her arm. After this
exploit miss was sent off to a boarding-school; here
she was no small favorite with the girls, whom she led
into all manner of scrapes, and no small plague to the
poor governess, whose tables were hacked, and beds
cut, and curtains set on fire continually. It is true
miss soon laid aside her romping airs and assumed a
very demure appearance; but she was always playing
one sly trick or another, and had learned to tell lies in
order to lay it upon the innocent. At length she was
discovered in writing anonymous letters by which
whole families in the town had been set at variance;
and she was then dismissed the school with ignominy.

She has since lived a very busy life in the world; seldom is there a great crowd of which she does not make one, and she has even frequently been taken up for riots and other disorderly proceedings very unbecoming to her sex.

The next I shall introduce to your acquaintance is a city lady, *Miss Management;* a very stirring, notable woman, always in a bustle and always behindhand. In the parlor she saves candle-ends; in the kitchen everything is waste and extravagance. She hires her servants at half wages and changes them at every quarter. She is a great buyer of cheap bargains; but as she cannot always use them, they grow worm and moth eaten on her hands. When she pays a long score to her butcher, she wrangles for the odd pence, and forgets to add up the pounds. Though it is her great study to save, she is continually outrunning her income; which is partly owing to her trusting a cousin of hers, *Miss Calculation,* with the settling of her accounts, — who, it is very well known, could never be persuaded to learn perfectly her multiplication-table, or state rightly a sum in the rule of three.

Miss Lay and *Miss Place* are sisters, great slatterns. When Miss Place gets up in the morning she cannot find her combs, because she has put them in her writing-box. Miss Lay would willingly go to work, but her housewife is in the drawer of the kitchen dresser, her bag hanging on a tree in the garden, and her thimble anywhere but in her pocket. If Miss Lay is going a journey, the keys of her trunk are sure to be lost. If Miss Place wants a volume out of her bookcase, she is certain not to find it along with the rest of the set. If you peep into Miss Place's dressing-room, you find drawers filled with foul linen, and her best cap hanging upon the carpet-broom. If you call Miss Lay to take a lesson in drawing, she is so long in gathering together her pencils, her chalk, her india-rubber, and her drawing-paper, that her master's hour is expired before she has well got her materials together.

Miss Understanding. This lady comes of a respectable family, and has a half-sister distinguished for her good sense and solidity ; but she herself, though not a little fond of reasoning, always takes the perverse side of the question. She is often seen with another of her intimates, *Miss Representation,* who is a great talebearer, and goes about from house to house telling people what such a one and such a one said of them behind their backs. Miss Representation is a notable story-teller, and can so change, enlarge, and dress up an anecdote, that the person to whom it happened shall not know it again. How many friendships have been broken by these two, or turned into bitter enmities ! The latter lady does a great deal of varnish-work which wonderfully sets off her paintings, — for she pretends to use the pencil; but her productions are such miserable daubings, that it is the varnish alone which makes them pass to the most common eye. Though she has all sorts, black varnish is what she uses most. As I wish you very much to be on your guard against this lady whenever you meet her in company, I must tell you she is to be distinguished by an ugly leer; it is quite out of her power to look straight at any object.

Miss Trust, a sour old creature, wrinkled and shaking with palsy. She is continually peeping and prying about, in the expectation of finding something wrong. She watches her servants through the keyhole, and has lost all her friends by little shynesses that have arisen no one knows how. She is worn away to skin and bone, and her voice never rises above a whisper.

Miss Rule. This lady is of a very lofty spirit, and, had she been married, would certainly have governed her husband; as it is, she interferes very much in the management of families, and, as she is very highly connected, she has as much influence in the fashionable world as amongst the lower classes. She even interferes in political concerns; and I have heard it whispered that there is scarcely a cabinet in Europe where she has not some share in the direction of affairs.

Miss Hap and *Miss Chance.* These are twin sisters, so like as scarcely to be distinguished from each other. Their whole conversation turns on little disasters; one tells you how her lap-dog spoiled a new Wilton carpet, the other how her new muslin petticoat was torn by a gentleman's setting his foot upon it. They are both left-handed, and so exceedingly awkward and ungainly, that, if you trust either of them with but a cup and saucer, you are sure to have them broken. These ladies used frequently to keep days for visiting; and as people were not very fond of meeting them, many used to shut themselves up and see no company on those days, for fear of stumbling on either of them. Some people even now will hardly open their doors on Friday for fear of letting them in.

Miss Take. This lady is an old, doting woman, who is purblind and has lost her memory. She invites her acquaintances on wrong days, calls them by wrong names, and always intends to do just the contrary thing to what she does.

Miss Fortune. This lady has the most forbidding look of any of the clan, and people are sufficiently disposed to avoid her as much as it is in their power to do; yet some pretend that, notwithstanding the sternness of her countenance on the first address, her physiognomy softens as you grow more familiar with her, and though she has it not in her power to be an agreeable acquaintance, she has sometimes proved a valuable friend. There are lessons which none can teach so well as herself; and the wisest philosophers have not scrupled to acknowledge themselves better for her company. I·may add that, notwithstanding her want of external beauty, one of the best poets of our language fell in love with her, and wrote a beautiful ode to her praise.

THE FOUR SISTERS.*

I AM one of four sisters; and, having some reason to think myself not well used, either by them or by the world, I beg leave to lay before you a sketch of our history and characters. You will not wonder that there should be frequent bickerings amongst us, when I tell you, that, in our infancy, we were continually fighting; and, so great was the noise and din and confusion, in our constant struggles to get uppermost, that it was impossible for anybody to live amongst us in such a scene of tumult and disorder. These brawls, however, by a powerful interposition, were put an end to; our proper place was assigned to each of us; and we had strict orders not to encroach on the limits of each other's property, but to join our common offices for the good of the whole family.

My first sister (I call her the first, because we have generally allowed her the precedence in rank) is, I must acknowledge, of a very active, sprightly disposition; quick and lively, and has more brilliancy than any of us; but she is hot: everything serves for fuel to her fury, when it is once raised to a certain degree;

* Evenings at Home.

and she is so mischievous, whenever she gets the upper
hand, that, notwithstanding her aspiring disposition,
if I may freely speak my mind, she is calculated to
make a good servant, but a very bad mistress.

I am almost ashamed to mention, that, notwithstanding her seeming delicacy, she has a most voracious
appetite, and devours everything that comes in her
way; though, like other eager, thin people, she does no
credit to her keeping.   Many a time has she consumed
the product of my barns and storehouses; but it is all
lost upon her.   She has even been known to get into
an oil-shop or tallow-chandler's, when everybody was
asleep, and lick up, with the utmost greediness, whatever she found there.   Indeed, all prudent people are
aware of her tricks; and, though she is admitted into
the best families, they take care to watch her very
narrowly.   I should not forget to mention that my sister was once in a country where she was treated with
uncommon respect.   She was lodged in a sumptuous
building, and had a number of young women of the
best families to attend on her, and feed her, and watch
over her health; in short, she was looked upon as
something more than a common mortal.   But she
always behaved with great severity to her maids; and
if any of them were negligent of their duty, or made a
slip in their own conduct, nothing would serve her but
burying the poor girls alive.   I have myself had some

dark hints and intimations, from the most respectable authority, that she will some time or other make an end of me. You need not wonder, therefore, if I am jealous of her motions.

The next sister I shall mention to you has so far the appearance of modesty and humility that she generally seeks the lowest place. She is, indeed, of a very yielding, easy temper, generally cool, and often wears a sweet, placid smile upon her countenance. But she is easily ruffled; and when worked up, as she often is, by another sister, whom I shall mention to you by and by, she becomes a perfect fury. Indeed, she is so apt to swell with sudden gusts of passion that she is suspected, at times, to be a little lunatic. Between her and my first-mentioned sister there is a more settled antipathy than between the Theban pair; and they never meet without making efforts to destroy one another. With me she is always ready to form the most intimate union, but it is not always to my advantage. There goes a story in our family, that, when we were all young, she once attempted to drown me. She actually kept me under a considerable time; and though, at length, I got my head above water, my constitution is generally thought to have been essentially affected by it. From that time she has made no such atrocious attempt, but she is continually making encroachments upon my property; and, even when she

appears most gentle, she is very insidious, and has such
an undermining way with her that her insinuating arts
are as much to be dreaded as open violence. I might,
indeed, remonstrate; but it is a known part of her
character that nothing makes any lasting impression
upon her.

As to my third sister, I have already mentioned the
ill offices she does me, with my last-mentioned one,
who is entirely under her influence. She is, besides,
of a very uncertain, variable temper; sometimes hot,
and sometimes cold, nobody knows where to find her.
Her lightness is even proverbial; and she has nothing
to give those who live with her more substantial than
the smiles of courtiers. I must add that she keeps in
her service three or four rough, blustering bullies, with
puffed cheeks, who, when they are let loose, think they
have nothing to do but to drive the world before them.
She sometimes joins with my first sister, and their violence occasionally throws me into such a trembling,
that, though naturally of a firm constitution, I shake
as if I was in an ague-fit.

As to myself, I am of a steady, solid temper; not
shining, indeed, but kind and liberal, quite a Lady
Bountiful. Every one tastes of my beneficence; and I
am of so grateful a disposition, that I have been known
to return a hundred-fold for any present that has been
made me. I feed and clothe all my children, and

afford a welcome home to the wretch who has no other
shelter. I bear, with unrepining patience, all manner
of ill usage; I am trampled upon, I am torn, and
wounded with the most cutting strokes; I am pillaged
of the treasures hidden in my most secret chambers;
notwithstanding which I am always ready to return
good for evil, and am continually subservient to the
pleasure or advantage of others; yet, so ungrateful is
the world, that, because I do not possess all the airi-
ness and activity of my sisters, I am stigmatized as
dull and heavy. Every sordid, miserly fellow is called,
by way of derision, one of *my* children; and if a person, on entering a room, does but turn his eyes upon
me, he is thought stupid and mean, and not fit for good
company. I have the satisfaction, however, of finding
that people always incline towards me as they grow
older; and that those who seemed proudly to disdain
any affinity with me are content to sink, at last, into
my bosom. You will probably wish to have some
account of my person. I am not a regular beauty;
some of my features are rather harsh and prominent,
when viewed separately; but my countenance has so
much variety of expression, and so many different attitudes of elegance, that those who study my face with
attention find out continually new charms.

Though I have been so long a mother, I have still a
surprising air of youth and freshness, which is assisted

by all the advantages of well-chosen ornament, for I dress well, and according to the season.

This is what I have chiefly to say of myself and my sisters. To a person of your sagacity, it will be unnecessary for me to sign my name. Indeed, one who becomes acquainted with any one of the family cannot be at a loss to discover the rest, notwithstanding the difference in our features and characters.

LETTER OF A YOUNG KING.

MADAM,—Amidst the mutual compliments and kind wishes which are universally circulated at this season, I hope mine will not be the least acceptable; and I have thought proper to give you this early assurance of my kind intentions towards you, and the benefits I have in store for you: for, though I am appointed your sovereign, though your fates and fortune, your life and death, are at my disposal, yet I am fully sensible that I was created for my subjects, not my subjects for me; and that the end of my very existence is to diffuse blessings on my people.

My predecessor departed this life last night precisely at twelve o'clock. He died of a universal decay; nature was exhausted in him, and there was not vital heat sufficient to carry on the functions of life; his hair was fallen, and discovered his smooth, white, bald head; his voice was hoarse and broken, and his blood froze in his veins: in short, his time was come. And to say truth he will not be much regretted; for of late he had been gloomy and vaporish, and the sudden gusts of passion he had long been subject to were worked up into such storms it was impossible to live under him with comfort.

With regard to myself, I am sensible the joy expressed at my accession is sincere, and that no young monarch has ever been welcomed with warmer demonstrations of affection. Some have ardently longed for my coming, and all view my approach with pleasure and cheerfulness; yet such is the uncertainty of popular favor, that I well know that those who are most eager and sanguine in expressing their joy will soonest be tired of my company. You yourself, madam, though I know that at present you regard me with kindness, as one from whom you expect more happiness than you have yet enjoyed, will probably after a short time wish as much to part with me, and transfer the same fond hopes and wishes to my successor. But though your impatience may make me a very troublesome companion, it will not in the least hasten my departure; nor can all the powers of earth oblige me to resign a moment before my time. In order, therefore, that you may form proper expectations concerning me, I shall give you a little sketch of my temper and manners, and I will acknowledge that my aspect at present is somewhat stern and rough; but there is a latent warmth in my temper which you will perceive as we grow better acquainted, and I shall every day put on a milder and more smiling look: indeed, I have so much

fire, that I may chance sometimes to make the house
too hot for you; but in recompense for this inequality
of temper I am kind and bountiful as a giving God: I
come full-handed, and my very business is to dispense
blessings; — blessings of the basket and the store;
blessings of the field and of the vineyard; blessings
for time and eternity. There is not an inhabitant of
the globe who will not experience my bounty; yet
such is the ingratitude of mankind, that there is
scarcely one whom I shall not leave in some degree
discontented.

Whimsical and various are the petitions which are
daily put up to me from all parts; and very few of the
petitioners will be satisfied; because they reject and
despise the gifts I offer them with open hand, and set
their minds on others which certainly will not fall to
their share. Celia has begged me on her knees to find
her a lover: I shall do what I can; I shall bring her
the most magnificent shawl that has appeared in
Europe. For Dorinda, who has made the same petition,
I have two gifts, — wisdom and gray hairs; the former
I know she will reject, nor can I force her to wear it;
but the gray hairs I shall leave on her toilette, whether
she will or no. The curate of Sopron expects I shall
bring him a living: I shall present him with twins as
round and rosy as an apple. Nor can I listen to the
entreaty of Dorimant, whose good father being a little

asthmatic, he has desired me to push him into his
grave as we walk up May hill together: but I shall
marry him to a handsome, lively girl, who will make a
very pretty step-mother to the young gentleman.   It is
in vain for poor Sylvia to weary me as she does with
prayers to restore to her her faithless lover: but I shall
give her the choice of two, to replace him.   Codrus
has asked me if he may bespeak a suit of black: but
I can tell him his little wife will outlive me and him
too: I have offered the old man a double portion of
patience, which he has thrown away very pettishly.
Strephon has entreated me to take him to Scotland
with his mistress: I shall do it; and he will hate my
very name all his life after.

The wishes of some are very moderate; Fanny begs
two inches of height, and Cloe that I would take away
her awkward plumpness; Carus a new equipage, and
Philida a new ball-dress. A mother brought me her
son the other day, made me many compliments, and
desired me to teach him everything; at the same time
begging the youth to throw away his marbles, which
he had often promised to part with as soon as he saw
me : but the boy held them fast, and I shall teach him
nothing but to play at taw. Many ladies have come
to me with their daughters in their hands, telling me
they hope their girls, under me, will learn prudence:
but the young ladies have as constantly desired me to

teach prudence to their grandmothers, whom it would
better become, and to bring them new dances and new
fashions. In short, I have scarcely seen any one with
whom I am likely to agree, but a stout old·farmer who
rents a small cottage on the green. He was leaning
on his spade when I approached him. As his neighbor
told him I was coming, he welcomed me with a cheerful countenance ; but at the same time bluntly told me
he had not expected me so soon, being too busy to pay
much attention to my approach. I asked him if I
could do anything for him. He said he did not believe
me better or worse than those who had preceded me,
and therefore should not expect much from me ; that
he was happy before he saw me, and should be very
well contented after I left him : he was glad to see me,
however, and only begged I would not take his wife
from him, a thin, withered old woman who was eating a
mess of milk at the door. "And I shall be glad too," said
he, "if you will fill my cellar with potatoes." As he
applied himself to his spade while he said these words,
I shall certainly grant his request.

I shall now tell you, that, great and extensive as my
power is, I shall possess it but a short time. However
the predictions of astrologers are now laughed at, nothing is more certain than what I am going to tell you.
A scheme of my nativity has been cast by the most
eminent astronomers, who have found, on consulting

the stars and the aspect of the heavenly bodies, that Capricornus will be fatal to me; I know that all the physicians in the world cannot protract my life beyond that fatal period. I do not tell you this to excite your sensibility, — for I would have you meet me without fondness and part with me without regret, — but to quicken you to lay hold on those advantages I am able to procure you; for it will be your own fault if you are not both wiser and better for my company. I have likewise another request to make to you, — that you will write my epitaph : I may make you happy, but it depends on you to make me famous. If, after I am departed, you can say my reign was distinguished by good actions and wise conversations, and that I have left you happier than I found you, I shall not have lived in vain. My sincere wishes are, that you may long outlive me, but always remember me with pleasure. I am, if you use me well,

Your friend and servant,

THE NEW YEAR.

ON THE USES OF HISTORY.

LETTER I.

MY DEAR LYDIA, — I was told the other day that you have not forgotten a promise of mine to correspond with you upon some subjects which might be worth discussing, and relative to your pursuits. I have often recollected it also; and as promises ought not only to be recollected but fulfilled, I will without further preface throw together some thoughts on *History*, — a study that I know you value as it deserves; and I trust it will not be disagreeable to you, if you should find some observations which your own mind may have suggested, or which you may recollect to have heard from me in some of those hours which we spent together with mutual pleasure.

Much has been said of the uses of history. They are no doubt many, yet do not apply equally to all; but it is quite sufficient to make it a study worth our pains and time, that it satisfies the desire which naturally arises in every intelligent mind to know the transactions of the country, of the globe, in which he lives. Facts, as facts, interest our curiosity and engage our attention.

Suppose a person placed in a part of the country where he was a total stranger; he would naturally ask who are the chief people of the place, what family they are of, whether any of their ancestors have been famous, and for what. If he see a ruined abbey, he will inquire what the building was used for; and if he be told it is a place where people got up at midnight to sing psalms, and scourged themselves in the day, he will ask how there came to be such people, or why there are none now. If he observes a dilapidated castle which appears to have been battered by violence, he will ask in what quarrel it suffered, and why they built formerly structures so different from any we see now. If any part of the inhabitants should speak a different language from the rest, or have some singular customs among them, he would suppose they came originally from some remote part of the country; and would inform himself, if he could, of the cause of their peculiarities.

If he were of a curious temper, he would not rest till he had informed himself who every estate in the parish belonged to, what hands they had gone through, how one man got this field by marrying an heiress, and the other lost that meadow by a ruinous lawsuit. As a man of spirit he would feel delighted on hearing the relation of the opposition made by an honest yeoman to an overbearing rich man, on the subject of an accustomed path-

way or right of common. If he should find the town or
village divided into parties, he would take some pains to
trace the original cause of their dissension, and to find
out, if possible, who had the right on his side. Circumstances would often occur to excite his attention.
If he saw a bridge, he would ask when and by whom it
was built. If in digging in his garden he should find
utensils of a singular form and construction, or a pot of
money with a stamp and legend quite different from
the common coin, he would be led to inquire when
they were in use, and to whom they had belonged.
His curiosity would extend itself by degrees. If a
brook ran through the meadows, he would be pleased
to trace it till it swelled into a river, and the river till
it lost itself in the sea. He would be asking whose
seat he saw upon the edge of a distant forest, and what
sort of country lay behind the range of hills that
bounded his utmost view. If any strangers came to
visit or reside in the place where he lived, he would be
questioning them about the country they came from,
their connections and alliances, and the remarkable
transactions that had taken place within their memory
or that of their parents. The answers to these questions
would insensibly grow up into *History;* which, as you
see, does not originate in abstruse speculation, but
grows naturally out of our situation and relative connections. It gratifies a curiosity which all feel in some

degree, but which spreads and enlarges itself with the
cultivation of our powers, till at length it embraces the
whole globe which we inhabit. To know is as natural
to the mind as to see is to the eye; and knowledge
is itself an ultimate end. But though this may be
esteemed an ultimate and sufficient end, the study of
history is important to various purposes. Few pursuits
tend more to enlarge the mind. It gives us, and it
only can give us, an extended knowledge of human
nature ; not human nature as it exists in one age or
climate or particular spot of earth, but human nature
under all the various circumstances by which it can be
affected. It shows us what is radical and what is
adventitious. It shows us that man is still man, in
Turkey and in Lapland, as a vassal in Russia, or a member of a wandering tribe in India, in ancient Athens or
modern Rome ; yet that his character is susceptible of
violent changes, and becomes moulded into infinite
diversities by the influence of government, climate, civilization, wealth, and poverty. By showing us how
man has acted, it shows us to a certain degree how he
will ever act in given circumstances ; and general rules
and maxims are drawn from it for the service of the
lawgiver and the statesman.

Here I must observe, however, with regard to *events*,
that a knowledge of history does not seem to give us
any great advantage in foreseeing and preparing for

them. The deepest politician, with all his knowledge
of the revolutions of past ages, could probably no more
have predicted the course and termination of the late
French revolution than a common man. The state of
our own national debt has baflled calculation, — the
course of ages has presented nothing like it. Who
could have pronounced that the struggle of the Ameri-
cans would be successful, that of the Poles unsuccessful? Human characters, indeed, act always alike ; but
events depend upon circumstances as well as characters, and circumstances are infinitely various and
changed by the slightest causes. A battle won or lost
may decide the fate of an empire ; but a battle may be
won or lost by a shower of snow being blown to the
east or the west, by a horse (the general's) losing his
shoe, by a bullet or an arrow taking a direction a tenth
part of an inch one way or the other. — The whole
course of the French affairs might have been changed
if the king had not stopped to breakfast, or if the post-
master of Varennes had not happened to know him.
These are particulars which no man can foresee ; and
therefore no man can with precision foresee events.

The rising up of certain characters at particular periods ranks among those unforeseen circumstances that
powerfully influence events. Often does a single man,
as Epaminondas, illustrate his country, and leave a
long track of light after him to future ages ; and who

can tell how much even America owed to the *accident* of being served by such a man as Washington? There are always many probable events. All that history enables the politician to do is to predict that one or other of them will take place. If so and so, it will be this; if so and so, it will be that; but which, he cannot tell. There are always combinations of circumstances which have never met before from the creation of the world, and which mock all power of calculation. But let the circumstances be known, and the characters upon the stage, and history will tell what to expect from them. It will tell him with certainty, for instance, that a treaty extorted by force from distress will be broken when opportunity offers; that if the church and the monarch are united they will oppress, if at variance they will divide, the people; that a powerful nation will make its advantage of the divisions of a weaker which applies for its assistance.

It is another advantage of history that it stores the mind with facts that apply to most subjects which occur in conversation among enlightened people; whether morals, commerce, languages, polite literature, be the object of discussion, it is history that must supply her large storehouse of proofs and illustrations. A man or a woman may decline without blame many subjects of literature; but to be ignorant of history is not permitted to any of a cultivated mind. It may be

reckoned among its advantages, that this study naturally increases the love of every man to his country.
We can only love what we know; it is by becoming
acquainted with the long line of patriots, heroes, and
distinguished men, that we learn to love the country
which has produced them.

But I must conclude this letter, already perhaps too
long, though I have not got to the end of my subject;
it will give me soon another opportunity of subscribing
myself

Your ever affectionate friend.

LETTER II.

I LEFT off, my dear Lydia, with mentioning, among
the advantages of an acquaintance with history, that it
fosters the sentiments of patriotism.

What is a man's country ? To the unlettered peasant, who has never left his native village, that village is
his country, and consequently all of it he can love.
The man who mixes in the world, and has a large
acquaintance with the characters existing along with
himself upon the stage of it, has a wider range. His
idea of a country extends to its civil polity, its military
triumphs, the eloquence of its courts, and the splendor
of its capital. All the great and good characters he is

acquainted with swell his idea of its importance, and
endear to him the society of which he is a member;
but how wonderfully does this idea expand, and how
majestic a form does it put on, when History conducts
our retrospective view through the past ages! How
much more has the man to love, how much to interest
him in his country, in whom her image is identified
with the virtues of an Alfred, with the exploits of the
Henrys and Edwards, with the fame and fortunes of
the Sydneys and Hampdens, the Lockes and Miltons,
who have illustrated her annals! Like a man of noble
birth who walks up and down in a long gallery of por-
traits, and is able to say, " This my progenitor was
admiral in such a fight; that, my great-uncle, was
general in such an engagement ; he on the right hand
held the seals in such a reign ; that lady in so singular
a costume was a celebrated beauty two hundred years
ago ; this little man in the black cap and peaked beard
was one of the luminaries of his age, and suffered for
his religion"; — he learns to value himself upon his
ancestry, and to feel interested for the honor and prosperity of the whole line of descendants. Could a
Swiss, think you, be so good a patriot, who had never
heard the name of William Tell ? or the Hollander
who should be unacquainted with the glorious struggle which freed his nation from the tyranny of the
Duke of Alva ?

The Englishman conversant in history has been long acquainted with his country. He knew her in the infancy of her greatness; has seen her, perhaps, in the wattled huts and slender canoes in which Cæsar discovered her; he has watched her rising fortunes, has trembled at her dangers, rejoiced at her deliverances, and shared with honest pride triumphs that were celebrated ages before he was born; he has traced her gradual improvement through many a dark and turbulent period, many a storm of civil warfare, to the fair reign of her liberty and law, to the fulness of her prosperity and the amplitude of her fame.

Or should our patriot have his lot cast in some age and country which has declined from this high station of pre-eminence; should he observe the gathering glooms of superstition and ignorance ready to close again over the bright horizon; should Liberty lie prostrate at the feet of a despot, and the golden stream of commerce, diverted into other channels, leave nothing but beggary and wretchedness around him, — even then, in these ebbing fortunes of his country, History, like a faithful metre, would tell him how high the tide had once risen; he would not tread unconsciously the ground where the Muses and the Arts had once resided, like the goat that stupidly browses upon the fane of Minerva. Even the name of his country will be dear and venerable to him. He will muse over her

z

fallen greatness, sit down under the shade of her never-dying laurels, build his little cottage amidst the ruins of her towers and temples, and contemplate with tenderness and respect the decaying age of his once illustrious parent.

But if an acquaintance with history thus increases a rational love of our country, it also tends to check those low, illiberal, vulgar prejudices which adhere to the uninformed of every nation. Travelling will also cure them: but to travel is not within the power of every one. There is no use, but a great deal of harm, in fostering a contempt for other nations; in an arrogant assumption of superiority, and the clownish sneer of ignorance at everything in laws, government, or manners, which is not fashioned after our partial ideas and familiar usages. A well-informed person will not be apt to exclaim at every event out of the common way, that nothing like it has ever happened since the creation of the world, that such atrocities are totally unheard of in any age or nation;—sentiments we have all of us so often heard of late on the subject of the French revolution: when in fact we can scarcely open a page of their history without being struck with similar and equal enormities. Indeed, party spirit is very much cooled and checked by an acquaintance with the events of past times.

When we see the mixed and imperfect virtue of the

most distinguished characters; the variety of motives, some pure and some impure, which influence political conduct; the partial success of the wisest schemes, and the frequent failure of the fairest hopes; — we shall find it more difficult to choose a side, and to keep up an interest towards it in our minds, than to restrain our feelings and language within the bounds of good sense and moderation. This, by the way, makes it particularly proper that *ladies* who interest themselves in the events of public life should have their minds cultivated by an acquaintance with history, without which they are apt to let the whole warmth of their natures flow out, upon party matters, in an ardor more honest than wise, more zealous than candid.

With regard to the moral uses of history, what has just been mentioned may stand for one. It serves also by exercise to strengthen the moral feelings. The traits of generosity, heroism, disinterestedness, magnanimity, are scattered over it like sparkling gems, and arrest the attention of the most common reader. It is wonderfully interesting to follow the revolutions of a great state, particularly when they lead to the successful termination of some glorious contest. Is it true? — a child asks, when you tell him a wonderful story that strikes his imagination. The writer of fiction has the unlimited command of events and of characters; yet that single circumstance of truth, that the events re-

lated really came to pass, that the heroes brought upon
the stage really existed, counterbalances, with respect to interest, all the privileges of the former, and in
a mind a little accustomed to exertion will throw the
advantage on the side of the historian.

The more History approaches to Biography the more
interest it excites. Where the materials are meagre
and scanty, the antiquarian and the chronologer may
dwell upon the page; but it will seldom excite the
glow of admiration or draw the delicious tear of sensibility. I must acknowledge, however, in order to be
candid, that the emotions excited by the actions of our
species are not always of so pleasing or so edifying a
nature. The miseries and the vices of man form a
large part of the picture of human society: the pure
mind is disgusted by depravity, the existence of which
it could not have imagined to itself; and the feeling
heart is cruelly lacerated by the sad repetition of
wrongs and oppression, chains and slaughter, sack and
massacre, which assail it in every page : — till the mind
has gained some strength, so frightful a picture should
hardly be presented to it. Chosen periods of history
may be selected for youth, as the society of chosen
characters precedes in well-regulated education a more
indiscriminate acquaintance with the world. In favor
of a more extended view, I can only say that truth is
truth, — man must be shown as the being he really is,

or no real knowledge is gained. If a young person were to read only the *Beauties of History*, or, according to Madame Genlis's scheme, stories and characters in which all that was vicious should be left out, he might as well, for any real acquaintance with life he would gain, have been reading all the while Sir Charles Grandison or the Princess of Cleves.

One consoling idea will present itself with no small degree of probability on comparing the annals of past and present times, — that of a tendency to amelioration; at least it is evidently found in those countries with which we are most connected. But the only balm that can be poured with full effect into the feeling mind, which bleeds for the folly and wickedness of man, is the belief that all events are directed and controlled by supreme wisdom and goodness. Without this persuasion, the world becomes a desert, and its devastators the wolves and tigers that prowl over it.

It is needless to insist on the uses of history to those whose situation in life gives them room to expect that their actions may one day become the objects of it. Besides the immediate necessity to them of the knowledge it supplies, it affords the strongest motives for their conduct of hope and fear. The solemn award, the incorruptible tribunal, and the severe, soul-searching inquisition of Posterity, is calculated to strike an awe into their souls. They cannot take refuge in oblivion;

it is not permitted them to die : — they may be the
objects of gratitude or detestation as long as the world
stands. They may flatter themselves that they have
silenced the voice of truth ; they may forbid newspapers and pamphlets and conversation ; — an unseen
hand is all the while tracing out their history, and
often their minutest actions, in indelible characters ;
and it will soon be held up for the judgment of the
world at large.

Lastly, this permanency of human characters tends
to cherish in the mind the hope and belief of an existence after death. If we had no notices from the page
of history of those races of men that have lived before
us, they would seem to be completely swept away ;
and we should no more think of inquiring what human
beings filled our places upon the earth a thousand harvests ago, than we should think about the generations
of cattle which at that time grazed the marshes of the
Tiber, or the venerable ancestors of the goats that are
browsing upon Mount Hymettus ; — no vestige would
remain of one any more than of the other, and we
might more pardonably fall into the opinion that they
both had shared a similar fate. But when we see illustrious characters continuing to live on in the eye of
posterity, their memories still fresh, and their noble
actions shining with all the vivid coloring of truth and
reality ages after the very dust of their tombs is scat-

tered, high conceptions kindle within us; and, feeling one immortality, we are led to hope for another. We find it hard to persuade ourselves that the man who, like Antoninus or Socrates, fills the world with the sweet perfume of his virtue, the martyr or the patriot to whom posterity is doing the justice which was denied him by his contemporaries, should all the while himself be blotted out of existence, that he should be benefiting mankind and doing good so long after he is capable of receiving any, that we should be so well acquainted with him, and that he should never know anything of us. That one who is an active agent in the world, instructing, informing it, inspiring friendship, making disciples, should be nothing, — this does not seem probable; the records of time suggest to us eternity. — Farewell.

...

LETTER III.

MY DEAR LYDIA, — We have considered the uses of History , I would now direct your attention to those collateral branches of science which are necessary for the profitable understanding of it. It is impossible to understand one thing well without understanding to a certain degree many other things; there is a mutual dependence between all parts of knowledge. This is the reason that a child never fully comprehends what he is taught : he receives an idea, but not the full idea, perhaps not the principal, of what you want to teach him. But as his mind opens, this idea enlarges and receives accessory ideas, till slowly and by degrees he is master of the whole. This is particularly the case in History. You may recollect, probably, that the mere *adventure* was all you entered into, in those portions of it which were presented to you at a very early age. You could understand nothing of the springs of action, nothing of the connection of events with the intrigues of cabinets, with religion, with commerce ; nothing of the state of the world at different periods of society and improvement ; and as little could you grasp the measured distances of time and space which are set between them. This you could not do, not because the history was not related with clearness, but because you were destitute of other knowledge.

The first studies which present themselves as accessories in this light are *Geography* and *Chronology*, which have been called the two eyes of History. When was it done ? where was it done ? are the two first questions you would ask concerning any fact that was related to you. Without these two particulars there can be no precision or clearness.

Geography is best learned along with history ; for if the first explains history, the latter gives interest to geography, which without it is but a dry list of names. For this reason if a young person begin with ancient history, I should think it advisable, after a slight general acquaintance with the globe, to confine his geography to the period and country of which he is reading; and it would be a desirable thing to have maps adapted to each remarkable period in the great empires of the world. These should not contain any towns or be divided into any provinces which were not known at that period. A map of Egypt, for instance, calculated for its ancient monarchy, should have Memphis marked on it, but not Alexandria, because the two capitals did not exist together. A map of Judea for the time of Solomon, or any period of its monarchy, should not exhibit the name of Samaria, nor the villages of Bethany and Nazareth: but each country should have the towns and divisions, as far as they are known, calculated for the period the map was meant to illustrate. Thus geography, civil geography, would be seen to grow out of history; and the mere view of the map would suggest the political state of the world at any period.

It would be a pleasing speculation to see how the arbitrary divisions of kingdoms and provinces vary, and become obsolete, and large towns flourish and fall again into ruins; while the great natural features, the mountains, rivers, and seas, remain unchanged, by whatever names we please to call them, whatever empire encloses them within its temporary boundaries. We have, it is true, ancient and modern maps; but the one set includes every period from the Flood to the provinciating the Roman Empire under Trajan, and the other takes in all the rest. About half a dozen sets for the ancient states and empires, and as many for the modern, would be sufficient to exhibit the most important changes, and would be as many as we should be able to give with any clearness. The young student should make it an invariable rule never to read history without a map before him; to which should be added plans of towns, harbors, etc. These should be conveniently placed under the eye, separate if possible from the book he is reading, that by frequent glancing upon them the image of the country may be indelibly impressed on his imagination.

Besides the necessity of maps for understanding history, the memory is wonderfully assisted by the local association which they supply. The battles of Issus and the Granicus will not be confounded by those who have taken the pains to trace the rivers on whose banks they were fought: the exploits of Hannibal are connected with a view of the Alps, and the idea of Leonidas is inseparable from the straits of Thermopylæ. The greater accuracy of maps, and still more the facility, from the arts of printing and engraving, of procur-

ing them, is an advantage the moderns have over the
ancients. They have been perfected by slow degrees.
The Egyptians and Chaldeans studied the science of
mensuration; and the first map — rude enough no
doubt — is said to have been made by order of Sesostris when he became master of Egypt. Commerce
and war have been the two parents of this science.
Pharaoh Necho ordered the Phœnicians whom he sent
round Africa to make a survey of the coast. This
they finished in three years. Darius caused the Ethi-
opic Sea and the mouth of the Indus to be surveyed.
That maps were known in Greece you no doubt recollect from the pretty story of Socrates and Alcibiades.
Anaximander, a disciple of Thales, is said to have
made the first sphere, and first delineated what was
then known of the countries of the earth. He flourished 547 years before Christ. Herodotus mentions
a map of brass or copper which was presented by
Aristagoras, tyrant of Miletus, to Cleomenes, king of
Sparta, in which he had described the known world
with its seas and rivers. Alexander the Great in his
expedition into Asia took two geographers with him;
and from their itineraries many things have been
copied by succeeding writers.

From Greece the science of geography passed to
Rome. The enlightened policy of the Romans cultivated it as a powerful means of extending and

securing their dominion. One of the first things they
did was to make roads, for which it was necessary to
have the country measured. They had a custom when
they had conquered a country to have a painted map
of it always carried aloft in their triumphs. The great
historian Polybius reconnoitered under a commission
from Scipio Emilianus the coasts of Africa, Spain, and
France, and measured the distances of Hannibal's
march over the Alps and Pyrenees. Julius Cæsar
employed men of science to survey and measure the
globe; and his own Commentaries show his attention
to this part of knowledge. Strabo, a great geographer
whose works are extant, flourished under Augustus;
Pomponius Mela in the first century.

Many of the Roman itineraries which are still extant show the systematic care which they bestow on a
science so necessary for the orderly distribution and
government of their large dominions. But still it was
late before geography was settled upon its true basis,—
astronomical observations. The greater part of the
early maps were laid down in a very loose, inaccurate
manner; and where particular parts were done with
the greatest care, yet if the longitude and latitude were
wanting, their relative situation to the rest of the earth
could not be known. Some attempts had indeed been
made by Hipparchus and Possidonius, Greek philosophers, to settle the parallels of latitude by the length

of the days; but the foundation they had laid was neglected till the time of Ptolemy, who flourished at Alexandria about 150 years after Christ, under Adrian and Antoninus Pius. This is he from whom the Ptolemaic system took its name. He diligently compared and revised the ancient maps and charts, correcting their errors and supplying their defects by the reports of travellers and navigators, the measured or reputed distances of maps and itineraries, and astronomical calculations, all digested together; he reduced geography to a regular system, and laid down the situation of places according to minutes and degrees of longitude and latitude as we now have them. His maps were in general use till the last three or four centuries, in which time the progress of the moderns in the knowledge of the globe we inhabit has thrown at a great distance all the ancient geographers.

We are now, some few breaks and chasms excepted, pretty well acquainted with the outline of the globe, and with those parts of it with which we are connected by our commercial or political relations; but we are still profoundly ignorant of the interior of Africa, and imperfectly acquainted with that of South America and the western part of North America. We know little of Thibet and the central parts of Asia, and have as yet only touched upon the great continent of New Holland.

The best ancient maps are those of D'Anville. It has required great learning and proportionate skill to bring together the scattered notices which are found in various authors, and to fix the position of places which have been long ago destroyed; very often the geographer has no other guide than the relation of the historian that such a place is within six or eight days' journey from another place. In some instances the maps of Ptolemy are lately come into repute again,— as in his delineation of the course of the Niger, which is thought to be favored by modern discoveries. Major Rennel has done much to improve the geography of India.

There are many valuable maps scattered in voyages and travels, and many of the atlases contain a collection sufficient for all common purposes; but a complete collection of the best maps and charts, with plans of harbors, towns, etc., becomes an object of even princely expense. The French took the lead in this, as in some other branches of science. The late Empress of Russia caused a geographical survey to be taken of her dominions, which has much improved our knowledge of the northeastern regions of Europe and Asia. We have now, however, both single maps and atlases which yield to none in accuracy or elegance.

Yours affectionately.

LETTER IV.

DEAR LYDIA, — Geography addresses itself to the eye, and is easily comprehended ; to give a clear idea of Chronology is somewhat more difficult. It is easy to define it by saying it gives an answer to the question, When was it done ? but the meaning of the *when* is not quite so obvious. A date is a very artificial thing, and the world had existed for a long course of centuries before men were aware of its use and necessity. *When* is a relative term ; the most natural application of it is, How long ago, reckoning backwards from the present moment ? Thus if you were to ask an Indian when such an event happened, he would probably say, So many harvests ago, when I could but just reach the boughs of yonder tree ; in the time. of my father, grandfather, great-grandfather ; still making the time then present to him the date from which he sets out. Even where a different method is well understood, we use in more familiar life this natural kind of chronology, — The year before I was married, — when Henry, who is now five years old, was born, — the winter of the hard frost. These are the epochs which mark the annals of domestic life more readily and with greater clearness, so far as the real idea of time is concerned, than the year of our Lord, as long

as these are all within the circle of our personal recollection. But when events are recorded, the relater
may be forgotten, and the *when* again occurs: "When
did the historian live? I understand the relative
chronology of his narration; I know how the events
of it follow one another; but what is their relation to
general chronology, to time as it relates.to me and to
other events?"

To know the transactions of a particular reign — that
of Cyrus, for instance — in the regular order in which
they happened in that reign, but not to know where
to place them with respect to the history of other times
and nations, is as if we had a very accurate map of a
small island existing somewhere in the boundless ocean,
and could lay down all the bearings and distances of
its several towns and villages, but for want of its longitude and latitude were ignorant of the relative position
of the island itself. Chronology supplies this longitude
and latitude, and fixes every event to its precise point
in the chart of universal time. It supplies a common
measure by which I may compare the relater of an
event with myself, and his *now* or *ten years ago* with
the present *now* or *ten years*, reckoning from the time
in which I live.

In order to find such a common measure, men have
been led by degrees to fix upon some one known event,
and to make that the centre from which, by regular

distances, the different periods of time are reckoned, instead of making the present time, which is always varying, and every man's own existence, the centre.

The first approach to such a mode of computing time is to date by the reigns of kings; which, being public objects of great notoriety, seem to offer themselves with great advantage for such a purpose. The Scripture history, which is the earliest of histories, has no other than this kind of successive dates: "Now it came to pass in the fifth year of the king Hezekiah"; "And the time that Solomon reigned in Jerusalem over all Israel was forty years; and Solomon slept with his fathers, and Rehoboam his son reigned in his stead." From this method a regular chronology might certainly be deduced if we had the whole unbroken series; but unfortunately there are many gaps and chasms in history, and you easily see that if any links of the chain are wanting, the whole computation is rendered imperfect. Besides, it requires a tedious calculation to bring it into comparison with other histories and events. To say that an event happened in the tenth year of the reign of King Solomon gives you only an idea of the time relative to the histories of that king, but leaves you quite in the dark as to its relation with the time you live in, or with the events of the Roman history.

We want, therefore, an universal date, like a lofty

obelisk seen by all the country round, from and to which every distance should be measured. The most obvious that offers itself for this purpose is the creation of the world, an event equally interesting to all; to us the beginning of time, and from which, therefore, time would flow regularly down in an unbroken stream from the earliest to the latest generations of the human race. This would probably, therefore, have been made use of, if the date of the creation itself could be ascertained with any exactness; but as chronologers differ by more than a thousand years as to the time of that event, it is necessary previously to mention what system is made use of, which renders this era obscure and inconvenient. It has therefore been found more convenient, in fact, to take some known event within the limit of well-authenticated history, and to reckon from that fixed point backwards and forwards. As we cannot find the head of the river, and know not its termination, we must raise a pillar upon its banks and measure our distances from that, both up and down the stream. This event ought to be important, conspicuous, and as interesting as possible, that it may be generally received; for it would spare a great deal of trouble in computation, if all the world would make use of the same date. This, however, has never been the case, chance and national vanity having had their full share in settling them.

The Greeks reckoned by olympiads, but not till more than sixty years after the death of Alexander the Great. The Olympic games were the most brilliant assembly in Greece. The Greeks were very fond of them; they began 776 years before Christ, and each olympiad includes four years. Some of the earlier Greek historians digested their histories by ages, or by the succession of the priestesses of Juno at Argos; others by the archons of Athens, or the kings of Lacedæmon. Thucydides uses simply the beginning of the Peloponnesian war, the subject of his history; for, writing to his contemporaries, it seems not to have occurred to him that another date would ever be necessary. The Arundelian marbles, composed sixty years after the death of Alexander the Great, reckon backwards from the then present time.

The Roman era was the building of their city, — the eternal city, as they loved to call it.

The Mahometans date from the Hegira, or flight of Mahomet from Mecca — his birthplace — to Medina, A. D. 622; and they have this advantage, that they began almost immediately to use it.

The era used all over the Christian world is the birth of Christ. This was adopted as a date about A. D. 360; and though there is an uncertainty of a few years, which are in dispute, the accuracy is sufficient for any present purpose.

The reign of Nabonassar, the first king of Babylon, of Yesdigerd, the last king of Persia, — who was conquered by the Saracens, — and of the Seleucidæ of Syria, have likewise furnished eras.

Julius Scaliger formed an era which he called the *Julian period ;* being a cycle of 7980 years, produced by multiplying several cycles into one another, so as to carry us back to a period 764 years before the creation of the world. This era, standing out of all history like the fulcrum which Archimedes wished for, and independent of variation or possibility of mistake, was a very grand idea ; and in measuring everything by itself, measured it by the eternal truth of the laws of the heavenly bodies. But it is not greatly employed, the common era serving all ordinary purposes. In modern histories the olympiads, Roman eras, and others, are reduced in the margin to the year of our Lord, or of the creation.

Such is the nature of eras, now in such common use that we can with difficulty conceive the confusion in which, for want of them, all the early part of history is involved, and the strenuous labors of the most learned men, which have been employed in arranging them, and reducing history to the order in which we now have it.

The earliest history which we possess, as we have before observed, is that of the Jewish Scriptures ; these carry us from the creation to about the time of Herodotus. Having no date, we are obliged to compute from generations, and to take the reigns of kings where they are given. But a great schism occurs at the very outset. The Septuagint translation of the Mosaic history into Greek, which was made by order of Ptolemy Philadelphus, differs from the Hebrew text by 1400 years from the creation to the birth of Abraham.

The chronology of the Assyrian and Babylonish monarchies is involved in inextricable difficulties; nor are we successful in harmonizing the Greek with the Oriental writers of history. The Persian historians make no mention of the defeat of Xerxes by the Greeks, or that of Darius by Alexander. All nations have had the vanity to make their origin mount as high as possible; and they have often invented series of kings, or have reckoned the contemporary individuals of different dynasties as following each other in regular succession, as if one should take the kings of the Heptarchy singly instead of together.

You will perhaps ask, If we have no eras, what have we to reckon by? We have generations and successions of kings. Sir Isaac Newton, who joined wonderful sagacity to profound learning and astronomical skill, made very great reforms in the ancient chronology. He pointed out the difference between generations and successions of kings. A generation is not the life of a man, it is the time that elapses before a man sees his successor; and this, reckoning to the birth of the eldest son, is estimated at about thirty years. The succession of kings would seem at first sight to be the same, and so it had been reckoned; but Newton corrected it, on the principle that kings are often cut off prematurely in turbulent times, or are succeeded either by their brothers or by their uncles, or others older than themselves. The lines of kings of France, England, and other countries within the range of exact chronology, confirmed this principle; he therefore rectified all the ancient chronology according to it, and with the assistance of astronomical observations he found reason to allow, as the average length of a reign, about eighteen or twenty years.

But, after all, great part of the chronology of ancient history is founded upon conjecture and clouded with uncertainty.

Although I recommend to you a constant attention to chronology, I do not think it desirable to load your memory with a great number of specific dates, both because it would be too great a burden on the retentive powers, and because it is, after all, not the best way of attaining clear ideas on the subject of history. In order to do this it is necessary to have in your mind the relative situation of other countries at the time of any event recorded in one of them. For instance, if

you have got by heart the dates of the accession of the
kings of Europe, and want to know whether John lived
at the time of the Crusades, and in what state the
Greek empire was, you cannot tell without an arith-
metical process, which, perhaps, you may not be quick
enough to make. You cannot tell whether Constanti-
nople had been taken by the Turks when the Sicilian
Vespers happened; for each fact is insulated in your
mind, and, indeed, your dates give you only the dry
catalogue of accessions. Nay, you may read separate
histories, and yet not bring them together, if the
countries be remote. Each exists in your mind separately, and you have at no time the state of the world.
But you ought to have an idea at once of the whole
world, as far as history will give it. You do not see
truly what the Greeks were, except you know that the
British Isles were then barbarous.

A few dates, therefore, perfectly learned, may suffice,
and will serve as landmarks to prevent your going far
astray in the rest; but it will be highly useful to connect the histories you read in such a manner in your
own mind that you may be able to refer from one to the
other, and form them all into a whole. For this purpose it is very desirable to observe and retain in your
memory certain coincidences which may link, as it
were, two nations together. Thus you may remember
that Haroun al Raschid sent to Charlemagne the first

clock that was seen in Europe. If you are reading the history of Greece when it flourished most, and want to know what the Romans were doing at the same time, you may recollect that they sent to Greece for instruction when they wanted to draw up the laws of the Twelve Tables. Solon and Crœsus connect the history of Lesser Asia with that of Greece. Egbert was brought up in the court of Charlemagne. Philip Augustus of France and Richard I. of England fought in the same crusade against Saladin. Queen Elizabeth received the French ambassador in deep mourning after the massacre of St. Bartholomew.

It may be desirable to keep one kingdom as a metre for the rest. Take for this purpose first the Jews, then the Greek, the Romans, and, because it is so, our own country; then harmonize and connect all the other dates with these.

That the literary history of a nation may be connected with the political, study also biography, and endeavor to link men of science and literature, and artists, with political characters. Thus Hippocrates was sent for to the plague of Athens; Leonardo da Vinci died in the arms of Francis I. Often an anecdote, a smart saying, will indissolubly fix a date.

Sometimes you may take a long reign, as that of Elizabeth or Louis XIV., and, making that the centre, mark all the contemporary sovereigns, and also the men of letters. Another way is to make a line of life, composed of distinguished characters who touch each other. It will be of great service to you in this view to study Dr. Priestley's biographical chart; and of still greater to make one for yourself, and fill it by degrees as your acquaintance with history extends. Marriages connect the history of different kingdoms; as those of Mary Queen of Scots and Francis II., Philip II. and Mary of England.

These are the kind of dates which make everything lie in the mind in its proper order; they also take fast hold of it. If you forget the exact date by years, you have nothing left; but of circumstances you never lose all idea. As we come nearer to our own times, dates must be more exact. A few years more or less signify little in the destruction of Troy, if we knew it exactly; but the conclusion of the American war should be accurately known, or it will throw other events near it into confusion.

In so extensive a study no auxiliary is to be neglected: poetry impresses both geography and history in a most agreeable manner upon those who are fond of it; thus:—

> ". . . . fair Austria spreads her mournful charms,
> The queen, the beauty, sets the world in arms."

A short, lively character in verse is never forgotten:—

> " From Macedonia's madman to the Swede."

Historic plays deeply impress, but should be read with caution. We take our ideas from Shakespeare more than history; he, indeed, copied pretty exactly from the chroniclers, but other dramatic writers have taken great liberties both with characters and events.

Painting is a good auxiliary; and though in this country history is generally read before we see pictures, they mutually illustrate one another. Painting also shows the costume. In France, where pictures are more accessible, there is more knowledge generally diffused of common history. Many have learned Scripture history from the rude figures on Dutch tiles.

I will conclude with the remark, that, though the beginner in history may and ought to study dates and epochs for his guidance, chronology can never be fully possessed till after history has been long studied and carefully digested.

Farewell; and believe me

Yours affectionately.

FASHION.

A VISION.

YOUNG as you are, my dear Flora, you cannot but have noticed the eagerness with which questions relative to civil liberty have been discussed in every society. To break the shackles of oppression and assert the native rights of man is esteemed by many among the noblest efforts of heroic virtue; but vain is the possession of political liberty if there exists a tyrant of our own creation, who, without law or reason, or even external force, exercises over us the most despotic authority; whose jurisdiction is extended over every part of private and domestic life; controls our pleasures, fashions our garb, cramps our motions, fills our lives with vain cares and restless anxiety. The worst slavery is that which we voluntarily impose upon ourselves; and no chains are so cumbrous and galling as those which we are pleased to wear by way of grace and ornament. — Musing upon this idea gave rise to the following dream or vision : —

Methought I was in a country of the strangest and most singular appearance I had ever beheld : the rivers were forced into *jets d'eau* and wasted in artificial water-works; the lakes were fashioned by the hand of art; the roads were sanded with spar and gold-dust; the trees all bore the marks of the shears, they were bent and twisted into the most whimsical forms, and connected together by festoons of ribbon and silk fringe; the wild flowers were transplanted into vases of fine china, and painted with artificial white and red.

The disposition of the ground was full of fancy, but grotesque and unnatural in the highest degree; it was all highly cultivated, and bore the marks of wonderful industry; but among its various productions I could hardly discern one that was of any use.

My attention, however, was soon called off from the scenes of inanimate life by the view of the inhabitants, whose form and appearance was so very preposterous, and, indeed, so unlike anything human, that I fancied myself transported to the country of

> "The Anthropophagi, and men whose heads
> Do grow beneath their shoulders":

for the heads of many of these people were swelled to an astonishing size, and seemed to be placed in the middle of their bodies. Of some, the ears were distended till they hung upon the shoulders; and of others, the shoulders were raised till they met the ears: there was not one free from some deformity, or mon-

strous swelling, in one part or other; either it was
before, or behind, or about the lips, or the arms were
puffed up to an unusual thickness, or the throat was
increased to the same size with the poor objects once
exhibited under the name of the monstrous Craws:
some had no necks; others had necks that reached
almost to their waists; the bodies of some were bloated
up to such a size that they could scarcely enter a pair
of folding doors; and others had suddenly sprouted up
to such a disproportionate height that they could not
sit upright in their loftiest carriages.

Many shocked me with the appearance of being
nearly cut in two, like a wasp; and I was alarmed at
the sight of a few, in whose faces, otherwise very fair
and healthy, I discovered an eruption of black spots,
which I feared was the fatal sign of some pestilential
disorder.

The sight of these various and uncouth deformities
inspired me with much pity; which, however, was soon
changed into disgust, when I perceived, with great surprise, that every one of these unfortunate men and
women was exceeding proud of his own peculiar deformity, and endeavored to attract my notice to it as
much as possible. A lady, in particular, who had a
swelling under her throat, larger than any goitre in the
Valais, and which, I am sure, by its enormous projection, prevented her from seeing the path she walked in,

brushed by me with an air of the greatest self-complacency, and asked me if she was not a charming
creature.

But by this time I found myself surrounded by an
immense crowd, who were all pressing along in one
direction; and I perceived that I was drawn along
with them by an irresistible impulse, which grew
stronger every moment. I asked whither we were
hurrying with such eager steps, and was told that we
were going to the court of Queen Fashion, the great
Diana whom all the world worshippeth. I would have
retired, but felt myself impelled to go on, though without being sensible of any outward force.

When I came to the royal presence, I was astonished at the magnificence I saw around me. The
queen was sitting on a throne, elegantly fashioned in
the form of a shell, and inlaid with gems and mother-
of-pearl. It was supported by a camelion, formed of a
single emerald. She was dressed in a light robe of
changeable silk, which fluttered about her in a profusion of fantastic folds, that imitated the form of clouds,
and like them were continually changing their appearance. In one hand she held a rouge-box, and in the
other one of those optical glasses which distort figures
in length or in breadth according to the position in
which they are held. At the foot of the throne was
displayed a profusion of the richest productions of

every quarter of the globe, tributes from land and sea,
from every animal and plant; perfumes, sparkling
stones, drops of pearl, chains of gold, webs of the finest
linen; wreaths of flowers, the produce of art, which
vied with the most delicate productions of nature; forests of feathers waving their brilliant colors in the air
and canopying the throne; glossy silks, network of
lace, silvery ermine, soft folds of vegetable wool, rustling paper, and shining spangles; — the whole inter-
mixed with pendants and streamers of the gayest tinctured ribbon.

All these together made so brilliant an appearance
that my eyes were at first dazzled, and it was some
time before I recovered myself enough to observe the
ceremonial of the court. Near the throne, and its
chief supports, stood the queen's two prime ministers,
Caprice on one side and Vanity on the other. Two
officers seemed chiefly busy among the attendants.
One of them was a man with a pair of shears in his
hand and a goose by his side, — a mysterious emblem,
of which I could not fathom the meaning: he sat cross-
legged, like the great lama of the Tartars. He was
busily employed in cutting out coats and garments;
not, however, like Dorcas, for the poor, — nor, indeed,
did they seem intended for any mortal whatever, so ill
were they adapted to the shape of the human body.
Some of the garments were extravagantly large, others

as preposterously small: of others, it was difficult to guess to what part of the person they were meant to be applied. Here were coverings, which did not cover; ornaments, which disfigured; and defences against the weather, more slight and delicate than what they were meant to defend; but all were eagerly caught up, without distinction, by the crowds of votaries who were waiting to receive them.

The other officer was dressed in a white succinct linen garment, like a priest of the lower order. He moved in a cloud of incense more highly scented than the breezes of Arabia; he carried a tuft of the whitest down of the swan in one hand, and in the other a small iron instrument, heated red-hot, which he brandished in the air. It was with infinite concern I beheld the Graces bound at the foot of the throne, and obliged to officiate as handmaids under the direction of these two officers.

I now began to inquire by what laws this queen governed her subjects, but soon found her administration was that of the most arbitrary tyrant ever known. Her laws are exactly the reverse of those of the Medes and Persians, for they are changed every day and every hour: and what makes the matter still more perplexing, they are in no written code, nor even made public by proclamation: they are only promulgated by whispers, an obscure sign or turn of the eye, which

those only who have the happiness to stand near the
queen can catch with any degree of precision: yet the
smallest transgression of the laws is severely punished;
not indeed by fines or imprisonment, but by a sort
of interdict similar to that which in superstitious times
was laid by the Pope on disobedient princes, and
which operated in such a manner that no one would
eat, drink, or associate with the forlorn culprit, and he
was almost deprived of the use of fire and water.

This difficulty of discovering the will of the goddess
occasioned so much crowding to be near the throne,
such jostling and elbowing of one another, that I was
glad to retire and observe what I could among the
scattered crowd; and the first thing I took notice of
was various instruments of torture which everywhere
met my eyes. Torture has, in most other governments
of Europe, been abolished by the mild spirit of the
times; but it reigns here in full force and terror. I
saw officers of this cruel court employed in boring
holes with red-hot wires in the ears, nose, and various
parts of the body, and then distending them with the
weight of metal chains or stones, cut into a variety
of shapes; some had invented a contrivance for cramp-
ing the feet in such a manner that many are lamed
by it for their whole lives. Others I saw, slender and
delicate in their form and naturally nimble as the
young antelope, who were obliged to carry constantly

about with them a cumbrous, unwieldy machine of a pyramidal form, several ells in circumference.

But the most common, and one of the worst instruments of torture, was a small machine armed with fishbone and ribs of steel, wide at top but extremely small at bottom. In this detestable invention the queen orders the bodies of her female subjects to be enclosed: it is then, by means of silk cords, drawn closer and closer at intervals, till the unhappy victim can scarcely breathe; and they have found the exact point that can be borne without fainting, which, however, not unfrequently happens. The flesh is often excoriated, and the very ribs bent, by this cruel process. Yet, what astonished me more than all the rest, these sufferings are borne with a degree of fortitude which, in a better cause, would immortalize a hero or canonize a saint. The Spartan who suffered the fox to eat into his vitals did not bear pain with greater resolution; and as the Spartan mothers brought their children to be scourged at the altar of Diana, so do the mothers here bring their children, — and chiefly those whose tender sex one would suppose excused them from such exertions, — and early inure them to this cruel discipline. But neither Spartan, nor Dervise, nor Bonze, nor Carthusian monk, ever exercised more unrelenting severities over their bodies than these young zealots: indeed, the first lesson they are taught is a surrender of their own inclinations and an implicit obedience to the commands of the Goddess.

But they have, besides, a more solemn kind of dedication, something similar to the rite of confirmation. When a young woman approaches the marriageable age, she is led to the altar: her hair, which before fell loosely about her shoulders, is tied up in a tress, sweet oils drawn from roses and spices are poured upon it; she is involved in a cloud of scented dust, and invested with ornaments under which she can scarcely move. After this solemn ceremony, which is generally concluded by a dance round the altar, the damsel is obliged to a still stricter conformity than before to the laws and customs of the court, and any deviation from them is severely punished.

The courtiers of Alexander, it is said, flattered him by carrying their heads on one side, because he had the misfortune to have a wry neck; but all adulation is poor compared to what is practised in this court. Sometimes the queen will lisp and stammer, — and then none of her attendants can speak plain; sometimes she chooses to totter as she walks, — and then they are seized with sudden lameness: according as she appears half undressed, or veiled from head to foot, her subjects become a procession of nuns, or a troop of Bacchanalian nymphs. I could not help observing, however, that those who stood at the greatest distance from the throne were the most extravagant in their imitation.

I was by this time thoroughly disgusted with the character of a sovereign at once so light and so cruel, so fickle and so arbitrary, when one who stood next me bade me attend to still greater contradictions in her character, and such as might serve to soften the indignation I had conceived. He took me to the back of the throne and made me take notice of a number of industrious poor, to whom the queen was secretly distributing bread. I saw the Genius of Commerce doing her homage, and discovered the British cross woven into the insignia of her dignity.

While I was musing on these things a murmur arose among the crowd, and I was told that a young votary was approaching. I turned my head and saw a light figure, the folds of whose garment showed the elegant turn of the limbs they covered, tripping along with the step of a nymph. I soon knew it to be yourself: — I saw you led up to the altar, — I saw your beautiful hair tied in artificial tresses, and its bright gloss stained with colored dust, — I even fancied I beheld produced the dreadful instrument of torture; — my emotions increased, — I cried out, "O spare her! spare my Flora!" with so much vehemence that I awaked.

DESCRIPTION OF TWO SISTERS.

D EAR COUSIN, — Our conversation last night upon beauties put me in mind of two charming sisters, with whom I think you must be acquainted as well as I, though they were not in your list of belles. Their charms are very different, however. The youngest is generally thought the handsomest, and yet other beauties shine more in her company than in her sister's, whether it be that her gay looks diffuse a lustre on all around, while her sister's beauty has an air of majesty which strikes with awe, or that the younger sets every one she is with in the fairest light, and discovers perfections which were before concealed, whilst the elder seems only solicitous to set off her own person and throw a shade upon every one else; yet — what you will think strange — it is she who is generally preferred for a confidant; for her sister, with all her amiable qualities, cannot keep a secret.

O what an eye the younger has! as if she could look a person through; yet modest is her countenance, even and composed her pace, and she treads so softly, — "smooth sliding without step," as Milton says. She

seldom meets you without blushing, — her sister cannot blush. She dresses very gayly, sometimes in
clouded silks, which, indeed, she first brought into fashion ; but blue is her most becoming color, and she generally appears in it. Now and then she wears a very
rich scarf or sash braided with all manner of colors.

The elder, like the Spanish ladies, dresses in black,
in order to set off her jewels, of which she has a
greater number than Lady ——, and, if I might judge,
much finer. I cannot pretend to give you a catalogue
of them ; they are of all sizes, and set in all figures.
Her enemies say she does well to adorn her dusky
brow with brilliants, and that without them she would
be but little taken notice of ; but certain it is, she has
inspired more serious and enthusiastic passions than
her sister, whose admirers are often fops more in love
with themselves than with her. A learned clergyman
some time ago fell deeply in love with her, and wrote a
fine copy of verses on her ; and, what was worst, her sister could not go into company without hearing them.

One thing they quite agree in, — not to go out of
their way or alter their pace for anybody. Once or
twice, indeed, I have heard that the younger . . . . but
it was a great while ago, and she was not so old then,
and so was more complaisant. She is generally waked
with a fine concert of music ; the other prefers a good
solo. . . . .

But see! the younger beauty looks pale and sick! She faints, — she is certainly dying! a slight blush still upon her cheek! it fades, fast, fast. — She is gone, yet a sweet smile overspreads her countenance. Will she revive? Shall *I* ever see her again? Who can tell me?

ON FRIENDSHIP.

FRIENDSHIP is that warm, tender, lively attachment which takes place between persons in whom a similarity of tastes and manners, joined to frequent intercourse, has produced an habitual fondness for each other. It is not among our duties, for it does not flow from any of the necessary relations of society; but it has its duties when voluntarily entered into. In its highest perfection it can only, I believe, subsist between two; for that unlimited confidence and perfect conformity of inclinations which it requires cannot well be found in a larger number. Besides, one such friendship fills the heart, and leaves no want or desire after another.

Friendship, where it is quite sincere and affectionate, free from affectation or interested views, is one of the greatest blessings of life. It doubles our joys, and it lessens our sorrows, when we are able to pour both into the bosom of one who takes the tenderest part in all our interests, who is to us another self. We love to communicate all our feelings; and it is in the highest degree grateful where we can do it to one who will

enter into them all; who takes an interest in everything that befalls us; before whom we can freely
indulge even our little weaknesses and foibles, and
show our minds, as it were, undressed; who will take
part in all our schemes, advise us in any emergency;
who rejoices in our company, and who, we are sure,
thinks of us in our absence.

With regard to the choice of friends, there is little to
say; for a friend was never chosen. A secret sympathy, the attraction of a thousand nameless qualities, a
charm in the expression of the countenance, even in
the voice or the manner, a similarity of circumstances,
— these are the things that begin attachment, which is
fostered by being in a situation which gives occasion
for frequent intercourse; and this depends upon
chance. Reason and prudence have, however, much to
do in restraining our choice of improper or dangerous
friends. They are improper if our line of life and pursuits are so totally different as to make it improbable
we shall long keep up an intimacy, at least without
sacrificing to it connections of duty; they are dangerous if they are in any respect vicious.

It has been made a question whether friendship can
subsist among the vicious. If by vicious be meant
those who are void of the social, generous, and affectionate feelings, it is most certain it cannot, because
these make the very essence of it. But it is very pos-

19 *

sible for persons to possess fine feelings without that steady principle which alone constitutes virtue; and it does not appear why such may not feel a real friendship. It will not, indeed, be so likely to be lasting, and is often succeeded by bitter enmities.

The duties of friendship are, first, sincere and disinterested affection. This seems self-evident; and yet there are many who pretend to love their friends, when at the same time they only take delight in them, as we delight in a fine voice or a good picture. If you love your friend, you will love him when his powers of pleasing and entertaining you have given way to malady or depression of spirit. You will study *his* interest and satisfaction; you will be ready to resign his company, to promote his advantageous settlement at a distant residence, to favor his connection with other friends. These are the tests of true affection; without such a disposition you may enjoy your friend, but you do not love him.

Next, friendship requires pure sincerity and the most unreserved confidence. Sincerity every man has a right to expect from us, but every man has not a right to our confidence. This is the sacred and peculiar privilege of friendship; and so essential is it to the very idea of this connection, that even to serve a friend without giving him our confidence is but going halfway; it may command gratitude, but will not produce love. Above all things, the general tenor of our thoughts and feelings must be shown to our friends exactly as they are ; without any of those glosses, colorings, and disguises, which we do, and partly must, put on in our commerce with the world.

Another duty resulting from this confidence is inviolable secrecy in what has been intrusted to us. To every one, indeed, we owe secrecy in what we are formally intrusted with; but, with regard to a friend, this extends to the concealing everything which in the fulness of his heart and in the freedom of unguarded conversation he has let drop, if you have the least idea it may in any manner injure or offend him. In short, you are to consider yourself as always, to him, under an implied promise of secrecy; and should even the friendship dissolve, it would be in the highest degree ungenerous to consider this obligation as dissolved with it.

In the next place, a friend has a right to our best advice on every emergency ; and this, even though we run the risk of offending him by our frankness. Friends should consider themselves as the sacred guardians of each other's virtue ; and the noblest testimony they can give of their affection is the correction of the faults of those they love. But this generous solicitude must be distinguished from a teazing, captious, or too officious notice of all the little defects and frailties which their close intercourse with each other brings continually into view: these must be overlooked or borne with; for as we are not perfect ourselves, we have no right to expect our friends should be so.

Friends are most easily acquired in youth, but they are likewise most easily lost; the petulance and impetuosity of that age, the eager competitions and rivalships of an active life, and more especially the various changes in rank and fortune, connections, party, opinions, or local situations, burst asunder or silently untwist the far greater part of those friendships which, in the warmth of youthful attachment, we had fondly promised ourselves should be indissoluble.

Happy is he to whom in the maturer season of life there remains one tried and constant friend. Their affection, mellowed by the hand of time, endeared by the recollection of enjoyments, toils, and even sufferings shared together, becomes the balm, the consolation, and the treasure of life. Such a friendship is inestimable, and should be preserved with the utmost care; for it is utterly impossible for any art ever to transfer to another the effect of all those accumulated associations which endear to us the friend of our early years.

These considerations should likewise induce us to show a tender indulgence to our friends, even for those faults which most sensibly wound the feeling heart, —

a growing coldness and indifference. These may be brought on by many circumstances which do not imply a bad heart; and provided we do not by bitter complaints and an open rupture preclude the possibility of a return, in a more favorable conjuncture the friendships of our youth may knit again, and be cultivated with more genuine tenderness than ever.

I must here take occasion to observe, that there is nothing young people ought to guard against with more care than a parade of feeling and a profusion of exaggerated protestations. These may sometimes proceed from the amiable warmth of a youthful heart; but they much oftener flow from the affectation of sentiment, which is both contemptible and morally wrong.

All that has been said of the duties or of the pleasures of friendship in its most exalted sense is applicable in a proportionate degree to every connection in which there exists any portion of this generous affection. So far as it does exist in the various relations of life, so far it renders them interesting and valuable; and were the capacity for it taken away from the human heart, it would find a dreary void, and starve amidst all the means of enjoyment the world could pour out before it.

CONFIDENCE AND MODESTY:

A FABLE.

WHEN the Gods, knowing it to be for the benefit of mortals that the few should lead and that the many should follow, sent down into this lower world Ignorance and Wisdom, they decreed to each of them an attendant and guide, to conduct their steps and facilitate their introduction. To Wisdom they gave Confidence, and Ignorance they placed under the guidance of Modesty. Thus paired, the parties travelled about the world for some time with mutual satisfaction.

Wisdom, whose eye was clear and piercing, and commanded a long reach of country, followed her conductor with pleasure and alacrity. She saw the windings of the road at a great distance; her foot was firm, her ardor was unbroken, and she ascended the hill or traversed the plain with speed and safety.

Ignorance, on the other hand, was short-sighted and timid. When she came to a spot where the road branched out in different directions, or was obliged to pick her way through the obscurity of the tangled thicket, she was frequently at a loss, and was accustomed to stop till some one appeared, to give her the necessary information, which the interesting countenance of her companion seldom failed to procure her.

Wisdom in the mean time, led by a natural instinct, advanced towards the temple of Science and Eternal Truth. For some time the way lay plain before her, and she followed her guide with unhesitating steps: but she had not proceeded far before the paths grew intricate and entangled; the meeting branches of the trees spread darkness over her head, and steep mountains barred her way, whose summits, lost in clouds, ascended beyond the reach of mortal vision. At every new turn of the road her guide urged her to proceed; but after advancing a little way, she was often obliged to measure back her steps, and often found herself involved in the mazes of a labyrinth which, after exercising her patience and her strength, ended but where it began.

In the mean time Ignorance, who was naturally impatient, could but ill bear the continual doubts and hesitation of her companion. She hated deliberation, and could not submit to delay. At length it so happened that she found herself on a spot where three ways met, and no indication was to be found which might direct her to the right road. Modesty advised her to wait; and she had waited till her patience was exhausted. At that moment Confidence, who was in disgrace with Wisdom for some false steps he had led her into, and who had just been discarded from her presence, came up, and offered himself to be her guide. He was accepted. Under his auspices Ignorance, naturally swift of foot, and who could at any time have outrun Wisdom, boldly pressed forward, pleased and satisfied with her new companion. He knocked at every door, visited castle and convent, and introduced his charge to many a society whence Wisdom found herself excluded:

Modesty, in the mean time, finding she could be of no further use to her charge, offered her services to Wisdom. They were mutually pleased with each other, and soon agreed never to separate. And ever since that time Ignorance has been led by Confidence, and Modesty has been found in the Society of Wisdom.

PICNIC.

PRAY, mamma, what is the meaning of *picnic?* I have heard lately once or twice of a *picnic supper,* and I cannot think what it means; I looked for the word in Johnson's Dictionary and could not find it.

I should wonder if you had; the word was not coined in Johnson's time: and if it had, I believe he would have disdained to insert it among the legitimate words of the language. I cannot tell you the derivation of the phrase; I believe picnic was originally a cant word, and was first applied to a supper or other meal in which the entertainment is not provided by any one person, but each of the guests furnishes his dish. In a picnic supper one supplies the fowls, another the fish, another the wine and fruit, etc.; and they all sit down together and enjoy it.

A very sociable way of making an entertainment.

Yes, and I would have you observe that the principle of it may be extended to many other things. No one has a right to be entertained gratis in society; he must expend if he wishes to enjoy. Conversation,

o c

particularly, is a picnic feast, where every one is to contribute something, according to his genius and ability. Different talents and acquirements compose the different dishes of entertainment, and the greater variety the better; but every one must bring something, for society will not tolerate any one long who lives wholly at the expense of his neighbors. Did not you observe how agreeably we were entertained at Lady Isabella's party last night?

Yes: one of the young ladies sung, and another exhibited her drawings; and a gentleman told some very good stories.

True: another lady who is very much in the fashionable world gave us a great deal of anecdote; Dr. R., who is just returned from the Continent, gave us an interesting account of the state of Germany; and in another part of the room a cluster was gathered round an Edinburgh student and a young Oxonian, who were holding a lively debate on the power of galvanism. But Lady Isabella herself was the charm of the party.

I think she talked very little; and I do not recollect anything she said which was particularly striking.

That is true. But it was owing to her address and attention to her company that others talked and were heard by turns; that the modest were encouraged and drawn out, and those inclined to be noisy restrained and kept in order. She blended and harmonized the

talents of each; brought those together who were
likely to be agreeable to each other, and gave us no
more of herself than was necessary to set off others.
I noticed particularly her good offices to an accomplished but very bashful lady and a reserved man of
science, who wished much to be known to one another,
but who would never have been so without her introduction.   As soon as she had fairly engaged them
in an interesting conversation, she left them, regardless of her own entertainment, and seated herself
by poor Mr. ——, purely because he was sitting in a
corner and no one attended to him.   You know that
in chemical preparation two substances often require
a third to enable them to mix and unite together.
Lady Isabella possesses this amalgamating power: this
is what she brings to the picnic.   I should add, that
two or three times I observed she dexterously changed
topics, and suppressed stories which were likely to
bear hard on the profession or connections of some of
the company.   In short, the party which was so agreeable under her harmonizing influence would have had
quite a different aspect without her.   These merits,
however, might easily escape a young observer.   But
I dare say you did not fail to notice Sir Henry B——'s
lady, who was declaiming with so much enthusiasm,
in the midst of a circle of gentlemen which she had
drawn round her, upon the *beau idéal*.

No, indeed, mamma, I never heard so much fire and feeling : and what a flow of eloquent language ! I do not wonder her eloquence was so much admired.

She has a great deal of eloquence and taste : she has travelled, and is acquainted with the best works of art. I am not sure, however, whether the gentlemen were admiring most her declamation, or the fine turn of her hands and arms. She has a different attitude for every sentiment. Some observations which she made upon the beauty of statues seemed to me to go to the verge of what a modest female will allow herself to say upon such subjects, — but she has travelled. She was sensible that she could not fail to gain by the conversation while beauty of form was the subject of it.

Pray what did ——, the great poet, bring to the picnic, for I think he hardly opened his mouth ?

He brought his fame. Many would be gratified with merely seeing him who had entertained them in their closets ; and he who had so entertained them had a right to be himself entertained in that way which he had no talent for joining in. Let every one, I repeat, bring to the entertainment something of the best he possesses, and the picnic table will seldom fail to afford a plentiful banquet.

LETTER FROM GRIMALKIN TO SELIMA.

MY DEAR SELIMA, — As you are now going to quit the fostering cares of a mother, to enter, young as you are, into the wide world, and conduct yourself by your own prudence, I cannot forbear giving you some parting advice in this important era of your life.

Your extreme youth, and, permit me to add, the giddiness incident to that period, make me particularly anxious for your welfare. In the first place, then, let me beg you to remember that life is not to be spent in running after your own tail. Remember you were sent into the world to catch rats and mice. It is for this you are furnished with sharp claws, whiskers to improve your scent, and with such an elasticity and spring in your limbs. Never lose sight of this great end of your existence. When you and your sister are jumping over my back and kicking and scratching one another's noses, you are indulging the propensities of your nature, and perfecting yourselves in agility and dexterity; but remember that these frolics are only preparatory to the grand scene of action. Life is long,

but youth is short. The gayety of the kitten will most
assuredly go off. In a few months, nay, even weeks,
those spirits and that playfulness, which now exhilarate
all who behold you, will subside; and I beg you to
reflect how contemptible you will be, if you should
have the gravity of an old cat without that usefulness
which alone can insure respect and protection for your
maturer years.

In the first place, my dear child, obtain a command
over your appetites, and take care that no tempting
opportunity ever induces you to make free with the
pantry or larder of your mistress. You may possibly
slip in and out without observation; you may lap a little cream or run away with a chop without its being
missed; but, depend upon it, such practices sooner or
later will be found out; and if in a single instance you
are discovered, everything which is missing will be
charged upon you. If Betty or Mrs. Susan chooses to
regale herself with a cold breast of chicken which was
set by for supper, — you will have clawed it; or a rasp-
berry cream, — you will have lapped it. Nor is this
all. If you have once thrown down a single cup in
your eagerness to get out of the store-room, every china
plate and dish that is ever broken in the house, you
will have broken it; and though your back promises to
be pretty broad, it will not be broad enough for all the
mischief that will be laid upon it. Honesty, you will
find, is the best policy.

Remember that the true pleasures of life consist in the exertion of our own powers. If you were to feast every day upon roasted partridges, from off Dresden china, and dip your whiskers in syllabubs and creams, it could never give you such true enjoyment as the commonest food procured by the labor of your own paws. When you have once tasted the exquisite pleasure of catching and playing with a mouse, you will despise the gratification of artificial dainties.

I do not with some moralists call cleanliness a half virtue only. Remember it is one of the most essential to your sex and station ; and if ever you should fail in it, I sincerely hope Mrs. Susan will bestow upon you a good whipping.

Pray do not spit at strangers who do you the honor to take notice of you. It is very uncivil behavior, and · I have often wondered that kittens of any breeding should be guilty of it.

Avoid thrusting your nose into every closet and cupboard, — unless indeed you smell mice ; in which case it is very becoming.

Should you live, as I hope you will, to see the children of your patroness, you must prepare yourself to exercise that branch of fortitude which consists in patient endurance ; for you must expect to be lugged about, pinched, and pulled by the tail, and played a thousand tricks with, all which you must bear without putting out a claw; for you may depend upon it, if you attempt the least retaliation you will forever lose the favor of your mistress.

Should there be favorites in the house, such as tame birds, dormice, or a squirrel, great will be your temptations.   In such a circumstance, if the cage hangs low and the door happens to be left open, to govern your appetite I know will be a difficult task.   But remember that nothing is impossible to the governing mind; and that there are instances upon record of cats who in the exercise of self-government have overcome the strongest propensities of their nature.

If you would make yourself agreeable to your mistress, you must observe times and seasons.   You must not startle her by jumping upon her in a rude manner; and above all, be sure to sheathe your claws when you lay your paw upon her lap.

You have, like myself, been brought up in the country, and I fear you may regret the amusements it affords; such as catching butterflies, climbing trees, and watching birds from the windows, which I have done with great delight for a whole morning together. But these pleasures are not essential.   A town life has also its gratifications.   You may make many pleasant acquaintances in the neighboring courts and alleys.   A concert upon the tiles in a fine moonlight summer's evening may at once gratify your ear and your social feelings. Rats and mice are to be met with everywhere; and at any rate you have reason to be thankful that so creditable a situation has been found for you, without which you must have followed the fate of your poor brothers, and with a stone about your neck have been drowned in the next pond.

It is only when you have kittens yourself that you will be able to appreciate the cares of a mother. How unruly have you been when I wanted to wash your face! how undutiful in galloping about the room instead of coming immediately when I called you! But nothing can subdue the affections of a parent. Being grave and thoughtful in my nature, and having the advantage of residing in a literary family, I have mused deeply on the subject of education; I have pored by moonlight over Locke and Edgeworth and Mrs. Hamilton, and the laws of association; but after much cogitation I am only convinced of this, that kittens will be kittens, and old cats old cats. May you, my dear child, be an honor to all your relations, and to the whole feline race. May you see your descendants of the fiftieth generation; and when you depart this life, may the lamentations of your kindred exceed in pathos the melody of an Irish howl.

Signed by the paw of your affectionate mother,

GRIMALKIN.

ALLEGORY ON SLEEP.

MY DEAR MISS D * * * *, — The affection I bear you, and the sincere regard I have for your welfare, will, I hope, excuse the liberty I am going to take in remonstrating against the indulgence of a too partial affection which I see with sorrow is growing upon you every day.

You start at the imputation : but hear me with patience ; and if your own heart, your own reason, does not bear witness to what I say, then blame my suspicions and my freedom.

But need I say much to convince you of the power this favored lover, whose name I will not mention, has over you, when at this very moment he absorbs all your faculties, and engrosses every power of your mind to such a degree as leaves it doubtful whether this friendly admonition will reach your ear, lost as you are in the soft enchantment ? Is it not evident that in his presence you are dead to everything around you ? The voice of your nearest friend, your most sprightly and once-loved amusements, cannot draw your attention ; you breathe, you exist, only for him. And when at length he has left you, do not I behold you languid, pale, bearing in your eyes and your whole carriage the marks of his power over you? When we parted last night, did not I see you impatient to sink into his arms? Have you never been caught reclined on his bosom, on a soft carpet of flowers, on the banks of a purling stream, where the murmuring of the waters, the whispering of the trees, the silence and solitude of the place, and the luxurious softness of everything around you, favored his approach and disposed you to listen to his addresses? Nay, in that sacred temple which ought to be dedicated to higher affections, has he never stolen insensibly on your mind, and sealed your ears against the voice of the preacher, though never so persuasive? Has not his influence over you greatly increased within these few weeks? Does he not every day demand, do you not every day sacrifice to him, a larger portion of your time?

Not content with your devoting to him those hours

"When business, noise, and day are fled,"

does he not encroach upon the morning watches, break in upon your studies, and detain your mind from the pursuit of knowledge and the pursuit of pleasure, — of all pleasure but the enervating indulgence of your passion?

Diana, who still wishes to number you in her train,

invites you to join in her lively sports; for you Aurora bathes the new-born rose in dew, and streaks the clouds with gold and crimson; and Youth and Health offer a thousand innocent pleasures to your acceptance.

And, let me ask you, what can you find in the company of him with whom you are thus enamored, to make you amends for all that you give up for his sake? Does he entertain you with anything but the most incoherent rhapsodies, the most romantic and visionary tales? To believe the strange, improbable, and contradictory things he tells you requires a credulity beyond that of an infant. If he has ever spoken truth, it is mixed with so much falsehood and obscurity that it is estimated the certain sign of a weak mind to be much affected with what he says.

As I wish to draw a true portrait, I will by no means disguise his good qualities; and shall therefore allow that he is a friend to the unhappy and the friendless, that his breast is the only pillow for misfortune to repose on, and that his approaches are so gentle and insinuating as in some moments to be almost irresistible. If he is at all disposed to partiality, it is in favor of the poor and mean, with whom he is generally thought to associate more readily than with the rich. Yet he dispenses favors to all: and those who are most disposed to rebel against his power and treat him with contempt could never render themselves quite independent of him.

He is of a very ancient family, and came in long before the Conquest. He has a half-brother, somewhat younger than himself, who has made his name very famous in the world: he is a tall, meagre figure, with a ghastly air and a most forbidding countenance; he delights in slaughter, and has destroyed more men than Cæsar or Alexander.

He who is the subject of my letter is fond of peace, sleek and corpulent, with a mild heavy eye and a physiognomy perfectly placid; yet with all this opposition of feature and character, there is such a resemblance between them (as often happens in family likenesses), that in some lights and attitudes you can scarce distinguish the one from the other.

To finish the description of your lover, — he is generally crowned with flowers, but of the most languid kind, such as poppies and cowslips; and he is attended by a number of servants, thin and light-footed, to whom he does not give the same livery; for some are dressed in the gayest, others in the most gloomy habits imaginable, but all fantastic.

He is subject to many strange antipathies, and as strange likings. The warbling of the lark, to others so agreeable, is to him the harshest discord, and Peter could not start more at the crowing of a cock. The slightest accident, the cry of an infant, a mouse behind the wainscot, will oftentimes totally disconcert and put him to flight, and at other times he will not regard the loudest thunder. His favorite animal is the dormouse, and his music the dropping of water, the low tinkling of a distant bell, the humming of bees, and the hollow sound of the wind rustling through the trees.

But I have now said enough to let you into the true character of this powerful enchanter. You will answer, I know, to all this, that he begins by enslaving every faculty that might resist him, and that his power must be already broken before Reason can exert herself. You will perhaps likewise tell me (and I must acknowledge the justice of the retort) that I myself, though my situation affords a thousand reasons to resist him which do not take place with you, have been but too sensible of his attractions.

With blushes I confess the charge. At this moment, however, the charm is broken, and Reason has her full empire over me. Let me exhort you therefore . . . . But why exhort you to what is already done ? for if this letter has made its way to your ear, if your eye is now perusing its contents, the spell is dissolved, and you are no longer sunk in the embraces of *Sleep*.

ON EXPENSE:

A DIALOGUE.

YOU seem to be in a revery, Harriet; or are you tired with your long bustling walk through the streets of London?

Not at all, papa; but I was wondering at something.

A grown person even cannot walk through such a metropolis without meeting with many things to wonder at. But let us hear the particular subject of your admiration; was it the height and circumference of St. Paul's, or the automatons, or the magical effect of the Panorama that has most struck you?

No, papa; but I was wondering how you who have always so much money in your pockets can go through the streets of London, all full of fine shops, and not buy things; I am sure if I had money I could not help spending it all.

As you never have a great deal of money, and it is given you only to please your fancy with, there is no harm in your spending it in anything you have a mind to; but it is very well for you and me too that the

money does not *burn* in my pocket as it does in
yours.

No, to be sure you would not spend all your money
in those shops, because you must buy bread and meat;
but you might spend a good deal. But you walk past
just as if you did not see them: you never stop to
give one look. Now tell me really, papa, can you
help *wishing* for all those pretty things that stand in
the shop windows?

For all! Would you have me wish for all of them?
But I will answer you seriously. I do walk by these
tempting shops without wishing for anything, and indeed in general without seeing them.

Well, that is because you are a man, and you do not
care for what I admire so very much.

No, there you are mistaken; for, though I may not
admire them so very much as you say you do, there are
a vast number of things sold in London which it would
give me great pleasure to have in my possession. I
should greatly like one of Dollond's best reflecting
telescopes. I could lay out a great deal of money, if
I had it to spare, in books of botany and natural
history. Nay, I assure you I should by no means be
indifferent to the fine fruit exposed at the fruit-
shops; the plums with the blue upon them as if
they were just taken from the tree, the luscious
hot-house grapes, and the melons and pine-apples.

Believe me, I could eat these things with as good a relish as you could.

Then how can you help buying them, when you have money; and especially, papa, how can you help thinking about them and wishing for them?

London is the best place in the world to cure a person of extravagance, and even of extravagant wishes. I see so many costly things here which I know I could not buy, even if I were to lay out all the money I have in the world, that I never think of buying anything which I do not really want. Our furniture, you know, is old and plain. Perhaps if there were only a little better furniture to be had, I might be tempted to change it; but when I see houses where a whole fortune is laid out in decorating a set of apartments, I am content with chairs whose only use is to sit down upon, and tables that were in fashion half a century ago. In short, I have formed the habit of *self-government*, one of the most useful powers a man can be possessed of. Self-government belongs only to civilized man, — a savage has no idea of it. A North American Indian is temperate when he has no liquor; but as soon as liquor is within his reach, he invariably drinks till he is first furious and then insensible. He possesses no power over .himself, and he literally can no more help it than iron can help being drawn by the loadstone.

But he seldom gets liquor, so he has not a habit of drinking.

You are right; he has not the habit of drinking, but he wants the habit of self-control: this can only be gained by being often in the midst of temptations, and resisting them. This is the wholesome discipline of the mind. The first time a man denies himself anything he likes and which it is in his power to procure, there is a great struggle within him, and uneasy wishes will disturb for some time the tranquillity of his mind. He has gained the victory, but the enemy dies hard. The next time he does not wish so much, but he still thinks about it. After a while he does not think of it; he does not even see it. A person of moderate fortune, like myself, who lives in a gay and splendid metropolis, is accustomed to see every day a hundred things which it would be madness to think of buying.

Yes; but if you were very rich, papa, — if you were a lord?

No man is so rich as to buy everything his unrestrained fancy might prompt him to desire. Hounds and horses, pictures and statues and buildings, will exhaust any fortune. There is hardly any one taste so simple or innocent but what a man might spend his whole estate in it, if he were resolved to gratify it to the utmost. A nobleman may just as easily ruin himself by extravagance as a private man, and indeed many do so.

But if you were a king?

If I were a king, the mischief would be much greater; for I should ruin not only myself, but my subjects.

A king could not hurt his subjects, however, with buying toys or things to eat.

Indeed, but he might. What is a diamond but a mere toy? but a large diamond is an object of princely expense. That called the Pitt diamond was valued at £1,000,000. It was offered to George the Second, but he wisely thought it too dear. The dress of the queen of France was thought by the prudent Necker a serious object of expense in the revenues of that large kingdom; and her extravagance and that of the king's brothers had a great share in bringing on the calamities of the kingdom. As to eating, you could gratify yourself with laying out a shilling or two at the pastry-cook's; but Prince Potemkin, who had the revenues of the mighty empire of Russia at command, could not please his appetite without his dish of sterlet soup, which cost every time it was made above thirty pounds; and he would send one of his aids-de-camp an errand from Yassy to Petersburg, a distance of nearly seven hundred miles, to fetch him a tureen of it. He once bought all the cherries of a tree in a greenhouse at about half a crown apiece. The Roman empire was far richer than the Russian, and in the time of the emperors was all under the power of one man. Yet when they had such gluttons as Vitellius and Heliogabalus, the revenue of whole provinces was hardly sufficient to give them a dinner: they had tongues of nightingales, and such kind of dishes, the value of which was merely in the expense.

I think the throat of the poor little nightingales might have given them much more pleasure than the tongue.

True; but the proverb says, The belly has no ears. In modern Rome, Pope Adrian, a frugal Dutchman, complained of the expense his predecessor, Leo X., was at in peacock sausages. The expenses of Louis XIV. were of a more elegant kind; he was fond of fine tapestry, mirrors, gardens, statues, magnificent palaces. These tastes were becoming in a great king, and would have been serviceable to his kingdom if kept within proper limits; but he could not deny himself anything, however extravagant, that it came in his mind to wish for, and, indeed, would have imagined it beneath him to think at all about the expense; and therefore while he was throwing up water fifty feet high at his palaces of Versailles and Marli, and spouting it out of the mouths of dolphins and tritons, thousands of his people in the distant provinces were wanting bread.

I am sure I would not have done so to please my fancy.

Nor he neither, perhaps, if he had seen them; but these poor men and their families were a great way off, and all the people about him looked pleased and happy, and said he was the most generous prince the world had ever seen.

Well, but if I had Aladdin's lamp I might have everything I wished for.

I am glad at least I have driven you to fairyland. You might, no doubt, with the lamp of Aladdin, or Fortunatus's purse, have everything you wished for; but do you know what the consequences would be?

Very pleasant, I should think.

On the contrary, you would become whimsical and capricious, and would soon grow tired of everything. We do not receive pleasure long from anything that is not bought with our own labor; this is one of those permanent laws of nature which man cannot change, and therefore pleasure and exertion will never be separated even in imagination in a well-regulated mind. I could tell you of a couple who received more true enjoyment of their fortune than Aladdin himself.

Pray do.

The couple I am thinking of lived about a century ago in one of our rich trading towns, which was then just beginning to rise by manufacturing tapes and inkle. They had married because they loved one another; they had very little to begin with, but they were not afraid, because they were industrious. When the husband had come to be the richest merchant in the place, he took great pleasure in talking over his small beginnings; but he used always to add, that, poor as he was when he married, he would not have taken a thousand pounds for the table his dame and he ate their dinner from.

What! had he so costly a table before he was grown rich?

On the contrary, he had no table at all; and his wife and he used to sit close together, and place their dish of pottage upon their knees; their knees were the table. They soon got forward in the world, as industrious people generally do, and were enabled to purchase one thing after another; first, perhaps, a deal table; after a while a mahogany one; then a sumptuous sideboard. At first they sat on wooden benches; then they had two or three rush-bottomed chairs; and when they were rich enough to have an arm-chair for the husband and another for a friend, to smoke their pipes in, how magnificent they would think themselves! At first they would treat a neighbor with a slice of bread and cheese and a draught of beer; by degrees with a good joint and a pudding; and at length with all the delicacies of a fashionable entertainment.; and all along they would be able to say, "The blessing of God upon our own industry has procured us these things." By this means they would relish every gradation and increase of their enjoyments; whereas the man born to a fortune swallows his pleasures *whole*, he does not *taste* them. Another inconvenience that attends the man who is born rich is, that he has not early learned to deny himself. If I were a nobleman, though I could not buy everything I might fancy for myself, yet playthings for you would not easily ruin me, and you would probably have a great deal of pocket-money; and you would grow up with a confirmed habit of expense, and no ingenuity, for you would never try to make anything, or to find out some substitute if you could not get just the thing you wanted. That is a very fine cabinet of shells which the young heiress showed you the other day; it is perfectly arranged and mounted with the utmost elegance, and yet I am sure she has not half the pleasure in it which you have had with those little drawers of shells of your own collecting, aided by the occasional contributions of friends, which you have arranged for yourself, and display with such triumph. And now, to show you that I do sometimes think of the pleasures of my dear girl, here is a plaything for you which I bought while you were chatting at the door of a shop with one of your young friends.

A magic-lantern! How delightful! O thank you, papa! Edward, come and look at my charming magic-lantern.

THE END.

Cambridge : Electrotyped and Printed by Welch, Bigelow, & Co.